COINAGE IN ROMAN EGYPT

Erik Christiansen

COINAGE
IN ROMAN EGYPT

THE HOARD EVIDENCE

AARHUS UNIVERSITY PRESS

Coinage In Roman Egypt

© Copyright: The author and Aarhus University Press 2004
Cover illustration: "The Miser's Hoard". As fig. 2
Cover design: Lotte Bruun Rasmussen
Paper: 100 g Munken Pure
Type: Minion
Typeset and printed by Narayana Press, Gylling

ISBN 87 7288 964 0

AARHUS UNIVERSITY PRESS
Langelandsgade 177
DK-8200 Aarhus N

Fax: +45 89 42 53 80
www.unipress.dk

Published with financial support by
Aarhus University Research Foundation and
Dronning Margrethe and Prins Henrik's Fond

To Dorith

CONTENTS

List of Figures

LIST OF TABLES

LIST OF PLATES

PREFACE

Dubitando enim ad inquisitionem venimus; inquirendo veritatem percipimus.

(PIERRE ABELARD)

This is not a book about coins, but about coins as money, or more precisely stated, a book about the hoard evidence from Roman Egypt and what it may tell us about the use of coins in Egypt as a Roman province from the conquest by Augustus in 30 BC to Diocletian's currency reform in AD 296.

The Roman coins of Alexandria have been my main field of research for almost 30 years now, and when I began examining the hoard evidence afresh in connection with this present publication, I became aware of some important aspects which hitherto have remained unnoticed, or at least not sufficiently noticed. The ensuing investigations gave rise to a number of questions that by implication pertained to the present scholarly debate about coinage in the Ancient World and in the Roman economy. This is how I hope readers will receive the result.

I am indebted to so many for their support: Churchill College, Cambridge, accepted me as Visiting Fellow during Michaelmas Term 2000, and the Carlsberg Foundation financed the costs. I profited from the atmosphere and facilities of my new college and enjoyed being 'back home' in Cambridge. Unfortunately, I suffered a stroke during my stay, but the support I received from fellows and staff made it possible for me to return to my work. In the same vein, I owe thanks to Margaret and Dick Whittaker.

During my sojourn in Cambridge I also had access to the library of the Coin Room in the Fitzwilliam Museum, and discussed many points and even whole chapters in draft with colleagues, foremost T.V. Buttrey, Dorothy Thompson and Peter Spufford; furthermore with Chistopher Howgego (Oxford) and Dominic Rathbone (London). None of them can be made responsible for the views taken here, but I hope they will recognize their 'fingerprints'.

Sincere thanks to my Department at the University of Aarhus, not only for the sabbatical leave that made my stay at Cambridge possible, but also for the working conditions offered to me after my return to Aarhus. As usual, the Coin Cabinet in Copenhagen rendered very helpful service, including an invitation to participate in a seminar held in November 2001 on single finds/stray finds, with a contribution on 'the case of Egypt'.

For some twenty years, Richard Reece (Cirencester) has acted as my fastidious private peer reader. It is almost impossible for me to describe the instigating way in which his critical remarks have always improved my arguments and language! My former student, Peter F. Bang (then at Cambridge) also read the entire manuscript and helped with some keen comments. I hope they both enjoy the outcome.

Thanks also to one of my students, Jakob Drud, who worked out Figures 10-18 and Tables V-IX in a most diligent way. His salary was generously paid by the Advokat Axel Ernst's og frøken Alfrida Ernst's Legat. I am also very grateful to the Aarhus University Research Foundation and the Dronning Margrethe and Prins Henrik's Fond for their financial support, and to Aarhus University Press, especially Sanne Lind Hansen and Mary Waters Lund, for diligent work during the publication.

Last, but not least, I owe profound thanks to my wife. Not only has she followed the project from its first preliminary sketches to its completion, but has supported me during and after my illness in an inestimable way. This book is dedicated to her.

Erik Christiansen
2003

CHAPTER I

The Evidence of Coin Hoards

It was a strange collection, like Billy Bones's hoard for the diversity of coinage, but so much larger and so much varied that I think I never had more pleasure than in sorting them. English, French, Spanish, Portuguese, Georges and Louises, doubloons and double guineas and moidores and sequins, the picture of all the kings of Europe for the last hundred years, strange Oriental pieces stamped with what looked like wisps of string or bits of spider's web, round pieces and square pieces, and pieces bored through the middle, as if to wear them round your neck – nearly every variety of money in the world must, I think, have found a place in that collection; and for number, I am sure they were like autumn leaves, so that my back ached with stooping and my fingers with sorting them out.

(Robert Louis Stevenson, *Treasure Island*)

'Hoard', 'treasure' may immediately evoke vivid pictures of a wooden chest full of gold coins, jewellery and precious stones, secretly buried in an isolated island only known by pirates and now – found by the instructions in a brownish, half-burned, blood-stained document – lying glittering in the moonlight, feverishly being watched by eager eyes, behind which lurk insidious plans for getting sole possession of this large fortune. Readers who expect this book to be about such exciting stories should turn instead to Robert Stevenson's *Treasure Island*. Scholarly research is seldom so exciting!

Preamble

This chapter is no exhaustive treatment of the coin hoard evidence in general, nor of all the theoretical and methodological problems connected with investigation into it as a historical source. In order to be so, much more documentation and many more examples ought to have been induced. Nor does it bring new theories or sweeping new points of view. I will pose questions, and when discussing possible answers I will mainly take my examples from the period I know best, that is the Roman world before Diocletian's reforms.

The chapter is meant as a preamble to the following description and discussions of the hoard evidence from Roman Egypt, since that should be viewed in the light of the ongoing debate about ancient coinage in general, and the hoard evidence and the Roman coinage in particular. How far *Coinage in Roman Egypt* may contribute to this debate will be clear – I hope – from the chapters that follow.

By 'hoard' is meant 'at least two coins (or at least one coin and another object of value) apparently purposely buried together'[1] or lost – and preferably found together.[2] Most scholars today agree on such a definition,[3] which clearly distinguishes 'hoards' from 'stray finds', i.e. single coins lost by accident (or sacrifice).

There may be modifications to this definition. A single gold coin lost or buried by its owner may have represented his whole fortune and therefore a past treasure. Generally, however, stray finds represent less valuable coins, lost 'from the pocket' and not regained since the owner did not notice the loss or did not bother to retrieve it. Groups of stray-found coins may therefore offer a picture of small change used for daily transactions in a given area at a given period of time.

Others have argued for 'accumulated' losses as hoards of a specific category.[4] Undoubtedly, many single coins found at one place may provide an interesting picture of coins lost or sacrificed for centuries. Yet, they are unintentional accumulations – which were neither deposited nor lost as a whole – and therefore not hoards. Contrary to hoards, they do not provide their own chronological context.

A more important modification is the existence of 'composite' hoards, i.e. hoards to which later additions have been made. Thus the pirate could have returned to his island's treasure in order to refill his chest with newly robbed booty or to get some ready cash. Yet, what matters to us is the composition of the hoard when it last was found and therefore as it was at the latest time of its disposal, when it ceased to be at the owner's hand.

A composite hoard may be an 'encapsulated' or an 'extended' hoard. The encapsulated hoard is, by definition, not a hoard typical of the time of final burial, whereas an extended hoard may reflect older coinage still considered to be of value or be the result of additions made in a modern period.

We also have 'secondary' hoards, that is, groups of coins deposited or lost together in a modern period and not in their original past.

A definition of 'coin' is also needed:

Coins are defined as 'small struck pieces of metal carrying a value commonly accepted within the area of a 'ruler' or 'state' whose government is responsible for their production and whose authority guarantees their value'.[5]

It may be that neither the value nor the authority are explicitly stated on the coin itself, and therefore are questions for scholarly debate. What matters, however, is that people in a certain area ('city-state', country, empire, or province) at a certain period accepted the coin's value in the confidence that other people – and the government it-self! – would do the same. All forms of money depend on confidence. Coins represent a practical way of ensuring such confidence, based on confidence in the sovereign's authority. The Euro, for example, makes no difference, since confidence relies on a shared sovereignty and combined authority.

There may be 'private' coins as well. At times with an insufficient supply of ordin-ary coinage, private people may have made their own coins, which were accepted by other people although not by the government, at least not officially. This unofficial coinage does not distract from the fundamental notion that coins are – and have al-ways been – a mark of authority. The punishment for producing forgeries has always been severe. In the later Roman Empire counterfeiting coins was a 'sacrilege' in the same way as melting coins, and therefore a 'capital offence'[6] (meaning the death sen-tence).

Quite another story applies to coins that left their place of origin. Such 'foreigners' may have been accepted for many reasons, which will not be discussed here as they do not distract from the definition offered, based as it is on the 'homeland'.

A definition of coins will demonstrate quite clearly that coins are a specific form of money and in principle not different from, for example, cowrie shells in 'primitive' societies. Even in a society that made regular use of coins, such as the Greco-Roman world, other objects may also have served as money, being either a means of payment, a means of storing wealth, or merely accounting devices/reckoning units. Furthermore, we should not be surprised to find coin terms expressing a means of accounting and not actual coins in use. The former British 'guinea' (21 shillings) and the former Danish 'daler' (2 kroner) are well-known modern examples of this widespread phenomenon, but even terms for existing coins may be used as accounting units, whereas the actual sum was paid in an equivalent amount of other coins or merely represented an entry of credit or debit.

Reasons for hoarding

In *theory* at least, there are three main groups of hoards: 'savings hoards', 'emergency hoards', and 'accidentally lost hoards' (or 'purse hoards'). Their evidence may be said to differ as much as reasons for their hoarding.

A 'savings hoard' will represent the owner's conscious selection of the best coins available and not needed for daily use. The coins would have been set aside in readiness for later and perhaps larger transactions, or deposited on loan with another person, thus testifying to the most valuable coins available at the time of the hoard's disposal. It may even be a 'treasure', the value of which would depend on the saver: perhaps it is a child's moneybox or a tycoon's ready cash.

An 'emergency hoard' will represent the coins the owner was able to hide when in fear of theft, robbery, or looting. He may have been in hurry and therefore gathered as many coins as he could, some pieces being of considerable value, others less so. Partly a 'savings hoard', it may also testify to coins used for daily needs at the time of disposal, but in what proportions will be difficult to decide. A special version of this is a 'crisis hoard' resulting, for instance, from the – perhaps vain – efforts of an owner to rescue his fortune if his house caught fire.

An 'accidentally lost hoard' will represent the coins an owner carried with him when shopping, travelling, or the like. It may well be the contents of his saving box taken to the market, probably indicating coins for both smaller and larger transactions, and therefore is the best evidence we have for coins as a means of payment: in other words the circulation of coins at the time of loss of the hoard.

In *practice*, however, the distinctions are often blurred. The original owner took fright, sampled his best coins (now a 'savings hoard') or gathered all the coins he could (now an 'emergency hoard'), then, when fleeing, lost or was robbed of his 'purse of coins' (now an 'accidentally lost hoard'). The robber may then have hidden his booty for later use ('savings hoard'), hastily having buried it in fear of being caught ('emergency hoard'), or perhaps he lost it when running away from the place of misdeed ('accidentally lost hoard'), etc., etc.

By saying this, I am not trying to decry the theoretical distinction between such hoards, but merely to warn against any rigorous application of it. Even when circumstances of the find are well-known and the hoard was well contained (in a sealed pot, e.g.) – which quite often is not the case, we can rarely say which category we are dealing with, and a vicious circle of argument is near: hoard X contains many valuable coins, hoard X is a 'savings hoard', hoard X is yet another proof that 'savings hoards' consist of the most valuable coins at the time. Theory may be illuminating but also distorting!

There is a fourth group of hoards, which may be difficult to classify among the three main groups. We may call them 'debasement hoards' or 'waste hoards'. This group of coins has become almost worthless. Perhaps these coins were simply thrown away or given to children to play with. Perhaps, by accident, they were brought home from abroad, laid aside and forgotten without being exchanged into valid currency.

In this regard, one particular type of hoard would be of immense interest to us: for example, a new currency has been introduced by decree and all previous coins declared invalid. People in possession of such coins are ordered to bring them to a money-changer. Unfortunately, the money has been earned in an illegal way, and in order not to be discovered, it has been hidden away, perhaps in the hope that the government will rescind the decree at a later time. This happened in many European countries after World War II, and it goes without saying how much such a hoard could tell us, not only about the previous currency, but also about the effects of the decree. But again, how can we tell that this was the case?

Another category of hoards is clearer. Called 'deposit hoards' (or 'sacrificial hoards'), we find them in temples as offerings to the gods, in building foundations for commemoration, or in a grave as coins for the afterlife. The wider conclusions are less satisfying. Coins needed by the gods in their eternal life (if any?) or by the dead for display in the underworld entail little exact information about coinage needed in the earthly world, and however much foundation coins can be revealing in matters of dating, little more can be expected.

When the 'Lohe Hoard' was found in Stockholm, Carl-Frederik Palmstierna in 1938 gave the ingenious explanation that the owner of the house, count Conrad Lohe had buried the hoard 'to avoid its passing by inheritance into the hands of a much-hated nephew'.[7] The explanation was soon discarded, but on the whole 'disinheritance hoards' cannot be excluded from consideration and tell us that only imagination limits possible interpretations.

This being so, it is understandable why many an excavator has offered a vivid interpretation of the hoard under publication.[8] But caution is needed: we do not know what hoarders were thinking!

Recovery of hoards

It may seem a truism – although at times insufficiently attended to – that hoards of the past were not meant for us. In most cases, the original owner's intention was to regain the buried or lost hoard, but for some reason or another was not able to do so. Even 'deposit hoards' were not meant for an inquisitive posterity, apart perhaps from 'foundation' coins.

Actually, most hoards will have been found again either by the owner or by another. Although a few ended up in 'composite hoards', we only have the tip of an original iceberg, and this tip may not even be representative of the original hoarding pattern.

Anyone who has studied hoard evidence on a larger than one scale will deplore the fact that so many original hoards have vanished without a trace, apart perhaps from rumours. Many hoards have been – and still are – totally dispersed, many others have only been given a brief note or notice.

Compared to the many hoards known – not to speak of many hoards probably still lying unearthed – scholarly interest in their evidence is a newcomer, and it will cause no surprise to find Theodor Mommsen as one of the pioneers.[9] Until the middle of the 19th century even serious museum curators were thinking in terms of treasure or merely wanted to pick up rare specimens or new types not already present in the existing collection. Not only worn specimens but also common coins of good preservation were dispersed without due registration or with no registration at all. This we can deplore but not remedy, and it is – as always in history – useless to blame our predecessors for their attitudes.

More deplorable and difficult to remedy is the fact that treasure hunting is still going on – in some countries more than others. Even today, a finder of a hoard can profit from his find by selling it on the market. He can select the best specimens, one by one or group by group, and offer them at a high (and 'special') price to tourists or amateur collectors who are unaware of their provenance, or to antiquities dealers who, at best, pretend not to know. In some countries some of these finds will be detected and confiscated by the police according to law, hopefully complete. On the other hand, less experienced finders may be offered a fixed price for each and every specimen and therefore try to increase their profit by adding some other coins found in another context. If confiscated, such finds will cause problems for even a well-educated numismatist.

In recent years, metal detectors have increased the number of hoards found. Fortunately, many such finds have been reported to local museums or the like, but sadly, not always.

Our greatest concern is a full and reliable description not only of the hoard, but also of the find circumstances. Many hoard publications, especially of an earlier age, are defective in both respects. All necessary information may not have been available or not sufficiently explored.

Even archaeological excavations have not always produced the clear evidence we expect. Some excavators may not have the necessary training for handling coins. Such was the case at least some decades ago. We even have cases where archaeologists were not interested in coins not considered relevant to a specific excavation – and therefore discarded them! While no educated archaeologist would behave like that today, even the best modern excavations depend on what sites and layers are accessible for their results. Their accessibility might be due to concession or accident, or the threat of new construction plans, but due to present or past conditions some sites will offer promising hoards in a very good condition, others none at all, or perhaps only items in a hopelessly conserved condition.

An archaeological excavation should preferably result in a publication that is useful to others. Unfortunately, though, some publications – especially those of an earlier age – may not comprise a full description of the coins found, or indeed may not mention them at all, since the expedition had other aims.

Some readers may find this too pessimistic or even superfluous. I think not. I do think, however, that the lesson to learn – and not always learned – is that even under the most favourable conditions we must be well aware of all the defects and fallacies in recovery of the hoards we have at our disposal.

Making use of the hoards

Many coin hoards found in one area or from one period may leave the impression of prosperity or flourishing trade (which may not be the same). This may or may not be true. Prosperity may be contingent on other objects. Coins may be gifts and tributes offered from outside. They may even imply, for reasons we do not know, nothing but a high-standing status. Commercial transactions can generally be performed by other means of payment, even worthless tokens, or by systems of credit.

On the other hand, many coins found in hoards as well as stray finds, may testify to a widespread use of coins, which may reflect prosperity and trade, and few coins or no coins at all may reflect economic poverty and dwindling trade. However, as always, what has to be remembered is that absence of evidence is no evidence of absence. We do not need to explain the absence of hoards. We need to explain their existence.

Many years ago, Sture Bolin claimed that numerous hoards from a certain period did not prove a country to be prosperous, but rather was evidence of warfare and disturbances.[10] Not only did more people try to hide their fortunes in such vexed times, but fewer of them would have regained their hoards when peace arrived.

Bolin's thesis has gained much support from later investigations,[11] but caution is needed. Unless corroborated by other evidence, such as traces of fire or written communications, a large number of hoards not recovered in the past are not in themselves proof of warfare and devastation. Other modifications are at hand. Many hoards may just as well be the result of people leaving their fortunes at home when leaving to participate in warfare and disturbances abroad, from which they never returned, as Michael Crawford pointed out with regard to Italy during the late Roman republic.[12]

From other areas and periods other reasons might apply: a long-lasting plague with its death-toll; heavy exactions of extra burdens which the inhabitants tried to evade by concealing their valuables, never found again; or perhaps disturbances in the coinage system, to which people reacted by laying aside the coins they had (awaiting a change for the better?). And again, we cannot conclude that the absence of hoards today is clear evidence of peace and stability in the past. The concealed hoards may have been found again or not found at all.

Patterns of coin circulation in towns may differ from the countryside, or there again be similar. The hoard evidence is insufficient for discussing such questions, due to later circumstances. Hoards found in the countryside, not to speak of ruined towns, may be more easily discovered by posterity than hoards found in towns and cities with a continued existence. Nor can we exclude the possibility that a hoard found in the countryside was deposited by a nearby town dweller who considered it to be a more secure hiding-place, whereas most hoards originally deposited in town houses would have been regained in antiquity.

Stray finds constitute better evidence. At least from the many scattered coin finds in, for example, far remote Roman Britain,[13] it can be said with certainty today that the use of coins in the countryside was much more widespread than the previous *communis opinio* claimed.[14]

Theoretically at least, it is easy to distinguish between town and country, even in formal terms for the Roman period. This said, we might generally suppose that town dwellers needed small change for their many petty transactions. It is also tempting to suppose a picture of farmers, dependant or not, taking their harvested produce to the market, selling it for cash, spending some money on commodities normally bought in town, plus on immediate pleasure, and then taking the rest home to be saved for future payments of rents, taxes, dowries, and so on.[15] If in any way true, this may be what is reflected in the coin hoards found in the countryside, but then again the circulation of coins in the towns may also reflect the peasants.

A credit system may pose limits to the need for and use of currency, yet without excluding it. Credit, however, is not possible unless you are a known and trustworthy person; for example, a local resident of good reputation. To make an extreme case: a soldier cannot buy services in a brothel on credit! Any credit-system must be based on the confidence that the sum owed will be paid as agreed or on demand.

A further implication is that the existence of a credit-system relies on confidence in the current means of payment. Suppose a pattern of a higher number of coins in the urban sites than in the countryside. The explanation may be that people had no – or had lost – confidence in the existing coins. Townspeople preferred immediate cash, which they could just as quickly dispose of, whereas in the countryside larger payments were made in kind. Thus seen, neither a low nor a high amount of circulating coins is cogent proof of a sophisticated economy.

Apart from such general conclusions, hoards may be used to answer more specific questions. Hoards and sequences of hoards have been useful for establishing a relative chronology for coins and coin-series not otherwise datable.

Hoards and groups of single finds may be valuable for dating an archaeological site, or the archaeological surroundings may offer certain evidence for dating burial of a hoard. If the circumstances of find are unknown, we have generally to assume that the burial date is not much later than the latest datable coin in the hoard (even including illegible coins).[16] This may not always be true, of course, but unless we have certain clues for another date, it is – apart from pure guesswork – the only possible way of dating.

Ancient numismatists can only envy our colleagues in medieval numismatics who have access to royal charters on minting rights and the like, and – from the late medieval age – even mint accounts, listing coin outputs and so on.[17] We can only rely on the number of coins found when looking for the original coin production and possible fluctuations.

It may seem very simple. Just a mere glimpse may show various numbers of types and series of coins in a hoard. If we then take a selection of hoards – count totals and compare results – we may see patterns of some issues dominating totals, others being present in moderate or small numbers, and yet others rarely at all.[18]

However, it is rarely as easy as that. We have to ascertain – or presume – that the present hoard evidence is a representative sample of the original number of coins, pay due attention to survival rates and the possible withdrawal of coins. Having done this, we may suppose not to be far from having clues to factual variations in the original production of coins, and from this set about making statistics that show relative distribution in percentages.

The worry here is that such studies are based on the assumption that the hoard evidence does reflect the original production of coins in spite of possible and various preferences for hoarding in the past. To go 'behind' this assumption we need to study dies, and it is here that problems turn up.

Few, and even few of the completely known and fully described hoards, are preserved in their entirety today. To rely on one hoard will not be enough. In the extreme, it may be – or contain – a group of coins which, coming fresh from the mint, did not reach its destination without some loss. On a more general line, common sense will warn against drawing firm conclusions from a group of older coins in a hoard deposited very much later. Recently, Kris Lockyear has even argued for the paradox that 'it is much more informative when examining the coinage pool to have several hoards in the 100-300 range than it is to have a single hoard over, say, the 1,000 or 2,000 coin mark.'[19]

To make die studies of a large number of hoards – or even just the existing remains – may be an insurmountable affair. I willingly offer my own studies of Nero's Alexandrian billon coins as an example. I had to give up studying each of the 759 specimens in Toronto with reverse type Alexandria year 12, and ended with a stop-gap solution,[20] which proved to be less convincing than I thought it to be.[21]

Perhaps, computer technology will be the way out, but only perhaps. We still have to see if it can reveal the original details behind worn dies and worn coins. The simulated striking of ancient coins, published by L. Beer,[22] remains an admonitory illustration of how the continued use of a die can radically distort the impressions on the flan.

Attempting to work out estimates of the original size of any coin production from the number of dies found, presents even more serious problems. Most serious is the fact that we do not know with any certainty how many coins an ancient die was able to strike, nor can we know how many coins an actual die struck before it broke or was taken out of use. It may even differ from time to time, from mint to mint, and metal to metal, and we are not always better off with the better-documented medieval age.[23]

For such reasons T.V. Buttrey has disclaimed any such attempts as being based on uncertain, fictitious, and even wrong premises.[24] To some extent I agree. We cannot claim that any calculations represent the truth of the original number of coins struck and sent into circulation. To demand truth, however, is to demand too much. The 'scientific world is always a world of best guesses', to quote F. de Callataÿ from his convincing attempt to argue that the existence of bad calculations should not make us discard calculations which may be better founded.[25] Furthermore, as also argued by Adr. Savio[26] and – apparently – Kris Lockyear,[27] we may at least to some extent claim comparable estimates if our calculations are based on the same set of premises and variables. And that – at least to me – will suffice.

Certainly, we cannot make such estimates for every part of a long range of coinage and therefore have to rely on the sheer evidence of the hoards, which after all may be reliable for relative numbers and comparable sizes. At least, we should not forget that Bengt Thordeman proved a close relation between the known records of the coinage from the 17-18th centuries year by year, and not only the Lohe Hoard, but as many as 'about 30 coin-finds from different periods'.[28] From this he drew his famous 'law' that 'the content of each coin-find stands in a certain ratio to the amount of the coinage during the period covered by the find, and that … this proportion reaches increasing agreement the larger the find is numerically'.[29]

Taking the precautions Thordeman outlined concerning the same area, period, and monetary system, and considering the difference between 17-18th century Sweden as a single country and the multifarious Roman Empire, we cannot just exclude from consideration that this law may also apply to the ancient world (from which we have no similar documentary evidence); in other words, that the hoard evidence of ancient coins under *specific conditions* may give us a reliable picture of the original coinage. In practice, there are many problems to overcome in each particular case, but the end result will anyway be relative numbers, which can be compared to each other.

If such analyses show heavy fluctuations between, say, different Roman emperors, we are tempted to ask why apparently some emperors struck not only a higher number of coins than others, but even – as it seems – an extremely higher amount. We are thereby taken into a much more interesting question: which political and fiscal motives caused such effects?

Why did the Romans strike coins?

In 1990, C. Howgego published a stimulating article, entitled 'Why did Ancient States strike Coins?'[30] My concern in this section is to ask if – and if so, how far – the hoard evidence can make contributions to this discussion regarding the Roman world before Diocletian's reforms.

During the imperial period, the emperor (or other high ranking members of his family) was depicted on almost every obverse all over the Roman Empire. The intention must have been to make the emperor and his coin known, and at least we know from the New Testament that it worked. Otherwise, Jesus' famous saying: 'render unto Caesar what is Caesar's'[31] makes no sense. He knew, and the Pharisees and the readers of the Scripture knew the emperor from the denarii they had to use for paying some of their taxes to him. It is tempting to think that the emperor himself had to approve the effigy before it was brought into use. So at least it was – and still is today – the royal prerogative in European monarchies. Casually, the biography of Severus Alexander among the *Scriptores* tells us that 'he had himself depicted on many of his coins in the costume of Alexander the Great',[32] which is difficult to recognize from the existing coins.

A personal interest in the designs may also be inferred from Suetonius, according to whom Augustus 'issued a silver coin stamped with the sign of the constellation Capricorn, under which he was born',[33] and Nero 'had a coin struck', representing him in 'the guise of a lyre-player'.[34] These coins are recognizable today, but it does not follow that the emperor generally decided on the designs of his coinage.

There has been a vivid discussion about the choice and meaning of the reverse types. I still conclude that, as a rule, the Roman emperors did not mint coins to produce a message. It is the other way round: when they – for some reason or another – had decided to strike a coinage, they (or whoever it was) made a deliberate choice of which types to use.[35] Events created types, but we should not let types create events that are not otherwise documented.

There are exceptions. *Adventus* can be taken to mean a coin struck to celebrate the emperor's visit or expected visit to the town or the province, even if we have no other confirmation.[36] There are similar, albeit few, other cases. Anyway, what do large or small numbers of such coins found (in hoards or as stray finds) tell us about such an event, its scope of celebration, expenditure needed, or popularity?

If a relatively high number of such coins is found, it may be a product of local preferences for use or hoarding, which presupposes that a certain amount was available in circulation and had been struck, or the coins may merely have been kept as mementos. If another type is rarely found, does it mean that few people liked it – some even detested it? Or was it actually produced on a small scale?

This does not apply to specific 'event coins' only. In contrast to the rather stereotyped coinage of the classical Greek world, the early Roman Empire is characterized by a rich variety of reverse types. What do relative numbers in coin finds generally tell us about production, supply, circulation, and preferences? Were some types or group of types struck in high numbers or merely more popular than others and therefore more available or preferred for hoarding, whereas others were avoided? Do we find regional differences and therefore different attitudes among the subjects? Did the ordinary man know about the reverses in the same way as Jesus and his contemporaries immediately recognized the emperor on the obverse? Recognizing 'the Emperor' does not necessarily mean recognizing the actual ruling emperor.

A type or design may have had general connotations or specific importance, and the message may be obvious or hidden, either for contemporaries or for us. Furthermore, if a type is rarely found, how far can we talk about a message, if indeed a message was meant? The questions are legion. The answers may not be 'blowing in the wind', but are certainly more difficult to find than numerical proportions of the original coin production.

Some 25 years ago Michael Crawford, based on hoard evidence and die studies, argued for a close relationship between warfare and the irregular production of coins during the late Roman republic.[37] He earlier claimed that 'state payments' were the sole reason why the Romans struck coins.[38] Without denying the importance of public expenditure, Howgego's article, referred to above, was a forceful encounter with this influential view.

Crawford's general view seems more tenable for the republic than his critics will allow. At least the general connection between military events and the striking of denarii is too evident to be denied. For the imperial period, we may generally assume that military expenses were a great – probably even the greatest – part of public expenditure, as also claimed by some ancient authors (although mostly regarding the eventful 3rd century).[39]

There are, however, some major differences that must not be overlooked. Compared to the endemic warfare and conquests during the republic, the imperial period was a peaceful time until the reign of Marcus Aurelius. With Trajan's wars and the Jewish revolts during his and Hadrian's reign as outstanding exceptions, the imperial government's main concern was to feed a standing army not at war. How expensive this enormous task was and how far it was met by requisitions in kind or payment in cash has not been taken under systematic investigation, and perhaps cannot be.

Astonishingly, one thing seems to have been overlooked in the way military expenditure has been dealt with in recent research. According to military accounts in the papyri, soldiers in the imperial army did not receive their ordinary pay during service.[40] They received on request a small quantity of 'pocket-money' from time to time, and this – together with the expenses covering weapons, food and clothing – was deducted from the final and largest amount which was paid to the soldier when he *left the army* (after twenty years service for a legionary). Since, therefore, a soldier (or his heir) first received the bulk of his pay on leaving service, it is futile – not to say absurd – to include in any modern reconstruction of a possible imperial budget, exact amounts of yearly payments in coins to a supposed number of soldiers!

Of course, sufficient coins had to be ready when the soldiers retired, in addition to retirement bounties for veterans, but we do not know if they were stored with the legions or were sent on demand. Nor do we have sufficient records to enumerate when these requirements were met, and unless we make the preposterous assumption that all legionary soldiers were enlisted at one time and therefore discharged (apart from those dead in the meantime) at precise intervals of twenty years, we are left with the unhappy and irremediable situation that we cannot make any possible estimate of the amounts of coins actually needed and paid for this purpose each year.

Perhaps, the imperial government did not know either. Presumably, the soldiers were enlisted in groups as required, and from a modern point of view, we would expect an imperial bookkeeping capable of predicting the sums needed in advance. This may not have been necessary if the treasury had plenty of coins, or the mint could just be instructed to strike the amount of coins needed. No one can tell!

According to Suetonius,[41] Augustus' will, read in the Senate, included three rolls, one of which contained 'a summary of the conditions of the whole empire, how many soldiers there were in active service in all parts of it, how much money there was in the public treasury and in the privy-purse, and what revenues were in arrears. He added, besides, the names of the freedmen and slaves from whom the details could be demanded.' According to the summary accompanying his *Acts* (or Augustus' *Res Gestae*), Appendix 1, he spent a total of 600,000,000 denarii on payments to 'the treasury, to the Roman plebs or to discharged soldiers'.

The implications could be that Augustus – and his successors – had gross accounts of general expenditure. Whether such expenditure was made from their 'private' purse or the 'public' treasury is hardly relevant as a modern concept. Likewise, then, they presumably had some estimates of expected income.

Therefore, a crucial question for our theme will be if, and to what extent, they could estimate expected items of expenditure. Perhaps they did not need to do so. The prevailing principle was that expenditure should not exceed income. However sound this may be, it could easily be circumvented. An emperor might easily seem to increase his income by striking new coins from bullion at hand (bars in the treasury, magnificent equipment and adornment, or intensified mining). This was the way many kings of a later period 'converted assets into cash' (to phrase it in modern terms) if required. Their only problem was that they could not just continue to do so endlessly.

As long as the reserves were – or were considered to be – sufficient for the present needs, the emperors would have had no worries about a future monetary policy.[42] We cannot tell how Roman emperors reacted to a threatening deficit, but 'bad' emperors (like Nero) were vehemently blamed for tightening the tax screw,[43] whereas false parsimony was among the alleged accusations against Galba.[44] If true, both attitudes may be symptoms of the same financial thinking, not far from a hand to mouth economy.

Apart from ordinary payments, military expenditure comprised occasional rewards and donations, the bulk of which may even have been paid in cash to the soldiers (and spent on the spot?). We do have some coins, types and inscriptions, which may be indicative of the actual coins paid to the legions on such occasions, for example, LEGIO II TRAIANA. As far as I know, no systematic survey of these coins has been undertaken, but they seem to appear in less numbers than we would expect to find, reading the literary sources, even before AD 245.[45] During the unruly late 3rd century, though, their frequency and amounts may have been higher. However, this is of little relevance, as the soldiers may have been paid instead – or also – in other coins.

New coins for old?

This will take us to a vital point in the ongoing debate on coinage in the ancient world.[46] We do not know if the imperial government 'recognized some political responsibility... to maintain in circulation an adequate supply of the full range of denominations', as claimed by Dominic Rathbone.[47] Few today will subscribe to Parker's harsh judgement on the 'selfish and short-sighted policy of the emperors' for not supplying the trade with 'its necessary medium of exchange'.[48] Trade may flourish without coinage. On the other hand, once payments in coins to and from the government had been introduced, the same government would need to ensure that a sufficient amount was available to keep the system running. The effect would be that coinage was also available for private transactions, including trade. Public expenditure might, however, be defrayed by disbursing existing coinage, unless the government for some reason or another wanted – or needed – to strike new coins.

Coin hoards may be of much avail here. If, say, an emperor's coinage makes up a disproportionately high part of the evidence, it is tempting to conclude that the original production of coins also was disproportionately high. If, furthermore, some periods (or even years) show a very high proportion compared to others, and the literary sources tell about warfare going on or being planned during the same time, it seems obvious to claim this to be the reason.

There is more to that. If by comparison, the previous coinage constitutes a lower and even much lower proportion, the new coins may either have replaced the existing coinage or have been added to the pool. If a sequence of hoards shows the number of previous coins to be dwindling or even disappearing, the former explanation is the most evident, but nevertheless the amount of new coins may also have increased the pool as well. This latter explanation may be given further confirmation if the evidence shows that the new coinage has remained in substantial numbers during the following period, especially if that period is marked by low numbers of contemporary coins.

If the production of coins had been augmented on a very large scale, modern economic theories will tell us to look for repercussions on the economy, and even inflation, should production remain at the same level. However, it is not necessarily so. The coins may have been spent beyond the borders, financing trade, tributes to enemies for keeping peace, and even outright expenses for warfare abroad. Economies of the past were not as closely linked as the economies of present day societies.

The expected effects may also be absent even if all the coins were sent into circulation within the borders. Warfare may have increased the production or caused new exactions to be paid in coins. Such exactions may have provoked angry protests, but this does not imply an economic crisis.

An increased amount of coins may merely have been hoarded by wealthy people, but if sent into circulation may cause nothing more – or nothing less – than an increased monetization, meaning that the use of coins became more widespread for paying daily needs or storing wealth, compared to previous periods when other means of payment were common or a credit system prevailed. *Vice versa*, a heavy decrease in coin production may not have produced disastrous effects on the economy as such, but simply caused a reversal or change of habits. Anyway, what matters is not the actual amount of coins, but the prevailing impression of the monetary situation. Coinage is a part of the economy, and economy is not always ruled by crude facts.

Ancient coinage was minted in metals of an intrinsic value. So at least were the gold coins and originally the silver coins as well. If a government did not have the bullion needed for producing coins, it might decide on, or be forced to, debasement. This may have been caused by new and perhaps unexpected expenditure. It may also have been caused by a sheer wish to reap a profit, in order to increase the 'reserves' or make use of the metals for other purposes, such as jewellery or the exquisite ornamentation of palaces.

Debasement of coins is well attested from medieval Europe, called *renovatio monetae*, and Peter Spufford has claimed the following ideal conditions for it to succeed: 1) a government strong enough to enforce it; 2) a sufficiently developed coin-using economy; 3) a sufficiently small amount of coins in circulation; 4) no foreign coins allowed to circulate; 5) new types distinctly different from the previous.[49]

Condition No. 5 will have to be investigated in each particular case, and condition No. 3 is doubtful with regard to the Roman Empire (how can we measure 'sufficiently small'?). The other conditions do apply, however. Even in a weakened position the emperor was powerful and, with the precautions already stated, Roman society enjoyed a widespread use of coins. Without any doubt the emperor's coinages – or their equivalent – were valid currency all over the Empire and no foreign coinage was available for competitive use within the borders.

Coinage debasement was often met with opposition during the middle ages, and a somewhat similar attitude seems to have been taken by the senatorial aristocracy in Rome, although the evidence is scanty and only part of the story.[50] Pliny the Elder has a neutral remark on Nero's debasement of coins.[51] Dio Cassius merely states that Trajan 'caused all the money that was badly worn to be melted down'.[52] Dio's critical judgement of Caracalla's coinage is known in two abridged versions:[53] 'The gold that he gave them (sc. the barbarians) was of course genuine, whereas the silver and gold currency that he furnished to the Romans was debased; for he manufactured the one kind out of lead plated with silver and the other out of copper plated with gold' (LXXVIII.14.4). 'With Antoninus the coinage as well as everything was debased, both the silver and the gold that he furnished us' (LXXVIII.15.1).

Domitian's restoration of the silver denarius increased his financial difficulties,[54] not his popularity, whereas the subsequent debasement by Trajan[55] does not seem to have infringed his reputation as one of the 'good emperors'. Neither event is explicitly mentioned by our literary sources.

Our knowledge about coin debasements in the imperial period is almost exclusively based on modern measurements, and we cannot tell to what extent they were known among the Romans. Scholars seem to have overlooked the observation made by Sture Bolin many years ago that the specific weights of silver and copper lie so close together that the metallic content of the silver coins cannot be measured in that way.[56] In other words, if an ordinary Roman wanted to ascertain the intrinsic value, he had to melt down the coin. Paulus the jurist, writing shortly after AD 200, has a threatening warning about the terrible punishments for doing so (or in any other way damaging the emperor's gold or silver coin). It deserves to be quoted in full:

> … quiue nummos aureos argenteos adulterauerit lauerit conflauerit raserit corruperit uitiauerit, uultuue principum signatam monetam praetor adulterinam reprobauerit: honestiores quidem in insulam deportantur, humiliores autem in metallam dantur aut in crucem tolluntur: serui autem post admissum manumissi capite puniuntur.[57]

It may be argued that the existence of this provision shows us that melting down the silver coins did take place, and we cannot exclude that some dared the risk, for some reason or another, of being 'deported', 'sent to the mines', 'crucified', or 'decapitated' for being caught in and convicted of 'damaging' an emperor's gold or silver coin. It was hardly common within the empire, for which the emperor had an exclusive coin monopoly, also meaning that nothing could prevent him from debasing the coinage, as long as the soldiers and the other populace kept confidence in it.

How much this confidence depended on the actual silver value of the coins, and how much the Roman government cared for the relation to the market value of silver, is a matter of dispute. Contrary to Lo Cascio, according to whom it was an important determinant for the whole imperial period,[58] Dominic Rathbone has declared that it was of minor importance – even when the silver coins during the 3rd century had become a token coinage in relation to gold – as long as the government accepted its own coinage for tax payments 'at the same face value as it had been issued'.[59]

On the last assumption, a coin debasement – with or without an increase of the coinage – might even spiral the economy, and some may have profited if, for example, rents were paid in new coins at the same nominal value as the old. On the other hand, there can be no doubt that debasement had its limits. In the extreme, the Roman government could not, either by decree or in practice, force a population that was used to silver coins to accept mere leaden tokens in their stead. The consequences would have wrought chaos. As it was, successive and repeated reductions of weight and size might – in the long run at least – have caused uneasiness. Be that as it may, it should not be overlooked that, in the short run, adding other metals to a piece of silver may have the effect that the silver will concentrate on the outer surface,[60] thus making the new coin appear more lustrous than the old. However, if the coin ended up having a mere silver wash covering the surface which could easily be worn off, this deceit would be quite obvious to everyone and the psychological effects may perhaps be similar to those caused by the decisions taken between World War I and II to abandon the formal gold standard.

The coin evidence may be of greater worth in this regard than in the discussion of a possible increase in coins for expenditure. If a sequence of hoards shows an abrupt fissure between old and new coins, it may be reasonable to conclude that a debasement has taken place. If the new coins have a lower metal content, and/or lower weight, and are even of smaller size, there seems to be no doubt that a new standard drove good coins out for bad, according to Gresham's famous law, and probably back to the public treasury.

If many hoards were deposited at the same time, they can be interpreted as a reaction to the new coinage: in other words, they represent 'debasement hoards' (as mentioned above). If, furthermore, the new coins continue to dominate hoards of the following period, the debasement can be said to have worked. If, on the contrary, substantial numbers of later coins appear in hoards from the following period, they can be 'follow-up' coins, or be indications of new debasements that were effective to a greater or lesser extent.

We should not forget, however, that Gresham's law may also mean that bad coins may drive good coins into hoards. If, therefore, more than one hoard also contains a substantial – or even greater – number of older coins, the debasement may not have had its full effect. Whereas the new coins were spent on ordinary transactions, some people managed to keep older and better coins for a better bargain.

Ideal prescriptions

If we want a full survey of the variety of types or series from the past, we must go to the coin collections. Some coins are rarely, or not at all, found in the hoards, whereas almost every collection has been built up by the stamp-collecting principle. From that follows, however, what I have earlier claimed as a rule of thumb: 'The higher the number of coins of a given reign in collections, compared to their numbers in hoards, the scarcer the coinage will be'.[61]

If, therefore, we are interested in questions such as the original coin production and varying output, coin circulation and use of coins, public expenditure defrayed in coins and consequences for the economy, possible debasements and so on, we cannot rely on the collections but have to base our investigations on the coin finds, including the hoards.

Contrary to the history of medieval Europe, we have little or no documentary evidence with regard to these questions and therefore have to rely on the coins themselves.

Unfortunately, the hoard evidence suffers from grave defects caused by various infections found in original motives and preferences for hoarding, later survival rates and discoveries. We cannot cure these malaises, but we can remedy their effects by strict adherence to the following, ideal prescriptions:

1. Any investigation must be based upon all completely known and completely described hoards relevant in time and space.
2. Even incomplete evidence must be included, although with caution.
3. The hoards must vary in type and size and all the coins be correctly identified.
4. The hoards must have been deposited in various localities within the region in question and at different times within the investigated period.
5. The hoards must have been diligently retrieved from various sites and at different times of posterity.

Although it is seldom that all of these ideal prescriptions can be fulfilled, some of them may be fulfilled to a greater extent than others. The more these prescriptions are adhered to, the more we can offer possible answers to our questions. The less they are adhered to, the more cautious our answers should be.

One swallow doesn't make a summer, however beautiful it may be. One coin hoard allows no grand conclusions, however convincing they may seem.

NOTES

1. Christiansen (1985), p. 78, based on Mørkholm (1976), p. 102.
2. My additions. An original hoard may have been scattered by later accident or found piece-meal, meaning that the possible reconstruction has to be made with care.
3. See, e.g., Casey (1986), p. 51 and Grinder-Hansen (1992), p. 119. This chapter owes very much to their excellent treatment of the subject, although details and some conclusions may differ.
4. For example, Grierson (1965), pp. If.
5. Adapted from Thomsen (1994), p. 9; cf. also Casey (1986), pp. 11f.
6. *Codex Theodosianus* IX.23.1.
7. Thordeman (1948), p. 192.
8. No one mentioned, no one hurt.
9. Cf. Crawford (1990).
10. Bolin (1926), pp. 179ff.
11. For example, Blanchet (1936) generally; or Skovmand (1942) on Jutland during the Danish-Swedish wars in the 17th century, to mention just two.
12. Crawford (1969), pp. 76ff.
13. Reece (1987), pp. 71ff.
14. As Crawford (1970), p. 45.
15. Cf. Spufford (1988), pp. 382ff. for such a pattern in 13th century Europe.
16. Cf. Crawford (1969), p. 77, now generally accepted.
17. Thus, see Spufford (1988), *passim*.
18. See, e.g., Christiansen (1973/76).
19. Lockyear (1999), p. 220.
20. Christiansen (1988) II, p. 107.
21. Christiansen (1996), p. 93.
22. Beer (1979).
23. See Spufford (1988), p. 30.
24. Buttrey (1993) and (1994).
25. Calletaÿ (1995), quotation on p. 302.
26. Savio (1997).
27. Lockyear (1999). 'Apparently', since I do not understand a word of the underlying mathematics.

28. Thordeman (1948), esp. p. 200.

29. Same, p. 201.

30. Howgego (1990).

31. Luke 20.25, Mark 12.17; Matthew 22.21.

32. Scriptores, *Severus Alexander* XXV.9.

33. Suetonius, *The Deified Augustus* XCIV.12.

34. Suetonius, *Nero* XXV.2.

35. Christiansen (1988) I, pp. 98f.

36. As concluded by Casey (1986), p. 41. Some of his other cases are less convincing to me, but we seem to agree on the general line of argument.

37. Crawford (1974).

38. Crawford (1970), esp. p. 46.

39. Thus, Dio Cassius LII.6.5. and 28.1. Hopkins (1980), pp. 116f. with further references; restated by Hopkins (1995/96), p. 46. See recently Wolters (1999), pp. 211ff.

40. Fink (1971), pp. 241ff.; cf. Christiansen (1984), pp. 279f. See now also Wolters (1999), pp. 216ff. (although without the consequences drawn here).

41. Suetonius, *The Deified Augustus* CI.4.

42. For more details, yet in the same vein, see Wolters (1999), pp. 202ff. Cf. also Rathbone in *CAH2* X, p. 319.

43. Thus, see Tacitus, *Annales* XV.45 and Suetonius, *Nero* XXXVIII.

44. Tacitus, *Historiae* I.37.

45. See Campbell (1984), pp. 165ff.

46. See esp. Howgego (1992), to which I am much in debt for the following.

47. Rathbone in *CAH²* X, p. 319.

48. Parker (1935/1958), p. 280. Admittedly only criticizing Carausius and Allectus, but probably implying that other emperors had a 'better' policy.

49. Spufford (1988), p.94, cf. also p. 93.

50. See, generally, Walker's remarks in III (1978), pp. 107ff., esp. pp. 109f.

51. Pliny, *Naturalis Historiae* XXXIII.13: 'and most recently Nero brought it (sc. the weight of the gold denarius) down to 45 denarii to the pound.'

52. Dio Cassius LXVIII.15.3.

53. Cf. comments by Walker III (1978), p. 63.

54. Cf. Walker III (1978), pp. 117ff.

55. Walker II (1977), pp. 55f.

56. Bolin (1958), p. 197, note 2.

57. Paulus, *Sententiae* V.25.1, quoted from *Fontes iuris Romani antejustiniani* II. Florentinae 1940.

58. Lo Cascio (1981).

59. Rathbone (1993/96), pp. 324f. more or less restated in *CAH²* X, p. 119.

60. So, at least, is the case for the Alexandrian billon coins; see Christiansen (1988) I, p. 13 with references II, p. 29 note 48.

61. Christiansen (1983-84), p. 13.

CHAPTER II

CURRENCY IN ROMAN EGYPT

To Serapion, chief of police, from Orsenouphis son of Harpaesis, notable of the village of Euhemeria in the division of Themistes.[1] In the month Mesore of the past 14th year of Tiberius Caesar Augustus I was having some old walls on my premises demolished by the mason Petesouchos son of Petesouchos, and while I was absent from home to gain my living, Petesouchos in the process of demolition discovered a hoard which had been secreted by my mother in a little box as long ago as the 16th year of Caesar, consisting of a pair of gold earrings weighing 4 quarters, a gold crescent weighing 3 quarters, a pair of silver armlets of the weight of 12 drachmae of uncoined metal, a necklace with silver ornaments worth 80 drachmae, and 60 silver drachmae. Diverting the attention of his assistants and my people he had them conveyed to his own home by his maiden daughter, and after emptying out the aforesaid objects he threw away the box empty in my house, and he even admitted finding the box, though he pretends that it was empty. Wherefore I request, if you approve, that the accused be brought before you for the consequent punishment. Farewell.

Orsenouphis, aged 50, scar on left forearm.

(P. RYL. 119 = *Sel.Pap.* II, no. 278)

The evidence of the papyri

We do not know how Serapion reacted to this request from Orsenouphis dated to AD 28/29. Literally, 'the (items) put in store/hiding', the hoard probably represented Orsenouphis' mother's dowry and is a clear example of a 'savings hoard', one of the many – no doubt the majority of – hoards which were recovered during antiquity, although by another man than the owner. We have no similar examples among the other texts, unless O.Ashm.Shelton 195 is a declaration of the number of coins in the container,[2] which seems doubtful. Anyway, it does not belong to the Roman period, from which the only other sources we have for hoarding are the hoards themselves.

Fortunately, the papyrological material offers other evidence about coins and currency. The many thousands of papyri and scraps of papyri left from Roman Egypt offer a potential knowledge that we do not have for other parts of the Empire and makes it a tempting testing ground for much scholarly research.

In the beginning, modern interest for the papyri was aroused by the possibility of finding literary texts otherwise lost[3] – or indeed even hidden clues to the 'mysteries of Egypt' – and in this regard the Dane, Niels Iversen Schow's publication of the *Chartae Borgianae* in 1788 aroused disappointment by being nothing more than a tiresome account. It was not until later that German scholars in the 19th century (not least Th. Mommsen) and the 20th century (not least Ulrich von Wilcken) began to make other scholars of ancient history aware of the valuable information on daily life, economy, and so on, offered by the papyrus documents.

Whether official documents, private letters, or accounts – they were not meant for posterity, but were the remains of wastepaper baskets and paper being reused for other purposes (such as mummification). Each of them had its own purpose and therefore presupposes and inadvertently discloses knowledge of common phenomena. Orsenouphis complained to the police of robbery of a hoard and by doing so tells us that hoarding took place.

Yet, even today many historians of the ancient world seem to have more anxieties about the papyri than about coins! The papyrological evidence – with very good reason – is regarded as an intangible mess reserved for specialists. No ancient archivist ever arranged the documents neatly in reference files, and neither have they been gathered in modern central archives in which you can look for relevant papers in a special section of interest.

The story of papyrology partly resembles that of the story of numismatics. Since the late 19th century European and American scholars competed in their eager hunt for them. The Egyptian fellahîn soon learnt to increase their gain by tearing texts apart and selling piecemeal. The outcome has been that even original archives and whole papyrus scrolls are often found as scattered remains in many different collections today.

An unknown – but larger – number of texts and fragments have not been published yet, and many publications cause despair. It has not always been considered necessary to make a translation into a modern language, and even well-trained classicists may have difficulty in understanding a language which does not always adhere to modern educational standards, not to speak of strange words, bad grammar, scribal errors, holes caused by insect attacks, and so on. To this add the fact that not all libraries – not even all university libraries – have a full set of publications, or just a useful selection.

Computerization, especially the Duke Databank of Documentary Papyri, has already repaired this situation to a large extent, and there is no doubt that much more will follow. At the present stage, however, it may still be a difficult and time-consuming task to establish a survey of a relevant theme.

Of related interest for the study of coinage is the considerable information about prices and wages found in the papyri, private as well as official. The risk, however, is that information offered by only one, or just a few texts, may not reflect normality, but rather unusual situations such as good or bad inundations of the Nile. As with the coin hoards, we have to gather information from a variety of texts retrieved from different places and at different times. We cannot make a 'statistical yearbook' out of it, but may perhaps be able to discern and compare patterns and trends.

Of special interest is the occurrence of coins and coin terms. We must, however, be well aware that they may be mere accounting devices rather than actual coinage,[4] furthermore they may reflect economic transactions with no coins involved or no payments in cash. It may be clear from the context or the words used, such as *nomisma/nomismata* ('coin/coins'), *argyrion epishmon* ('minted silver'), or *dia cheiros* ('from hand to hand'), that payments were made in actual coins, but such cases are more rare than common, and even then it is not always clear which specific coins were meant nor how different denominations match with the coins we have. Anyway, to call the Alexandrian billon coin a 'tetradrachm' is a modern convention.

All this may sound unduly pessimistic, but like my remarks in Chapter I on the hoard evidence, it is meant as a warning against making too hasty conclusions based on the papyrological evidence, and should not overshadow the conclusions that seem to stand on firm ground. Some of these will be found as arguments in this book, and at least two are of general concern.

It has become increasingly clear that various systems of credit were in widespread use in Roman Egypt[5] (as was the case in the preceding Ptolemaic period).[6] It is also clear now that use of credit was rather sophisticated and implies at least two important consequences for the coinage. On the one hand it will have lessened the amount of coins needed for circulation, on the other hand – as stated earlier – it relies on confidence in valid currency. A system of payments 'on account' can only work if payments are made 'on demand'.

The papyri also leave the clear impression that – in contrast to Orsenouphis' mother – the usual habit was to deposit your money in a bank or with a friend.[7] The original owners would no doubt normally have regained their deposits on request and without problems. If this is true, the consequence will be that the hoards we have will generally reflect 'emergency hoards' and 'accidentally lost hoards' ('purse hoards') more than 'savings hoards'.

The evidence of the hoards

According to C.T. Currelly, who later founded what today is the Royal Ontario Museum in Toronto, the antiquities dealer Dattari told him 'that he had melted down two and a half tons of coins on a single day and at another time almost as many.'[8] Currel-ly's autobiography is not always reliable on details (as autobiographies rarely are), but in fact Dattari, who in the decades around 1900 almost monopolized the market in Egypt for ancient coins, openly declares in his letters to Milne (of whom more later)[9] that he often sends thousands of coins to the melting pot. In an article published in 1900 he claimed that two-thirds of the coins found in Egypt during the previous nine years had passed through his hands.[10]

The story of coin hoards from Roman (and Ptolemaic) Egypt is perhaps more de-pressing than elsewhere. An unknown number of hoards have for at least a century disappeared into the market (or the melting pot) without leaving any record,[11] in spite of legal measures and efforts by the Egypt Antiquities Service.[12]

When I published in 1985 my inventory of hoards of Alexandrian coins,[13] the first ten numbers listed hoards of which the composition is virtually unknown:

A1:   Several hoards (ca. 1850) from unknown sites in the Delta, some containing an unknown number of Alexandrian billon coins and several others containing a likewise unknown number of Alexandrian bronze coins.

A2:   Seven pottery jars (1905) from an unknown site, reported to have contained some 20,000 Alexandrian billon coins.

A3:   3,500 bronze coins (probably Alexandrian) found 1909 during excavations of the Roman baths in Benha (ancient Athribis).

A4:   4,000 Alexandrian bronze drachms[14] (from an unknown site), bought by Dat-tari in 1911.

A5:   An unknown number of Alexandrian bronze coins (from an unknown site), which Dattari heard of in 1918.

A6:   3,500 Alexandrian bronze drachms (from an unknown site), bought by Dattari in 1918.

A7:   3,500 Alexandrian bronze coins (from an unknown site in Faiyûm), bought by Dattari in 1918.

A8:   An unknown number of Alexandrian bronze coins (from an unknown site in Faiyûm), briefly mentioned by Dattari in 1918.

A9:   755 undescribed silver and bronze coins, found 1924 in Tell Sakha (ancient Xoïs).

A10: 80 bronze coins, partly Alexandrian, partly Roman, (otherwise undescribed), found 1925-31 in Alexandria.

Several coins from these hoards found their way into splendid collections, owned for example by Eddé, Huber and Dattari, but now dispersed, and therefore it will be impos-sible to reconstruct their original composition in any way. For an additional – higher

– number of hoards, also now dispersed, we have some brief descriptions, and their evidence will be induced in the relevant sections below.

Some of the other hoards may still lie dormant in Egyptian museums, as I personally noted in 1983 for the following, although some of them may represent accumulated finds more than actual hoards.

A11:   Ca. 900 Alexandrian undescribed billon coins from 1st century AD(?), found 1911 in a terracotta vase in Ihnasya el Madîna (ancient Heracleopolis Magna).

A12:   Ca. 1,508 Alexandrian undescribed billon coins from 1st century AD(?), found at an unknown site before 1969.

A40:   209+ Alexandrian billon coins (Claudius – Hadrian, incl. 142(+?) from Nero's reign) and one bronze coin, found at an unknown date in El-Ashmûnein (ancient Hermopolis Magna).

A56:   88+ Alexandrian billon coins (Nero (33+?) to Lucius Verus) found 1972-74 in Luxor (ancient Diospolis Magna) during clearance excavations at the Avenue of the Sphinxes.

A83:   32(+?) Alexandrian bronze coins (Vespasian – Julia Mamaea), found at an unknown site in the Delta on an unknown date.

A116: 202(+?) Alexandrian billon coins (Nero – the Tetrarchy) and 6(+?) Alexandrian bronze coins, found at an unknown site in the Delta on an unknown date.

A153: Ca. 495 Alexandrian billon coins (late 3rd century?), found at an unknown site before 1969.

A158: 6,427 Alexandrian billon coins (late 3rd century) plus 3 Alexandrian, 1 Macedonian, 63 Ptolemaic, 1 Roman Imperial, 15 late Roman-Byzantine, and 3 Ummayad bronze coins, found 1969 somewhere in Egypt.[15]

Some of these hoards may be published one day, as may some of the following, of which I have found traces and records during my visits to museums outside Egypt:

A18:   Ca. 160 Alexandrian billon coins (Tiberius – Nero), found ca. 1960 as a whole hoard somewhere in Egypt.

A24:   15(+?) Alexandrian billon coins (all Nero), probably part of a larger hoard found before 1940 somewhere in Egypt.

A39:   17 Alexandrian bronze coins (Trajan – Hadrian), found or bought at an unknown date somewhere in Egypt.

A44:   168 Alexandrian bronze drachms (Vespasian – Antoninus Pius), found 1923 in the ground at an unknown site in the Delta.

A50:   51 Alexandrian bronze drachms (Trajan – Antoninus Pius), probably a hoard found before 1934 somewhere in Egypt.

A121: 412(+?) Alexandrian billon coins (Valerian – the Tetrarchy), probably a hoard found or bought before 1866 somewhere in Egypt.

A126: Several hundred Alexandrian billon coins (Nero? to the Tetrarchy?), acquired 1905? somewhere in Egypt.

A151: Some 10,000(?) Alexandrian billon coins (Aurelian – the Tetrarchy), acquired at an unknown date somewhere in Egypt.

One main reason behind the sad story about the hoard evidence from Egypt is that originally the excavators were only looking for the Pharaonic remains, and on their way to them simply cleared the Greco-Roman layers, including possible coins and coin hoards.

Interest in the hoard evidence was mainly founded by one man, Joseph Grafton Milne, and we can date the start of his lifelong occupation with it. In connection with his participation in the Flinders Petrie excavations at Thebes, Milne in October 1895 bought two hoards of Alexandrian billon coins in the Cairo Bazaar. These hoards became mixed on the way to England and from then on have, by necessity, been treated as one hoard (A138).

Almost all the Alexandrian coins carry a Greek numeral (A, B, Γ, etc.) for the emperor's regnal year in Egypt (from late August to late August of the following year according to the Julian calendar). It is clear from Milne's first publication of the hoard[16] that he had become aware that the uneven distribution of the coins on emperors and years might reflect fluctuations in the original coin production.

Based on an additional number of 14 hoards (A36, A60-61, A63, A78, A86-87, A89, A97, A103-04, A109-10, and A140), Milne in 1911[17] was able to elaborate further on this question, adding valuable remarks on the composition and deposition of the hoards. However, no one seems to have been particularly interested.

Joseph Vogt's attempt in 1924[18] to let the Alexandrian coins establish a 'Grundlegung einer alexandrinischen Kaisergeschichte' became much more influential. With a few exceptions (when a type was only witnessed by hoard A92),[19] Vogt based his survey and discussions merely on coins found in collections. The relevance of such a survey is not in dispute, but the fact is that he created a distorted picture of the mint activity in Roman Alexandria and based some of his sweeping conclusions on false ground. Two examples may illustrate that. Anyone surveying his list of known coin-types from Nero's reign,[20] will get the impression that the Alexandrian mint had a much higher production of billon coins during years 3-5 than years 10-12, which is demonstrably untrue! Vogt declares the following concerning the Alexandrian coinage of Septimius Severus: 'Erstaunlich ist nun, dass während der wohl das ganze Jahr 200 ausfüllenden Anwesenheit des Kaisers in Ägypten die Bilder der Landesgötter fast ganz in der Prägung fehlen.'[21] From this he goes on to conclude that the emperor was not really concerned about life in the provinces. It would be more tenable to say, however, that the mint activity in Alexandria during the whole reign of Septimius Severus was astonishingly low, even during his visit to Egypt.

No one at the time seems to have noticed that Milne already had drawn two fundamental conclusions from the hoard evidence: 1) when the Alexandrian mint 'was busy striking tetradrachms, comparatively little bronze was coined', and 2) 'as a rule, the larger the coinage of tetradrachms in any year, the smaller was the number of distinct types used.'[22] From this follows – to which I have added further proof[23] – that several different types of a particular year found in the collections are no indication of a prolific activity and, in fact, may rather be the contrary! In years of large production the mint in Alexandria concentrated on a few specific issues, but in years of a parsimonious striking of coins had time for diversity.

Milne later became acquainted with another six hoards (A54, A69, A92, A98, A114, and A159), and for his catalogue of the Alexandrian coins in the Ashmolean Museum[24] he worked out two tables, listing the yearly distribution of the billon coins in each of the 21 hoards he now knew. The introduction to the catalogue included a section called 'Output of the Mint',[25] which he outlined emperor by emperor and often year by year. He did not make it clear, however, that the tables offered the evidence of his observations on the original fluctuations in the output of tetradrachms, nor that his observations on the bronze coinage were based on similar, although scantier information. Anyway, who cares about a coin catalogue apart from numismatists?

In the meantime, the University of Michigan had begun its excavations (1924-35) in Kôm Aushîm (ancient Karanis). Milne was entrusted with the publication of the first hoard found (A98),[26] but the rest – including 28 hoards of Alexandrian coins – were not published until 1964,[27] twelve years after Milne's death, and added almost a third of the evidence we have today.

Orsenouphis' mother secreted other valuables together with her coins. This habit is rarely confirmed by the evidence of the hoards normally containing nothing but coins. The exceptions are A29 (2 silver ingots and 8 silver bracelets in addition to 1,293 billon coins), A62 (1 ring in addition to 151 billon and 10 bronze coins), and A130 (a fragment of a bronze ring in addition to 33 billon coins), A82 (16 pieces of silverware in addition to 1,800? gold coins), A93 (16 articles of jewelry in addition to 26 gold coins), and A125 (20 gold medallions and 18 gold bars in addition to 600+ gold coins).

We cannot exclude the possibility that finders or museums separated such finds from the coins. On the other hand, the items of silver – other than coins – in hoard A29 (dated to the Roman period)[28] may not have been part of the hoard, but rather belonged to the gold- and silversmith from whom the police confiscated them. If that is the case, though, it is interesting that this phenomenon is virtually only found with gold coins.

Apart from the bronze coins in A62 – and apart from a few bronze coins often found in hoards of billon coins – any mixture of coins is very rare. The proportion between the 755 (Alexandrian?) silver and bronze coins in A9 is unknown. A10 and A124 are interesting examples of 'foreign' and Alexandrian coins found together, whereas A35 remains a riddle. We would not believe that 32 autonomous Greek silver coins had been deposited together with 262 imperial denarii (Nero – Trajan) and 5 silver coins from Roman Cyrenaica, unless Newell expressly stated 'that their patina and general appearance were absolutely identical, and, finally that in one case a Rhodian drachm was still adhering to a quinarius of Trajan.'[29]

The closed currency system

In *Res Gestae* (27.1) Augustus briefly states that he added Egypt to the 'dominion of the Roman people' (*imperio populi Romani*), but according to Tacitus,[30] he secluded it as one of the secrets of his power. Like his Ptolemaic predecessors he was Pharaoh in Egypt, which was administered by an equestrian prefect acting as a 'viceroy'[31] or invested with 'royal power'.[32] The prefect, however, got his command (*imperium*) by a Roman law (*lex*),[33] and Tacitus did call Egypt a Roman province (*provincia*).[34] Egypt was a 'segregated part of the Roman empire',[35] and a 'pocket borough of the emperor',[36] but there is an increasing awareness in present scholarship that Egypt may not be more unique than other provinces were, only that its uniqeness is much better attested by the evidence.[37] The Alexandrian coinage is part of that story.

Whereas previous publications had as a rule intermingled the Roman coins of Alexandria with other imperial coinage, Eckhel, the 'father of numismatics', classified the 'Alexandrian' coins as belonging to Roman Egypt during the imperial period from Augustus to Diocletian,[38] and stated Alexandria as the place of minting, for the plain – and cogent – reason that this was the seat of the Roman government.[39]

Behind Eckhel's assumption lies the fact that bronze drachms were by far the major part of Alexandrian coins known at his time, and among the reverses of these he would commonly have recollected 'Egyptian' or 'egyptianizing' types, such as sphinx or Nilus (see, for example, Plate II).[40] Furthermore, Zoëga in 1787 had entitled his publication of the Borgia Collection as *Numi Aegyptii*,[41] being well aware that Stefano Borgia had acquired the coins from Egypt itself.

On the other hand, that the Alexandrian coins belonged to the imperial issues was clear enough from the obverses, always having the portrait and the Greek names and titles of an emperor (or another member of the imperial house). And the 'Roman' part became much clearer when the billon tetradrachms became known in increasing numbers after around 1800. The majority of their reverses have Roman – or Greco-Roman

– types. By numismatic convention, the 'Roman coins of Alexandria' had become a separate group listed among the Greek series and discussed apart.

A papyrus from 258/57 BC (P.Cair.Zen. 59012)[42] informs us that people coming to Ptolemaic Egypt had to change their own coins and even older Ptolemaic coins into new currency. As stated by Mørkholm,[43] the hoard evidence makes clear that Egypt had become a closed currency system already around 305 BC.

Outside Egypt – or more properly, outside the Ptolemaic dominion – finds and even hoards of Ptolemaic coins are rare and isolated.[44] From this may follow that there was a general ban against bringing Ptolemaic coins out of Egypt (or at least the king's dominion). Since there are no silver ores in Egypt, this precious metal had to be imported, and the Ptolemies might have wanted to retain it within their realm.

Considering Egypt's special status within the Roman Empire, it would be no surprise to see the emperors continuing such a closed currency system. We have no papyrus testifying explicitly to this, but plenty of evidence of strict control at the borders,[45] and the hoards make clear that a currency exchange was entailed.

For my inventory in 1985 I found only 19 complete hoards found outside Egypt and containing Alexandrian coins (373 to be exact), in addition to nine incomplete or incompletely described hoards (containing 268+ Alexandrian coins).[46]

Two of these 28 hoards were definitely not buried during antiquity (A171 and A178), the following eight are doubtful for various reasons (and may even be 'secondary' finds): A163, A169-70, A173, A179, A181-82, and A184, whereas six contain a more or less curious mixture of Alexandrian and other coins (A161, A166, and A174-77).

The six billon tetradrachms (Nero – Lucius Verus) in A162[47] may be an interesting example of a purse lost by an Alexandrian merchant in Ceylon. Otherwise, the coin evidence makes clear that the Alexandrian coinage played no – or at least no direct – part in the eastern trade. In addition to the small hoard, nine stray find coins, reported from Ceylon (one bronze and eight billon, whereof seven from the late 3rd century)[48] and 23 from India (all billon, late 3rd century)[49] do not carry any weight.

Actually there are only three hoards, which, according to the circumstances of find were certainly buried in antiquity:

A171:   Eight Alexandrian billon coins (Nero – Commodus) in addition to one Ptolemaic silver and two Roman imperial bronze coins, found 1896 (or shortly before) in a tomb in a Roman settlement in Buchau, Germany.[50]

A180:   One Alexandrian bronze coin (Augustus) in addition to 39 early and two late Ptolemaic bronze coins, found 1967-68 during excavations in Mirgissa, Sudan.[51]

A185:   Six Alexandrian billon coins (Probus to the Tetrarchy), found 1961 in a late Roman tomb during excavations in Secovlje, Istria.[52]

It may be no coincidence that there is a preponderance of late billon Alexandrian coins among the eastern finds as well as among the western.[53] Irregularities are common in an unruly period; movements of soldiers became more frequent; the small late tetradrachms may easily escape attention; apparently the Alexandrian coinage may have become worthless in Egypt itself following Diocletian's currency reform (see below Chapter 8).

The 13 Alexandrian tetradrachms (Claudius – Hadrian) originally belonging to Louis-Gabriel COR's collection (now in the Musée municipal de Cognac) may be an original small hoard.[54] In 1994 I received a report on a hoard found during underwater excavations at Atlit in Israel, containing three Alexandrian billon (Trajan – Elagabalus) and one bronze drachm (Hadrian) plus three *tesserae* among 35 imperial, five 'provincial' silver and bronze coins and 42 'city coins'.[55] There have been constant oral reports about other hoards of Alexandrian coins found outside Egypt, but even if the reports about 'large numbers' are true, and even if A164-65, A167-68, A183, and A186-88 are original hoards deposited in antiquity, they count for little. Much more revealing is the group of coins bought by the Wiesbaden Museum in 1916: five republican denarii, 10 Alexandrian tetradrachms, two Byzantine 'folles', in addition to some illegible, and even medieval, pieces which were reported to have been found at 'Baustellen', but the composition causes considerable doubt as to the authenticity of the finds ('ganz erhebliche Zweifel'), as remarked by J. Gorecki.[56]

The conclusion is not to deny that some Alexandrian coins left Roman Egypt in antiquity. The conclusion is that they did not do so in *any substantial number* compared to the other evidence we have.

Turning to Egypt itself, Dattari claimed that the majority of the few imperial denarii found and circulating there belong to the Severan period.[57] He published only one hoard (A80) in support of this claim, which may have been prompted by his knowledge of the rarity of Alexandrian coinage from the same period.

In my inventory of 1985 I listed four complete hoards of Roman silver coins (A35, A66, A80, and A122, with end dates AD 117-290s), making a total of 687 coins (of which 150 – in three hoards – or 21.83% from Trajan's reign, and 142 – in one hoard – or 20.67% from the reign of Septimius Severus).[58]

The inclusion of 32 autonomous Greek coins from 322 to 43 BC in hoard A35 remains a mystery.[59] The main point here, however, is that it may have been buried in AD 117 (or shortly after) and also contained five silver coins struck in Cyrenaica.[60] Did it belong to a man who had fled from the Jewish revolt there and was killed during the ensuing unrest in Egypt?[61] If so, a somewhat similar hoard reported found in Egypt and offered on the London market in 1990 or 1991[62] may be explained likewise.

Similarly, the small hoard(?) of seven Judaic coins, including three coins from the Jewish revolt in AD 67-70 (A30) may have belonged to a rebel who in vain had tried to evade his doomed fate, and the 191 small Palmyrene bronze coins in A124 (together with 21 Alexandrian billon coins, Philip – the Tetrarchy) may have belonged to an unfortunate fugitive from Palmyra.

A70 (102 imperial silver coins, Vespasian – Clodius Albinus) is not sufficiently described to allow any conclusions, and the same is true for A10 (80 undescribed Alexandrian and imperial bronze coins), A71-72 (unknown numbers of bronze Greek imperials, especially of Septimius Severus), and A74 (an unknown number of imperial sesterces from the 3rd century AD(?)). Also inconclusive is the one bronze coin of Elagabalus from Antioch in A81 in addition to one Alexandrian bronze coin (Vespasian) and six leaden tokens.

Among the stray finds in Egypt, Milne noted some – although few – Roman bronze coins, especially from Gallienus onwards.[63] They may be accidental losses of no importance (but see below). He also stated, however, that he had never noticed a stray-found silver denarius.[64] Previously, Dattari claimed that Upper Egypt provided Roman bronze coins 'in quantità', most often in 'bellisima conservazione', from the reign of Aurelian to the Tetrarchy.[65] The situation may have changed now, and many more 'foreign' coins – even hoards – may have been found, although they remain unpublished (at least according to my knowledge). Yet, the conclusion is clear: some 'foreign' silver and bronze coins did enter Egypt in the period from Augustus to Diocletian, but *never in any substantial number* compared to the other evidence we have.[66] The stray find groups offer the same picture,[67] which is valid even for reigns, such as Septimius Severus, when the Alexandrian mint struck denarii,[68] which – by implication – were meant for use outside Egypt.

In 1984 I listed 131 papyri (AD 71/72-293/304) mentioning *denarius/denarii*.[69] Several new texts have been published, but none of them has shaken the general picture then given: seven to nine texts originate from outside Egypt; in another 102 texts (mostly military accounts) the denarius is clearly an accounting device; 20 cases remain uncertain. The papyrological evidence thus confirms that the denarius did not circulate in Egypt during this period, and in some texts the *denarius* merely seems to be a reckoning unit, meaning 'four silver drachmae' (the Alexandrian tetradrachm).

We rarely have proof of anything in the ancient world, but taken together, the present numismatic and papyrological evidence makes it more than probable that Roman Egypt before Diocletian's reforms had a closed currency similar to its Ptolemaic predecessor, at least regarding the silver coins. When arriving in Egypt at the border station, you had to change your 'own' coins into Alexandrian tetradrachms, which was the only valid currency inside Egypt itself, and when you left Egypt, you had to change the coins back.

It could be argued against the last point that no one would care to keep such 'billon' coins anyway, since they would not be accepted outside Egypt. I disagree. The many,

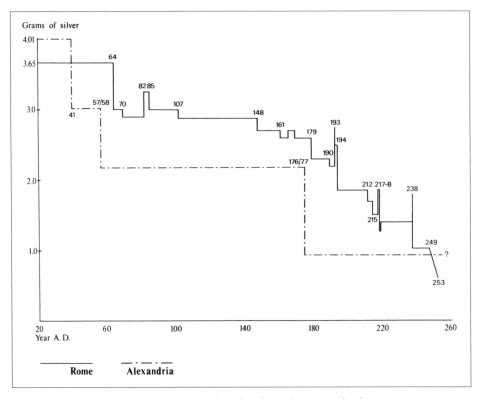

FIG. 1. *Grams of silver in the denarius and in the Alexandrian tetradrachm.*

small, and utterly debased tetradrachms from the late 3rd century should not make us
believe that the tetradrachm of the early period was regarded as valueless by contemporaries.

When the Alexandrian tetradrachm was introduced during the reign of Tiberius,
its weight (around 13 gram) and diameter (ca. 25 mm) was approximately the same as
the Ptolemaic predecessor. Modern measurements have shown *us* that it had less silver,
and that the silver content from the reign of Claudius was even lower than the contemporary denarius of a much lower weight (3.67 gram) and size.[70] To *them*, however,
it might have looked like a good silver coin, considering its size, weight, and shining
surface.

The equation of one imperial denarius to one Alexandrian tetradrachm was an
artificial exchange rate. The earliest evidence we have for that rate of exchange are re-
ceipts for the Jewish tax, issued during the reign of Vespasian,[71] but the rate may have
been introduced during the reign of Claudius.[72] There can be no doubt that this was
made possible by the closed currency system. The Roman government was able to pro-

vide Egypt with a certain amount of silver coins, without spending as much bullion as otherwise necessary. At the same time, the mere size and weight of the tetradrachms clearly marked them as a special coinage.

Contemporaries may not have known and did not need to care about the actual value of the coins as long as the Roman authority guaranteed their nominal value within the area, but even here confidence could be shaken if they were taken outside of the area and their actual inferiority was disclosed. Any closed currency system is built on fiction, its existence may be rumoured but the actual extent undisclosed. Knowledge about the naked facts behind the glittering surface may perhaps be inferred from Midrash Genesis Rabah XXXVII.5: 'The entire coinage of Egypt is thoroughly debased',[73] but the text is late (ca. AD 425?), and it is unclear if any specific coinage is meant, or just the traditionally Jewish dislike of anything Egyptian.

Peter Spufford's 'ideal' conditions for a debasement to succeed (see Chapter 1, p. 27) can now be tested on another ground. Our general knowledge of Roman Egypt gives the impression that the Romans were able to enforce what they wanted, as long as they did not in a too outrageous way offend what were thought to be Pharaonic traditions (and coinage was not part of Pharaonic Egypt, but a foreign element introduced by the Ptolemies). The Alexandrian tetradrachms were distinctly different from the Ptolemaic silver coins in that the obverse carried the portrait of the Roman emperor (or a member of his house), and different from the imperial denarii by sheer size and weight. The numismatic as well as the papyrological evidence make it clear that: a) foreign coins were not allowed to circulate, and b) Roman Egypt enjoyed a developed coin-using economy.

The 3rd condition ('a sufficiently small amount of coins in circulation') is more difficult to test. On the one hand, a widespread system of credit requires a lesser amount of coins available than a system of cash, but presupposes at least a certain amount in circulation. On the other hand, some taxes, especially the poll tax (*laographia*), were to be paid in coins,[74] and this could only be enforced if every fellah had access to actual coins. The coin finds (stray finds as well as hoards) testify to use of coins, although it will remain a 'qualified' guess to compare the actual amount struck and circulating with a total inhabitant figure of perhaps eight million (according to ancient figures).[75] Furthermore, the coinage exchange at the border stations could only work if the supply of coins was 'sufficient'.

We do not know how the system worked before the reign of Claudius nor what happened after the introduction of the 'antoninianus' under Caracalla, but the striking thing is that the Alexandrian tetradrachm, according to modern measurements, kept its own silver rate – always lower than the imperial denarius – also following the debasement under Marcus Aurelius and at least to the middle of the 3rd century (see *fig. 1*). It is still true to claim, as done by West and Johnson: 'This policy of monetary isolation, followed consistently for approximately 300 years, probably represents the longest-lived experiment with a purely fiduciary coinage that the world has seen',[76] or even to describe Roman Egypt as recently done by Kenneth Harl as 'a laboratory where [the emperor] could experiment freely in manipulation and debasing coins'. [77] It does not follow, of course, that this was the aim from the beginning.

The gold coins

Scholars today have become increasingly aware that the Romans may have made use of gold coins for paying or storing high amounts of money. During the reign of Septimius Severus, for example, the Alexandrian mint struck aurei for use outside Egypt,[78] but no gold coins for special use in Egypt. It would therefore be reasonable to see imperial aurei being used; in other words being exempt from, or added to, the closed silver currency system.

We have the following hoard evidence:

A55   (Karanis Hoard No. 4[79]): 60 Roman aurei, all belonging to the reign of Antoninus Pius, found in the courtyard of a house and originally stored in a cloth bag.

A93:   26 Roman aurei from the reign of Antoninus Pius to Gallienus (whereof 16 of Gordian III), found 1930 in 'the Jewish district' of ancient Alexandria together with 16 articles of jewellery.[80]

A125:   600+ Roman aurei from the reign of Severus Alexander to the Tetrarchy (from which at least 572 pieces), found 1902 in the ruins of a temple for Zeus Sarapis in Abu Qîr (ancient Canopus) together with 20 gold medallions and 18 gold bars.[81]

For my survey in 1985 I failed to notice the following hoard:

Ca. 38 aurei from the reign of Septimius Severus, reported found in 1930 near Suez.[82]

To these four hoards, with a total of 724+ gold coins, can be added the following – more or less – insufficient evidence:

A67:   Great hoards, whereof one containing ca. 800 Roman aurei from the reign of Hadrian to Commodus, reported to have been discovered in or around Mallawi in 1901-03.

A68:   Thousands of Roman aurei, found 1930 in Tell Sakha (ancient Xois), the main part of which had been dispersed before the remaining 299 coins – Nero to Commodus, with apparently a preponderance of Antoninus Pius and Marcus

Aurelius – were confiscated and brought to the museum in Alexandria.[83] It is probably the same hoard as the one Regling reported found during spring 1930 somewhere in Egypt,[84] and which according to his report contained some 1,200 aurei from the reign of Tiberius to Commodus, whereof almost 300 were confiscated 'für ein ägyptisches Museum' and ca. 580 sold to America. The Coin Cabinet in Berlin has in its possession 765 plaster casts of these coins,[85] whereof 629 can be dated to the Antonine period, mainly AD 177/178. Most of them derive from the same few dies, which may mean that the main part of the hoard had come directly from the mint and not by way of circulation.

A75:   Four Roman aurei (Antoninus Pius-Septimius Severus) left from a probable hoard found 1897 in El Minya.

A82:   1,800+ Roman aurei from the reign of Galba to Elagabalus (the majority belonging to Septimius Severus) found 1901-02 in two amphorae to the north of the great Ammon temple in Karnak (ancient Diospolis Magna) together with 16 pieces of silverware.

The editors of Karanis Hoard 4 (A55) guessed that it belonged to a Roman officer, 'who brought it with him when he left Italy for his station in Egypt.'[86] It certainly derives from a private settlement, as may also be the case for A93, and the 86 aurei in these two hoards together had a value of three times the total of 687 Roman silver coins in the four completely known hoards referred to above (one aureus = 25 denarii).

We cannot exclude, however, that the gold coins belonged to a public purse or were on transit to India. It may, though, be of more significance that A93 also contained 16 articles of jewelry and that the two largest hoards, both deriving from temple ruins, also contained a substantial number of other precious objects.

The papyrological evidence was summarized by West and Johnson in the following way: 'In view of the fairly large numbers of Roman aurei found in Egyptian hoards, the paucity of references to gold coins in the papyri is surprising.'[87] Even so, P.Mich. 121 verso (AD 42) and BGU 1045 (AD 154) both need a closer analysis for clarification, and the inscriptions referred to (CIG, Nos. 5001-03, 5005, 5007, and 5009-10, dated between AD 232 and 248) belong to a Nubian sanctuary in Kerdassi and not to Egypt itself.[88]

The number of gold coins found in hoards may seem neither greater or smaller than in other provinces, and we cannot tell how much further evidence has vanished into the market without being noticed (although finds of gold coins are prone to rumours at least). Nor can we exclude that the key may be discovered one day among the unpublished papyri. On the present evidence, however, it does seem unclear what part – if any considerable – gold coins or their standard may have played in the economy of Roman Egypt during the period considered here. But one final thing should be added:

even when we know of purchases of gold and gold jewellery being paid for in coins,[89] this does not in itself testify to the intrinsic value of the coins used.

The bronze coins

Judging from size and weight combined, Roman Egypt had five – perhaps six[90] – denominations from Nero's reign onwards.[91] There is almost unanimous agreement on stating the largest size (size I, 34 mm., ca. 24 grs.) to represent a drachm. I have suggested a system equivalating the Alexandrian and the imperial bronze coinage, as T.V. Buttrey has done for the local bronze coins of Cyrenaica.[92] If my system is valid, size III (24 mm., 8.55 grs.) represents 1½ obol unit (cf. Plate II). This is the rate of the *prosdiagraphomena* (the surcharge imposed when paying tax in coins), which was introduced during the reign of Claudius,[93] from which period onwards coins of this size are frequent.[94]

Since, however, the bronze coinage was a minor part of the closed currency system, there might have been no need for an equivalence to the imperial bronze coinage, and it will remain a question of debate how – and if – we should rather associate the four(five) known sizes smaller than the drachm with terms of *oboloi* mentioned by the papyri.[95]

The papyri seem to reveal three systems at work for payments in bronze:[96] a 'silver standard' (directly convertible into the tetradrachm), a 'bronze standard', and another bronze or 'demotic standard' (which died out during the first century AD). Quite honestly, though, I must admit that I cannot understand how this actually functioned.

For my inventory in 1985 I was able to list only 11 complete bronze hoards, found in Egypt. The scantiness and fragility of the evidence is shown by the fact that if hoard A31 is included, we have a total of 627 coins, whereof 343 (or 54.7%) are from the reign of Vespasian. If it is excluded, the total of coins is 323, whereof 62 (19.19%) are from the reign of Antoninus Pius.

A closer scrutiny of the Karanis Hoard 37 (A49)[97] disclosed, however, that it is not a billon hoard, but contained seven bronze coins, one drachm of Hadrian, three of Antoninus Pius, and three undescribed pieces ('kept in Egypt').[98] It was found 'secreted in the wall' of a storage room in a granary, in which were also found many papyri of the late 1st and first half of the 2nd century AD, and refutes the editor's claim that hoard 27 (A51) is 'the only hoard of drachms of Karanis'[99] (see below chap. 3, p. 69.).

As far as I know, only two hoards have been published since then:

During the recent Polish excavations in Alexandria a hoard was found above a late Roman level ('au-dessus d'un niveau romain tardif') in a house of Kôm el-Dikka.[100]

It contained the following – very corroded – 19 coins of the smallest three sizes: one Ptolemaic, five Augustus, two Tiberius, four Claudius, one Nero, one Claudius or Nero, one Domitian, and four illegible pieces. Thus it adds little to our scanty evidence.

In 1987 Michel Amandry published a hoard of bronze drachms from Tanis,[101] which probably derives from the French excavations there in 1935/36. It was found 'dans une construction de brique crue du grand temple…non loin de la chapelle d'Houroun'. Due to their mediocre state, the coins are hardly identifiable from the photographs, and only the following distribution has been given: Trajan = 2+, Hadrian = 6+, Aelius = 1, Antoninus Pius = 18+, Faustina II = 3, Marcus Aurelius = 2, unidentifiable = 8.

Recently, another two hoards were discovered in the Greco-Roman Museum in Alexandria:[102]

A hoard of 65 bronze coins (whereof Cleopatra VII: 12 and the reign of Augustus: 53), found in Armant (ancient Hermonthis) and donated to the museum in 1936.

A hoard of 11 bronze coins (whereof Cleopatra VII: 5, the reign of Augustus: 5, and Domitian: 1), contained 'in einem zerbrochenen Tongefäss' and found during construction work in el-Gaza'r (ancient?) in 1989 together with the right wing of a bronze figurine of Nike.

The known hoards of bronze coins may be divided into three groups. The first group comprises four hoards, which contain Ptolemaic bronze (39) in addition to early Alexandrian coins (116), almost all from the reign of Augustus. This combination will cause no surprise, since the early bronze coinage of Augustus (during whose reign no tetradrachms were struck) was clearly linked to the late Ptolemaic coins.[103] A32, which otherwise belong to the next group, may also have contained four Ptolemaic bronze coins. A62, which otherwise is a billon hoard with end date AD 166-67, contained as many as nine Ptolemaic bronze coins, whereto can be added one small coin in the Kôm el-Dikka hoard above, another in A84 (described below), and a trifle in some of the billon hoards. Apparently, the small Ptolemaic bronze coins had a long afterlife in the Roman period.

The hoards of the second group are bronze coins of size III. A16 contained one Agrippina (reign of Claudius) plus 32 illegible pieces, and A31-33 consisted almost exclusively of coins from the reign of Vespasian (341 out of 343, or 352 out of 363).

The third group comprises seven hoards, having a total of 226+ bronze drachms with the following distribution: Trajan 38+, Hadrian 59+, Antoninus Pius 81+, and Marcus Aurelius 4.

Hoard A84 is a mixture of all three groups, consisting of one late Ptolemaic, seven Alexandrian bronze coins of size III (Galba – Trajan?), and 11 drachms (Trajan(?) – Antoninus Pius), plus one of Severus Alexander. Contrary to the others, the last one was well preserved and therefore condemned as intrusive by Regling.[104] It may, however, testify to a long survival of the early drachms (whereto below).

The third group above gets further corroboration from the insufficiently known hoard evidence: A34, containing ca. 3,000+ bronze coins, mostly drachms Galba – Trajan; A44, containing 168 drachms Vespasian – Antoninus Pius; A46, containing ca. 650 drachms Trajan – Antoninus Pius; A57, containing 2,000 drachms and bronze coins of size III, predominantly from the reign of Trajan to Antoninus Pius; and A83, containing 32(+?) drachms Vespasian – Severus Alexander.

Somewhat more is known about A64 and A66, apparently also belonging to the third group. A64 was bought by Milne from Dattari in 1909 ('Dattari E'09') and contained 1,200 drachms and(?) 100 bronze coins of size III, from which Milne for his own collection selected three of size III (reign of Domitian) and 55 drachms of Trajan to Marcus Aurelius.[105] A66 was reported to have contained more than 2,000 bronze coins, whereof Milne bought 1,100 from Dattari in 1913 ('Dattari B'14') and for his own collection selected 557 drachms and one coin of size II (1 Domitian, 80 Trajan, 132 Hadrian, 269 Antoninus Pius, 75 Marcus Aurelius, and one Caracalla).[106]

Apart from 12 coins, probably donated to the British Museum,[107] the remaining parts of these two hoards were sent to Currelly in Toronto, together with an unknown number of stray finds from Egypt, and it may therefore be interesting to view the main composition of the bronze coins now in the Royal Ontario Museum:[108] Claudius 26 (13 undatable), Vespasian 54 (12 undatable), Trajan 158 (102 undatable), Hadrian 511 (257 undatable), Antoninus Pius 485 (275 undatable), and Marcus Aurelius 58 (39 undatable).

It would be interesting to know the composition of hoards A76 (700 bronze coins Commodus to Caracalla), A77 (3,000 drachms, including many from Caracalla's reign), A79 (85 bronze coins, deposited during the reign of Septimius Severus), and A3-8 (containing a total of at least 14,500 bronze, probably all drachms).

There are at least four reasons for the sad condition of the bronze hoards. The coins of smaller size will most probably have been used mainly for many small transactions and not considered worth hoarding to a considerable extent. Such hoards will have been of inferior interest for posterity. In his letters to Milne,[109] Dattari reported that the fellahîn preferred to sell the large pieces one by one to get a better price, and he furthermore said that he himself only picked out the better and rarer specimens of the lots he was offered. Milne did not make lists of the two hoards bought from Dattari.

Two points, however, are clear. Including the insufficient evidence, we more or less have certain knowledge of 32 hoards with a total of at least 28,200 bronze coins, far more than the seven+ hoards of 3,686 gold coins (including the insufficient evidence) mentioned in the preceding section, but less than 72 hoards with 68,187 billon tetradrachms (excluding the insufficient evidence), mentioned in the following section. Judging from this, the bronze coinage played a vital – but minor – part in the economy of Roman Egypt.

Apart from a small amount of coins of size III, the hoard evidence is dominated by bronze drachms from the reign of Trajan to Antoninus Pius (to a lesser extent, Marcus Aurelius as well). It would be interesting to see how far this reflects the original coin production. Milne found one instance of two bronze drachms that probably derive from the same obverse die,[110] whereas my die studies of bronze coins from Trajan's year 1 and 20 offered meagre results.[111]

Not only the Royal Ontario Museum's collection, but even the finest collections today have a high proportion of worn, undatable, and corroded bronze coins. Even according to the 'stamp collector's principle' (one coin of each type), it was often that only such specimens were available for selection. A main reason may be that these coins had been used again and again for a long period. How long we cannot tell. The latest hoards we know of are A83 and A84, both perhaps deposited in AD 230/31, and hereafter the minting of bronze coins virtually ceased.

Among the Karanis Hoards, which – apart from a few – all had an end date in the latter part of the 3rd century, there are three bronze hoards. Karanis Hoard 27 (= A51, referred to above), has an end date of AD 154/55, but contained a majority of illegible 33 coins,[112] and hoard 13 (= A16) contained only one legible coin (Agrippina/Claudius year 13) among a total of 32,[113] which makes the actual year of deposits highly questionable. Both were found in *insula* 33 and may have been lost during a fire in perhaps 295/296 (whereto see below, Chapter 3, p. 67ff.), and the former hoard was found in the same house as three hoards of billon coins: Karanis Hoards 28 (containing at least 23 tetradrachms with an end date of AD 268/269), 26 (containing 98 illegible pieces and four tetradrachms with an end date of AD 285/286), and 29 (containing at least 3,133 tetradrachms with an end date of AD 293/294).

If 'illegible' in the Karanis Publication actually means worn coins, these two hoards furnish further evidence of long-timed use of bronze coins and at least Hoard 27 may imply that they were available as late as the end of the 3rd century. If so, the billon tetradrachm of Carinus in hoard A53 of bronze coins may not be intrusive after all.

It has been a general assumption that the Alexandrian mint ceased to strike bronze coins when the billon tetradrachms had become so debased that there was no longer need for coins of lower value.[114] This may be true, but the question will be if – and if so, when – the debasement reached a point where the coins were only considered useful for minor transactions, and how then larger transactions were being made. Another explanation may be that the government needed the copper for the debased silver coins.

The need for small change may then have been met by still using the older bronze coins – including a few Ptolemaic, perhaps also some Roman, bronze coins – and probably by leaden tokens (*tesserae*).[115]

The leaden tokens are a difficult group (cf. plate II). Small and fragile as they are, they easily escape even the most attentive eye, and what we have today is no doubt just a tiny part of the original number. Milne published 172 pieces in his catalogue,[116] the vast majority of which derived from excavations in El Bahnasa (ancient Oxyrhynchus) 1897-1908. None of them carry a portrait of an emperor, 44 (Nos. 5276-5319) have inscriptions denoting a town (mainly Oxyrhynchus itself), 71 (Nos. 5320-5390) have types similar to the 'nome types' and therefore – contrary to them[117] – may be local issues, and 19 (Nos. 5391-5417) have dates of year. All of them may have been locally made and meant for local use, but other types have been reported from many other places.[118] In his catalogue Milne claimed that there was no trace of their use in Upper Egypt,[119] but thereby contradicted his own previous remarks on such provenance.[120]

We cannot tell whether they were purely private 'coins' or were authorized – or at least tolerated – by the Roman government. Some of them may have served as 'tickets' or the like.

The next and crucial question is when they were made, and when they were in normal use. We have evidence in two hoards. A15, found in a tomb in Abydos, contained five leaden tokens in addition to six Ptolemaic and two Alexandrian bronze coins, the last of which may give AD 52/53 as date of burial. They were of quite another type, however, and may have served as amulets or the like.[121] A81 contained six in addition to one Alexandrian bronze coin (Vespasian) and one ('a good deal worn') of Antioch from the reign of Elagabalus,[122] i.e. after the heavy debasement during the reign of Marcus Aurelius and the virtual cessation of striking bronze coinage. From the types of the tokens in general, Milne concluded that they were issued between 180 and 260.[123] There seems to be no certain clue to their possible nominal value.[124]

It seems safe to conclude that the bronze coins were a subsidiary, although important coinage, that the older specimens lingered on in use at least for a time after the cessation of striking new issues, but also that their role perhaps increasingly was taken over by the lead tokens.

The billon tetradrachms

In the introduction to his catalogue,[125] Milne declared that the tetradrachm circulated 'more extensively' among the Alexandrians than in the country: 'the peasantry would want bronze, so far as they wanted any coin at all.' This is an astonishing statement, since the stray find evidence, which Milne knew[126] almost as well as we do today, generally shows not only that Roman Egypt enjoyed a high level of monetization (defined as coins being used for money) but also that the tetradrachms were the coins mostly in use for daily transactions.[127] Actually, and paradoxically, Alexandria is one of the 'sites' for which the evidence is too meagre to allow definite conclusions. This is generally valid for the hoard evidence as well.

Milne had 21 hoards of billon tetradrachms at hand for analysis. The Karanis Expedition increased the number by 28. For my inventory of hoards in 1985,[128] I was able to add at least 18 completely known hoards found in Egypt. This resulted in a sum of 68 complete hoards with a total of 73,632 coins.[129]

On the other hand, A90 ('Dattari 3'), A101 ('Dattari 2'), A106 ('Dattari 5'), A139 ('Dattari 1'), and A141 ('Dattari 4') can be excluded, since later investigation has shown that these groups are neither hoards nor remains of hoards. As mentioned above, A49 (Karanis 37) is no billon hoard and has to be excluded as well.

In the *post scriptum* I was able to add one hoard of 15 coins, completely described,[130] and another three hoards with a total of 2,995 coins are sufficiently known to be included here (**A26-27 and A29**). I have recently got detailed information about a hoard of 233 tetradrachms, excavated in 1968 in Abu el-Gud.[131] This makes a total of 72 hoards (excluding **A14**, which is a special case) and – due to correction of totals – 73,638 coins (whereof 68,187 identified Alexandrian billon tetradrachms.

As usual, this is only part of the evidence we have. In the *post scriptum* I also added the Luxor Hoard from 1897 (41 coins) as inadequately published,[132] and there is incomplete evidence of another four hoards with 1,575(?) coins, perhaps deposited during the reign of Nero (A18-20 and A24), three hoards with 1,590+ coins, perhaps deposited between AD 68 and 160s (A29, A40, and A56), four hoards with at least 3,050 coins, perhaps deposited in mid-3rd century (A85, A91, A100, and A102), and eleven hoards containing at least 2,977 coins with end dates during the Tetrarchy (A116, A120-121, A123-124, A126, A129, A134, A137, A151, and A153).

There were at least 22,408 coins in 4+ totally undescribed hoards (A1-2 and A11-12). Of special interest would have been A2, described as seven pottery jars containing some 20,000 billon coins.[133]

Summing up, we have more or less certain evidence of some 100 hoards with a total of at least some 108,000 coins. These totals may be compared with the hoard evidence from the Ptolemaic period,[134] although this may be even more insufficiently known:

Ptolemaic period

Gold: 8 hoards with 488+ coins; silver: 33 hoards with 10,433+ coins; bronze: 17 hoards with 985+ coins.

Roman period

Gold: 7+ hoards with 3,600+ coins; 'silver': 100+ hoards with 108,000+ coins; bronze: 28 hoards with 28,000+ coins.

This precaution taken, Roman Egypt seems much more monetized than its Ptolemaic predecessor, especially regarding silver and 'silver' coins. Admittedly, another explanation could be that the Roman period was more unsettled – whether in political or economic terms – causing much more hoards to be lost. This may be true for the late 3rd century AD, but seems less likely for the early period.

When Milne claimed that 'the tetradrachms were wanted more for wholesale trade and for payment of troops than for the agricultural population',[135] he seems to have overlooked Huber's observation that the billon coins primarily were found in 'native towns' (whereas the early Alexandrian bronze coins were mostly found in Alexandria),[136] and Dattari's remark that he got the majority of his billon coins from Upper Egypt.[137]

Nor does the geographic distribution of known hoard sites (see *fig. 9*) allow for such a view. Admitted the difficulty in distinguishing between town and countryside in Roman Egypt, there seems to be no regional differences. I have no certain knowledge of later evidence of billon hoards than that presented here. In spite of all endeavours, I cannot exclude that some published hoards have escaped my attention, not to speak of hoards found – or rumoured to have been found – without any written notification,[138] and it does seem surprising that there are no reports nor rumours about recent finds. It will be clear, though, from the following chapters that the present evidence is large enough to allow safe conclusions. An additional number of hoards – even large hoards – will not substantially affect the patterns and trends now visible.

We may suspect errors and mistakes in identifying, describing and counting coins in the known hoards. They will not have crucial effects. I did have to rectify some attributions and numbers during the final preparations for this book and – if anything – had only to correct in the hundredths.

NOTES

1. Editor's error for Themistos.
2. As inferred by Foraboschi (1993), p. 333.
3. For the following, see in general, Turner (1968), pp. 17ff.
4. Cf. also Foraboschi – Gara (1982), p. 69.
5. As recently made clear by Rathbone (1991), pp. 331ff.

6. Cf. Samuel (1984).
7. See, e.g., *Sel. Pap.* I, Nos. 71 (P. Oxy. 1039, AD 210) and 177 (P. Fay. 100, AD 99).
8. Currelly (1956), p. 232.
9. On these letters see Christiansen/Easson (forthcoming).
10. Dattari (1900), p. 268.
11. Thus, see Huber (1871), pp. 280f., Milne (1903), p. 529, and Newell (1924) – all based on personal experience.
12. On this point see especially Eddé (1905), pp. 141ff. and Jungfleisch (1952-53).
13. Christiansen (1985). The A-numbers of this article will be used throughout this book for easy identification. In some cases, full or fuller references will be found there only and not repeated here. Bold-faced numbers mean that details will be found in Chapter III below.
14. The conventional term for the largest bronze coins of size I (see below).
15. The promised publication has never taken place due to Abdel Hady El Khafif's untimely death.
16. Milne (1903).
17. Milne (1911).
18. Vogt (1924).
19. Vogt (1924) II, pp. 84, 110, 113, 115, 123, 126, 128, and 137, referring to Breccia (1919) not as hoard-evidence, but for coins in the Museum in Alexandria.
20. Listed in Vogt (1924) II, pp. 8-10.
21. Vogt (1924) I, p. 166.
22. Milne (1911), p. 33.
23. Christiansen (1983-84), p. 12ff.
24. Milne (1933/1971).
25. Milne (1933/1971), pp. xixff.
26. Milne in Boak (1933), pp. 60ff.
27. Haatvedt & Peterson (1964).
28. Wainwright, 1925.
29. Newell (1924), p. 301.
30. *Annales* II.59.
31. Tacitus, *Historiae* I.11.
32. Strabo XVII.1.12 and Ammianus Marcellinus XXII.16.6.
33. *Digesta* I.17.1 (Ulpian).
34. Tacitus, *Historiae* I.11; so also Suetonius, *The Deified Augustus* XVIII.2 and Ammianus Marcellinus XXII.16.1; cf. *eparchia* in Strabo XVII.1.12.
35. Christiansen (1988) I, p. 11.
36. Lewis (1983/1999), p. 15.
37. Thus see Rathbone (1989) and Bowman & Rathbone (1992).
38. Eckhel (1794), pp. 26ff.
39. Eckhel (1775), p. 294.
40. See Christiansen (1988) and esp. (1992).
41. Zoëga (1787).

42. Translation and commentary by Préaux (1939), pp. 271ff.
43. Mørkholm (1982), p. 298.
44. Cf. Foraboschi (1994), pp. 180f.
45. Thus, BGU V 1210.68f. (*Gnomon Idios logos*); but Strabo remarks (II.2.3.5) from personal experience that the watch was 'considerably relaxed' under Roman control.
46. Christiansen (1985), pp. 88ff.
47. Still (1908).
48. Codrington (1924), pp. 36f.
49. Princep (1832), pp. 402ff.
50. Nestle (1896), pp. 57f.
51. Le Rider (1969), pp. 28ff. As stated p. 31, the two late Ptolemaic coins and the one of Augustus may not belong to the hoard at all.
52. Pegan (1969), pp. 259ff.
53. Christiansen (1985), p. 89; but Pegan's conclusions (1969), pp. 263f. are far-fetched.
54. Amandry (1986), pp. 9ff.
55. I am grateful to professor Ya'akov Meshorer (Jerusalem) for this information.
56. Gorecki in *FMRD* V.1.2 (19993/94), p. 414.
57. Dattari (1903), p. 285f. and (1906), pp. 58f.
58. Christiansen (1985), p. 88.
59. Weber's explanation (1932), pp. 5ff. does not sound convincing.
60. For this attribution see now Walker II (1977), p. 113.
61. As also suggested by Foraboschi (1993), p. 335.
62. Report by Richard Ashton in *NC* 158 (1998), pp. 288f.
63. Milne (1908), p. 307.
64. Milne (1914-16), p. 52.
65. Dattari (1900), p. 270.
66. *Pace* Callu (1969), pp. 179ff.
67. Christiansen (2002).
68. Mattingly (1932) and see now Savio (1985).
69. Christiansen (1984), pp. 272ff.
70. Walker I (1976), pp. 15 and 145f. The general conclusions are not affected by Hazzard (1990); se Christiansen (1996), p. 96.
71. Christiansen (1984), pp. 280f.
72. See Burnett in *RPC* I (1992), pp. 688f.
73. *Midrash Rahbah* I, p. 298. I am grateful to Professor Ya'akov Meshorer for this reference.
74. Cf. Wallace (1938), pp. 116ff. and Gara (1975), pp. 10ff. For other taxes paid in coin, see Wallace (1938), pp. 47ff., 135ff., 181ff., and 286ff.
75. Diodorus Siculus XVII.52.6 according to 'those who kept the census returns of the population', but according to I.31.8 the total population of Egypt was about seven million. Seven million, excluding Alexandria, according to Josephus, *Bellum Judaicum* II.16.4 (385), 'estimated from the poll-tax returns'. For a 'qualified' guess, see Christiansen (1988) I, p. 96. I still do not share the view taken by Hopkins (1980, p. 117, note 49) that the number may

be five million or even lower, nor am I quite convinced by the arguments in Rathbone (1990), pp. 103ff.

76. West & Johnson (1944), p. 1.

77. Harl (1996), p. 124.

78. Thus, see Bickford-Smith (1994/95), pp. 54f.

79. Haatvedt & Peterson (1964), pp. 14f.

80. Breccia (1932), pp. 27ff.

81. Among the references in Christiansen (1985), pp. 121f., Dressel Berlin 1926 should be corrected to 1906.

82. Regling (1931), p. 381

83. Breccia (1932), pp. 67f.

84. Regling (1931), p. 380.

85. Schultz (1982), p. 284.

86. Haatvedt & Peterson (1964), p. 14.

87. West & Johnson (1944), p. 70.

88. Cf. also discussion in Johnson (1951), pp. 12ff.

89. Cf. Foraboschi (1986), pp. 121f.

90. As suggested by Holm (1984).

91. For details and discussion see Christiansen (1988), II pp. 7ff.

92. Buttrey (1983).

93. Gara (1975), pp. 21ff.; cf. Christiansen (1979), p. 205.

94. Christiansen (1992b), pp. 101f.

95. Cf. Burnett in *RPC* I,1 (1992), p. 690.

96. See Rathbone (1997), pp. 188f.

97. Haatvedt & Peterson (1964), p. 92.

98. Christiansen (1985), p. 100 should be corrected accordingly.

99. Haatvedt & Peterson (1964), p. 58.

100. Lichocka (1995).

101. Amandry (1987), pp. 73f.

102. I am grateful to Professor Hans-Christoph Noeske (Frankfurt am Main) for lists.

103. See Gara (1984).

104. Regling (1912), pp. 115ff.; 'gut erhalten', p. 116.

105. Christiansen & Easson (forthcoming).

106. Christiansen & Easson (forthcoming).

107. Christiansen (1991), p. 132.

108. Christiansen & Easson (forthcoming).

109. Christiansen & Easson (forthcoming).

110. Milne (1933/71), nos. 2145 and 2156.

111. Christiansen (1988) II, pp. 126ff.

112. Haatvedt and Peterson (1964), p. 58.

113. Haatvedt & Peterson (1964), p. 20.

114. Lately stated by Savio 3 (1997), p. 22.

115. As suggested by Milne (1908), pp. 302ff. and (1922), p. 159.
116. Milne (1933/71), pp. 125ff. For further description and the question of provenance, see Milne (1908), pp. 287ff., (1915), pp. 107f., and (1930).
117. See discussion with further references in Christiansen (1988) I, pp. 227f.
118. Unfortunately, the 11 lead tokens found in Karanis (Haatvedt & Peterson (1964), p. 297, are of no avail, since there is no information about their circumstances of find.
119. Milne (1933/1971), p. xlv.
120. Milne (1930), p. 301.
121. Milne (1914).
122. Milne (1935), pp. 213f.
123. Milne (1908), pp. 301f. and (1922), p. 159.
124. In spite of Milne (1908), pp. 302f.; see Milne (1933/1971), p. xvii.
125. Milne (1933/1971), p. xxxvi.
126. E.g. especially Milne (1922) and (1935).
127. See Christiansen (2002).
128. Christiansen (1985).
129. Christiansen (1985), p. 81.
130. Visona (1983).
131. See chapter 4 below, p. 77.
132. Benson & Gourlay (1899), pp. 286f. and 381.
133. Eddé (1905), pp. 142f.
134. Gathered from *IGCH,* pp. 1664ff.
135. Milne (1933/1971), p. xxv.
136. Huber (1871), pp. 281f. 'im Schutte jener Städte ... deren Bevölkerung eine einheimische war'.
137. Dattari (1900), pp. 269f. Admittedly, Milne's distrust of Dattari's generalizations is well founded.
138. Any such information will be very welcome!

CHAPTER III

THE HOARDS OF TETRADRACHMS: KARANIS

FIG. 2.

Nick-named 'the Miser's Hoard', **A28** is nicely on display in the Royal Ontario Museum. Yet, we do not know the circumstances of its find, and actually the hoard evidence of the billon tetradrachms from Roman Egypt is far from fulfilling the ideal prescriptions outlined in the final section of Chapter One. In order to remedy the defects, I have divided the sufficiently known hoards into four groups: 1) the Karanis Hoards, 2) other excavation hoards, 3) the Dattari Hoards, and 4) other supposed hoards.

I have always been of the opinion that works on coinage ought to present the evidence, before it is analyzed, in such a way that readers may know and check its foundation. For this reason I will offer a brief description of each hoard, including the information we may have of its find. If these descriptions are too tedious to read, I hope they will be useful for reference and future research.

The order will be according to the latest datable coin in the hoards (the 'end date'), which of course is the *terminus post quem* for the deposit, but not necessarily the exact date of this. For each of the four groups, brief lists of contents are offered in Tables I-IV.

The 28 Karanis Hoards have a total of at least 23,222 Alexandrian billon tetradrachms. This is almost a third of the evidence we have in all and therefore deserves special treatment, which will be given in this chapter; the other three groups will be presented in the following chapter.

Apart from presenting the evidence, the main aim is to discuss and compare its general value and then present the scope of the inquiry to follow.

The publication of the coins found in Karanis

The hoards were found during the University of Michigan Excavations 1924-1935 in Kôm Aushîm (ancient Karanis) and all but one (Karanis 1 = **A98**) were published in 1964.[1] All information about each hoard will be reproduced from this publication, but a few general remarks are needed beforehand, mainly based on the preface (pp. V-VIII) and the introductions (pp. 1-9 and 10-12).

Apparently, the main aim of the expedition was to find papyri, the publication of which already began in 1931,[2] and has resulted in many volumes since then. A catalogue of the coins found was originally prepared in 1939 by R.A. Haatvedt as a dissertation. Years elapsed before the publication as a book was handed over to E.E. Peterson as part of his duties as Director of the Kelsey Museum of Archaeology, where the coins were deposited and still are present.

After Dr. Peterson's retirement, the work was resumed in 1964 by E.M. Hussselman, who – as she states herself – is 'a papyrologist, not a numismatist' (p. V). During her preparations for the final publication, she discovered 'many errors and inconsistencies' (p. V). When 'obvious', they were corrected, but some 'inconsistencies' were only changed in the list of types (pp. 361-389), and some incorrect transcriptions of the legends (pp. 390-399) were not corrected at all.

The main part of the publication is a catalogue (pp. 97-355), which gives detailed descriptions of all the coins found, including both 2,049 'single scattered specimens' (in other words, stray finds) and a total of 24,747 (*sic!*) in 38 hoards (p. 10) without distinction of provenance. Fortunately, a description of the composition of each hoard is offered on pp. 13-93, with references to the catalogue numbers, where one has to look for more details. This I have only done to a limited degree, and the main outcome was to discover that hoard 37 (A49) actually consists of bronze drachms, which is not stated in the text (p. 92).[3]

Several hoards contained many corroded or just illegible coins (some 4,500 according to p. 10), some of which a well-trained numismatist might have been able to identify, at least in general terms. Fortunately, their number – or approximate number – is stated for each hoard. Unfortunately, however, no description is given of the some 200(?) 'well-preserved coins, for the most part duplicates' (p. 1), left in Egypt for various museums.

It may be possible, although difficult, also to make a survey of the stray finds from Karanis. For this book, however, I will only make use of the hoard evidence.

The billon hoards

This section offers a brief description of the 28 billon hoards and the circumstances of their find. The order will be the 'end date' according to the latest datable coin in each hoard, and a summary is offered in Table I, listing the hoards by publication numbers.

Hoard 12 (**A17**), end date Nero year 12 (= AD 65/66), 50 coins: 40 Alexandrian tetradrachms Claudius to Nero and 10 illegible specimens.
The hoard was found at floor level, in a corner of a room, in a house within the precinct of a temple. It was originally stored in a small jar, which had been broken into pieces by the weight of the covering debris (pp. 18f.).

Hoard 30A (**A88**), end date Valerian year 5 (= AD 256/257), 40 coins: one Alexandrian bronze coin of Hadrian (size III), five Alexandrian tetradrachms Antoninus Pius to Valerian, six undescribed specimens left in Egypt, and 28 illegible pieces.
The hoard was found in the same *insula* as Nos. 13-36, at floor level in the same house as nos. 25-31, but in another room (p. 70).

Hoard 32 (**A94**), end date Gallienus year 10 (= AD 261/262), 747 coins: one Alexandrian bronze coin of Vespasian (size II), 472 Alexandrian tetradrachms Marcus Aurelius to Gallienus, three undescribed specimens left in Egypt, and 271 illegible pieces.
The hoard was found in the same *insula* as Nos. 13-31 and 33-36 in an underground

room of a house, lying in a pile on the floor without any protection; many coins had 'disintegrated completely' (pp. 72ff.).

*Hoard 14 (**A95**), end date Gallienus year 11 (= AD 262/263), 76 coins: 75 Alexandrian tetradrachms Nero to Gallienus and one illegible coin.

The hoard was found in the same *insula* as Nos. 13 and 15-36 at floor level of the same house as Nos. 15-24. It had been stored away in a cloth bag, which was only visible through the traces of the weave on the 'green patina that had accumulated on the coins', many of which had 'completely disintegrated' (pp. 20ff.).

*Hoard 15 (**A96**), end date Gallienus year 12 (= AD 263/264), 57 coins: 13 Alexandrian tetradrachms Hadrian to Gallienus, 20 undescribed specimens left in Egypt, and 24 illegible pieces.

The hoard was found in the same *insula* as nos. 13-14 and 16-36, in the same house as Nos. 14 and 16-24, and in the same underground room as Nos. 16-20, lying in an 'unprotected heap on the floor'; only a few specimens could be recovered (p. 23).

*Hoard 1 (**A98**), end date Claudius II year 2 (= AD 268/269), 860 coins: all Alexandrian tetradrachms Marcus Aurelius to Claudius II; 11 of these were left in Egypt (but are included in the publication).

The hoard was found under the floor of an underground room of a house (p. 13).[4]

*Hoard 28 (**A99**), end date Claudius II year 3 (= AD 269/270), 36 coins: 23 Alexandrian tetradrachms Gordianus I to Claudius II, four undescribed specimens left in Egypt, and nine illegible pieces.

The hoard was found in the same *insula* as Nos. 13-27 and 29-36, in the same house as Nos. 25-27 and 29-31, and in the same room as Nos. 26-27 and 29. It was contained in a jar, with the top level just beneath the floor level (pp. 58f.).

*Hoard 5 (**A105**), end date Aurelian year 4 (= AD 272/273), 31 coins: 17 Alexandrian tetradrachms Valerian to Aurelian and 14 illegible pieces.

The hoard was found in the same *insula* as hoards 6-7, in the same house and the same room as hoard no. 6. It had been stored in a pottery jar buried beneath the floor (pp. 15f.).

*Hoard 6 (**A107**), end date Aurelian year 6 (= AD 274/275), 192 coins: one Ptolemaic bronze coin, 181 Alexandrian tetradrachms all from the reign of Aurelian; one undescribed specimen left in Egypt, and nine illegible pieces.

The hoard was found in the same *insula* as hoards 5 and 7, in the same house and same room as hoard No. 5 in a 'pile' at floor level (p. 16).

Hoard 7 (A108), end date Aurelian year 6 (= AD 274/275), 22 coins: all Alexandrian tetradrachms from the reign of Aurelian.

The hoard was found in the same *insula* as Nos. 5-6, 'on the sill of the niche' in the wall of a room in a house (pp. 16f.).

Hoard 20 (A111), end date Carus year 1 (= AD 282/283), 127 coins: 55 Alexandrian tetradrachms Claudius II to Carus, 25 undescribed specimens left in Egypt, and 47 illegible pieces.

The hoard was found in the same *insula* as hoards Nos. 13-19 and 21-36, the same house as Nos. 15-19 and 21-24, and in the same underground room as Nos. 15-19. It had been placed 'on the floor without any protection', and an uncertain number of coins could not be 'recovered' (pp. 41f.).

Hoard 31 (A112), end date Carus year 1 (= AD 282/283), 416 coins: 379 Alexandrian tetradrachms Gordianus III to Carus and 37 illegible pieces.

The hoard was found in the same *insula* as Nos. 13-30A and 32-36, in the courtyard of the same house as Nos. 25-30A. It had been stored in a small amphora and 'placed in a bin' (pp. 71f.).

Hoard 26 (A115), end date Diocletian year 2 (= AD 285/286), 102 coins: four Alexandrian tetradrachms Aurelian to the Tetrarchy and 98 illegible pieces.

The hoard was found in the same *insula* as Nos. 13-25 and 27-36, in the same house as Nos. 25 and 27-31, and the same room as Nos. 27-29. It was found in a 'pile' at floor level along a wall (p. 57).

Hoard 36 (A117), end date Diocletian year 4 (= AD 287/288), 2,891 coins: 2,757 Alexandrian tetradrachms Claudius II to the Tetrarchy and 134 illegible pieces.

The hoard was found in the same *insula* as Nos. 13-35, in the same house and beneath the same passageway as hoards 33-35. Although stored in an amphora, many coins had 'completely disintegrated' (pp. 89ff.).

Hoard 30 (A118), end date Diocletian year 5 (= AD 288/289), 1,001 coins: 659 Alexandrian tetradrachms Marcus Aurelius to the Tetrarchy, six undescribed specimens left in Egypt, and 336 illegible pieces.

The hoard was found in the same *insula* as Nos. 13-29 and 30A-36 and in the same house as Nos. 25-29 and 30-31, at the foot of a stairway from the same room as

Nos. 25-29. It was 'stored in a heap', and many coins had 'disintegrated completely' (pp. 62ff.).

Hoard 25 (**A119**), end date Diocletian year 6 (= AD 289/290), 2,329 coins: 2,168 Alexandrian tetradrachms Aurelian to the Tetrarchy and 161 illegible pieces.

The hoard was found in the same *insula* as Nos. 13-24 and 26-36 and in the same house as Nos. 26-31, beneath the doorway between the courtyard and the same room as Nos. 26-29. It had been stored in a jar, broken 'into many fragments from the weight of the covering debris', and a number of coins had 'completely disintegrated' (pp. 54ff.).

Hoard 22 (**A131**), end date Diocletian year 9 (= AD 292/293), 523 coins: 462 Alexandrian tetradrachms Aurelian to the Tetrarchy, 16 undescribed specimens left in Egypt, and 45 illegible pieces.

The hoard was found in the same *insula* as Nos. 13-21 and 23-36, in the same house as Nos. 14-21 and 23-24 and the same underground room as No. 21. It had been stored in a jar 'hidden in a hole dug out beneath the mud floor' (pp. 46ff.).

Hoard 29 (**A133**), end date Diocletian year 10 (= AD 293/294), 4,500 coins: 3,133 Alexandrian tetradrachms Claudius II to the Tetrarchy and 1,367 illegible pieces.

The hoard was found in the same *insula* as Nos. 13-28 and 30-36, in the same house as Nos. 25-28 and 30-31 and the same room as Nos. 26-28. It was stored as a 'heap' on the floor, and hundreds of coins had 'entirely disintegrated' (pp. 59ff.).

Hoard 33 (**A136**), end date Constantius Caesar year 3 (= AD 294/295), 59 coins: one Alexandrian bronze coin from the reign of Vespasian (size III), 47 Alexandrian tetradrachms Probus to the Tetrarchy; two undescribed specimens left in Egypt, and nine illegible pieces.

The hoard was found in the same *insula* as Nos. 13-32 and 34-36, and in the same house as Nos. 34-36 beneath the floor of the same passageway. The coins were 'laid away in a heap', and only a minority could be recovered (pp. 79ff.).

Hoard 17 (**A143**), end date Maximian year 11 (= AD 295/296), 377 coins:[5] 320 Alexandrian tetradrachms Nero to the Tetrarchy, 50 undescribed specimens left in Egypt, and seven illegible pieces.

The hoard was found in the same *insula* as Nos. 13-16 and 18-36, in the same house as Nos. 14-16 and 18-24 and the same underground room as Nos. 15-16 and 18-20. It had been stored in 'a small amphora at floor level'. The editors suggested that 'the hoard was the work of an amateur coin collector of the late third century', which I very much doubt. They based this on the composition, being only one coin of Nero, single specimens Antoninus Pius – Marcus Aurelius, and then coins of almost every emperor 'with less than a third of the types being represented by more than one specimen'. More than two-thirds, however, are represented by two to nine specimens, which is very unlikely for a deliberate selection of coins (pp. 27ff.).

Hoard 18 (**A144**), end date Constantius/Galerius year 4 (= AD 295/296), 2,484 coins: 2,472 Alexandrian tetradrachms Aurelian to the Tetrarchy and 12 illegible pieces.

The hoard was found in the same *insula* as Nos. 13-17 and 19-36, in the same house as Nos. 14-17 and 19-24 and the same underground room as Nos. 15-17 and 19-20. It had been stored in a large jar (pp. 33ff.).

Hoard 19 (**A145**), end date Diocletian year 12 (= AD 295/296), 1,439 coins: 1,279 Alexandrian tetradrachms Claudius II to the Tetrarchy and 160 illegible pieces.

The hoard was found in the same *insula* as Nos. 13-18 and 20-36, in the same house as Nos. 14-18 and 20-24 and the same underground room as Nos. 15-18 and 20. It was 'laid away in a heap' (pp. 37ff.).

Hoard 21 (**A146**), end date Diocletian year 12 (= AD 295/296), 762 coins: 617 Alexandrian tetradrachms Aurelian to the Tetrarchy and 145 illegible pieces.

The hoard was found in the same *insula* as Nos. 13-20 and 22-36, in the same house as Nos. 14-20 and 22-24 and the same underground room as No. 22. It had been stored in a jar (pp. 42ff.).

Hoard 23 (**A147**), end date Diocletian year 12 (= AD 295/296), 1,486 coins: 1,010 Alexandrian tetradrachms Aurelian to the Tetrarchy and 476 illegible pieces.

The hoard was found in the same *insula* as Nos. 13-22 and 24-36, in an underground room of the same house as Nos. 14-22 and 24. It had been placed 'on the floor' in a cloth bag, 'leaving only a trace of the weave on the mass of the coins' (pp. 48ff.).

Hoard 24 (**A148**), end date Diocletian year 12 (= AD 295/296), 1,489 coins: 1,021 Alexandrian tetradrachms Aurelian to the Tetrarchy and 468 illegible pieces.

The hoard was found in the same *insula* as Nos. 13-23 and 25-36, in an underground room of the same house as Nos. 14-23. It lay in a 'heap' on the floor, and many of the coins had 'disintegrated completely' (pp. 51ff.).

Hoard 34 (**A149**), end date Maximian year 11 (= AD 295/296), 2,944 coins: 2,782 Alexandrian tetradrachms Aurelian to the Tetrarchy and 162 undescribed specimens left in Egypt.

The hoard was found in the same *insula* as Nos. 13-33 and 35-36, in the same passageway of the same house as Nos. 33 and 35-36. It had been stored in an amphora, and 'very few' of the coins had disintegrated.

Hoard 35 (**A150**), end date Diocletian year 12 (= AD 295/296), 1,479 coins:[6] 1,418 Alexandrian tetradrachms Aurelian to the Tetrarchy and 81 illegible pieces.

The hoard was found in the same *insula* as Nos. 13-34 and 36, in the same passageway of the same house as Nos. 33-34 and 36. It had been stored in an amphora placed 'below the floor'. A 'number of specimens were kept in Egypt', and it is unclear whether they are included in the described coinage or not.

Hoard 16 (**A152**), end date Diocletian year 12 (= AD 295/296), 1,103 coins: 931 Alexandrian tetradrachms Valerian to the Tetrarchy and 172 illegible pieces.

The hoard was found in the same *insula* as Nos. 13-15 and 17-36, in the same house as Nos. 14-15 and 17-24 and the same underground room as Nos. 15 and 17-20. It had been stored in a cloth bag, 'leaving only traces of the pattern of the weaving in the green deposit that covered the coins' (pp. 23ff.).

The setting of the hoards

B.P. Grenfell and A.S. Hunt had excavated in Karanis in 1896-97, which resulted among other things in hoard **A63** (containing 98 Alexandrian tetradrachms with an end date AD 169/170). After they left the place, the *sebakhin* moved in, digging for fertilizer, and when the Americans arrived, they discovered that this had almost completely destroyed 'the central and most ancient section of the city' (p. 1). According to the editor, this is the reason why so few Ptolemaic coins were found during the Michigan campaigns. There were two hoards (Nos. 10-11), found in 'a typical house of the late Ptolemaic period' and containing respectively 12 and 35 bronze coins, nearly all illegible (p. 18).

The same reason may be the explanation why so little coinage was found from the early Roman period. There were only three early hoards, found in three different places (see *fig. 3*): hoard 12 (**A17**), end date AD 65/66, containing 50 Alexandrian tetradrachms; hoard 37 (A49), end date AD 152/153, containing seven Alexandrian bronze drachms; hoard 4 (A55), end date AD 156/157, containing 60 imperial gold coins.

The editor concludes, from the excavations themselves and from the papyri found, that the city had 'attained its greatest growth by the middle or latter part of the second century', during the 3rd century had 'periods of decline and rebuilding', and 'suffered severely in the fourth century' (p. 2).

The evidence of the billon hoards is skewed. One hoard has an end date of AD 65/66, four have end dates between 256/57 and 263/64, seven between 268/69 and 282/83, and sixteen during the Tetrarchy (9 of these in AD 295/296), in other words 27 out of 28 hoards belong to the latter part of the 3rd century.

At a closer look, the picture narrows further. Whereas hoard 1 (A98), end date AD 268/269, and hoard 12 (A17), end date AD 65/66, are isolated hoards, hoards 5-7 (A 105 and A 107-108) were discovered in the same building complex (*insula* 27) in the northeastern section of the town, and Nos. 5-6 even in the same house. Judging from the many objects of glass, wood, cloth, rope, bronze, and pottery also recovered, the editors concluded that this had been 'the home of a comparatively well-to-do family' (p. 15). 31 and 192 coins in two hoards – all, except one Ptolemaic bronze coin, probably Alexandrian tetradrachms – do not sound like a high number, but may rather be two 'purses' for daily payments.

Hoard 7 was found in another house in a room, which was 'particularly productive of papyri, ostraca, wood, bronze, and other articles of daily household use'; a sum of 22 Alexandrian tetradrachms is compatible with this picture.

All three hoards have end dates during Aurelian's year 4-6 and may therefore belong to the same event.

All the other billon hoards were found in the same building complex (*insula* 33) in the southern section of the town (see *figs.* 3-4) during the excavation season of 1933-34. Ashes 'scattered throughout the rooms' and many of the mud brick walls being 'scorched red by fire' (p. 20) clearly show that the complex was destroyed by a heavy fire.

The hoards derive from four houses:

House 'B501'   11 hoards

'Room C': One hoard = No. 14 (A95), 75 tetradrachms from Nero to AD 262/263.
'Underground room G': Six hoards.
No. 15 (A96), at least 13 tetradrachms from Hadrian to AD 263/264.
No. 16 (A152), at least 931 tetradrachms from Valerian to AD 295/296.
No. 17 (A143), at least 320 tetradrachms from Nero to AD 295/296.
No. 18 (A144), at least 2,472 tetradrachms from Aurelian to AD 295/296.
No. 19 (A145), at least 1,279 tetradrachms from Claudius II to AD 295/296.
No. 20 (A111), at least 85 tetradrachms from Claudius II to AD 282/283.
'Underground room H': Two hoards.
No. 21 (A146), at least 617 tetradrachms from Aurelian to AD 295/296.
No. 22 (A131), at least 462 tetradrachms from Aurelian to AD 292/293.
'Underground room J': One hoard = No. 23 (A147), at least 1,010 tetradrachms from Aurelian to AD 295/296.
'Underground room N' One hoard = No. 24 (A148), at least 1,021 tetradrachms from Aurelian to AD 295/296.

If all these eleven hoards once belonged to the same owner, he must have been a wealthy man with a lot of money lying around.

'House B514' Seven hoards

'Room A': Three hoards.
No. 26 (**A115**), 102 coins (only four tetradrachms identified, from Aurelian to AD 285/286).
No. 28 (**A99**), at least 23 tetradrachms from Gordianus I to AD 269/270.
No. 29 (**A133**), at least 3,133 tetradrachms from Claudius II to AD 293/294.
Between 'Room A' and the courtyard: One hoard = No. 25 (**A119**), at least 2,168 tetradrachms from Aurelian to AD 289/290.
'Room A', at the foot of a stairway leading up to the second floor: One hoard = No. 30 (**A 118**), at least 659 tetradrachms from Marcus Aurelius to AD 288/289. Hoard No. 27 (bronze coins) was found in the same room.
'Room D': One hoard = No. 30A (**A88**), 40 coins, mostly illegible apart from five tetradrachms from Hadrian to AD 256/257.
The courtyard: One hoard = No. 31 (**A112**), at least 379 tetradrachms from Gordianus III to AD 282/283.

Here again, the owner must have been a wealthy man if all the hoards had belonged to him.

'House C414' One hoard

'Underground room F' = No. 32 (**A94**), at least 472 tetradrachms from Marcus Aurelius to AD 261/262.

'House C418', 'passageway' Four hoards

No. 33 (**A136**), at least 47 tetradrachms from Probus to AD 294/295.
No. 34 (**A149**), at least 2,782 tetradrachms from Aurelian to AD 294/295.
No. 35 (**A150**), at least 1,418 tetradrachms from Aurelian to AD 294/295.
No. 36 (**A117**), at least 2,757 tetradrachms from Claudius II to AD 287/288.

These four hoards may also have belonged to a wealthy man.

In spite of the different dates of the latest datable coin, it seems appropriate to suppose that the loss of all these hoards was caused by the same fire, which devastated the whole building complex. No other objects are reported to have been found – which sounds incredible – and we have only the hoards to date the fire. This may have taken place in – or perhaps shortly after – AD 295/296.

Even if the fire took place at a later date, all 23 hoards deriving from *insula* 33 may in any case represent the coinage available for hoarding at the time of Diocletian's coin reform. If that is right, it is particularly interesting to find two hoards of bronze coins along with them. Hoard 27 (A51) was found 'at floor level' in the same house as hoards Nos. 25-26 and 28-31 and in the same room as Nos. 26 and 28-29. As stated above (see Chap. 2, p. 51), it may represent older bronze coins still in use during the late 3rd century. Hoard 13 (A13), however, is an isolated hoard, found in 'the earliest level of occupation' in another house in 'a heap on the floor of an underground room' (p. 20).

A total overview of find circumstances can also be revealing. The twelve hoards found in underground rooms may reasonably be considered to be 'savings hoards', especially the six which had been stored in an amphora (No. 17), a cloth bag (Nos. 16 and 23), in a jar (No. 21), a large jar (No. 18), or even in a jar 'in a hole dug out beneath the mud floor' (No. 22, on p. 46). Their sizes vary from 320 to 2,472 coins, and all but one of the six are composed of tetradrachms from the latter part of the 3rd century, with a preponderance of coins from the Tetrarchy. The exception is the smallest one, No. 17, which contains a few early tetradrachms and has a preponderance of coins from the reign of Valerian.

The other six hoards from underground rooms were found in a 'heap' or 'pile' on the floor (as is the case for Nos. 13 (bronze coins), 15, 19-20, 24, and 32). One may guess that an original container (for instance a basket) had perished during the fire. Apart from the bronze hoard, they vary in size from 57 to 1,489 coins. No. 15, the smallest hoard, contains too few legible coins to be of value in this connection. Hoard 32 contains some early tetradrachms and has a preponderance of coins from the reign of Valerian. The other three hoards are composed of tetradrachms from the latter part of the 3rd century, with a preponderance of coins from the reign of Probus in No. 20 and of the Tetrarchy in the other two.

Thus a comparison between these two groups discloses no clear distinction between their composition.

The hoards discovered beneath the floor of a passageway may likewise have been 'savings hoards', especially the three that had been stored in an amphora (Nos. 34-36). Their sizes vary from 1,418 to 2,782 coins, and all three are composed of coins from the latter part of the 3rd century, with a preponderance of coins from the Tetrarchy. The same is true for No. 33, the small hoard found in 'a heap'.

Similar cases are jars, either buried beneath the doorway of a room and the courtyard (hoard No. 25) or just beneath floor level (hoard No 28), and a small amphora placed in a bin in the courtyard (No. 31). They vary in size from 23 to 2,168 and are

FIGS. 3. *Map of the Karanis excavations. Find sites of hoards 1-37.*

exclusively composed of coins from the latter part of the 3rd century, with a preponderance of coins of Claudius II (two hoards) or Probus (one hoard).

If all these hoards are 'savings hoards', it would be highly revealing to find so many
coins from the latter part of 3rd century AD deposited for such purpose. Another,
but less plausible explanation would be that the owners for some reason or another
took fright, in a hurry buried their coins ('emergency hoards') in as many safe places

as they could manage, and fled from the buildings, which were then destroyed by arson.

There remain the hoards found at floor level in an ordinary room, either in a cloth bag (No. 14) or simply as a 'pile' or a 'heap' (Nos. 26, 27 (bronze coins), 29-30, and 30A). Did they have an original container, which burnt? Had they fallen down from a more secret place in the upper stores when the fire destroyed the floor? Or should we rather imagine the owners feverishly gathering their coins but having to abandon their attempt? If so, the groups can be considered to represent 'emergency hoards'.

Hoards 26 and 30A contain too few legible coins to be of value in this connection, and No. 27 is a bronze hoard. The other three vary in size from 75 to 4,500 coins. The smallest hoard (No. 14) has a high percentage of tetradrachms from before the de-basement during the reign of Marcus Aurelius. The largest hoard (No. 29) exclusively contains coins from the latter part of the 3rd century, with a preponderance of coins from the reign of Probus and the Tetrarchy. The third hoard (No. 30) contained some early tetradrachms, but a majority from the 3rd century with a preponderance of coins from the reign of Valerian.

If early tetradrachms were considered to be more valuable than the coins from the 3rd century, then especially hoard 14 (found in 'a cloth bag') could be said to disclose signs of being a 'savings hoard'. However, composition and circumstances of find taken together, the general conclusion will be that the evidence of the 23 billon hoards from *insula* 33 in Karanis provides no certain basis for a distinction between different types of hoards.

A more puzzling question will be why so many hoards from one place remained unrecovered. Were all the inhabitants – or at least those who knew of the hoards – burnt to death during the fire, leaving only their ashes? Or did the scarce skeleton remains escape the excavators' attention? Had the inhabitants been killed or deported after the fire, or had they all been away and for some reason debarred from entering their houses on return? Were they not able to, or did they not care? Did they or maybe plunderers only remove the more valuable objects (of which there is no trace).

If the whole town had been destroyed at the same time, we would have had some plausible answers to such questions, but this is not the end date of Karanis, and there are no archaeological reports of other buildings caught by the fire.

A tempting idea would be to imagine the building complex as a bank or houses owned by three money-exchangers, who at the time of Diocletian's coin reform had received the now obsolete Alexandrian coins from their clients, but did not manage to make the exchange for the new coinage in due time, or were cheated by the govern-ment. If that is the right explanation, they probably represent the highest number of 'debasement hoards' ever found.

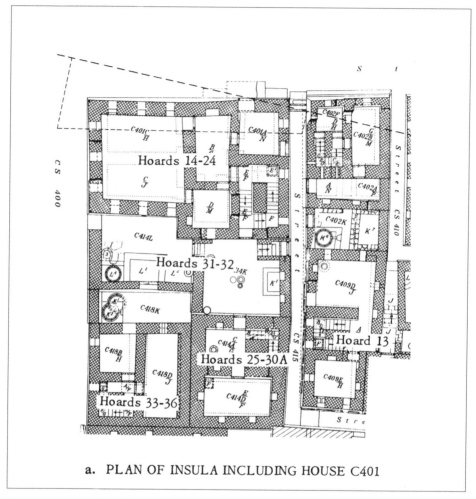

a. PLAN OF INSULA INCLUDING HOUSE C401

FIG. 4. *Karanis: plan of insula including house C401. Find sites of hoards 14-36.*

Concluding remarks

The 28 Karanis Hoards, containing at least 23,222 Alexandrian tetradrachms in varying totals, constitute a valuable group of coin evidence, not only due to sheer totals but also to the fact that the exact circumstances of find are well attested for each hoard.

There are a number of inconsistencies and errors in the publication, mainly due to the protractedness of completing a project performed by different hands. To this add the fact that the coins that are left in Egypt remain undescribed, and that a well-trained numismatist might have been able to identify a higher proportion of the coins labelled 'illegible'.

The evidence is skewed regarding period of time, which does not distract from its value for analysing the coinage of the late 3rd century AD.

The find circumstances, however, disclose a somewhat narrow picture. Three rather small billon hoards, from two neighboring houses, may belong to one event in AD 274/275. Another 23 derive from three houses – and perhaps from only three fairly wealthy men – all belonging to one building complex, which – according to the archaeological records – was destroyed by a heavy fire in AD 295/296 or shortly thereafter. A closer investigation of the original excavation reports may perhaps elucidate these questions further. For the purpose of this book, however, it will be enough to conclude that the original reports should make us cautious about coming to general conclusions from the Karanis evidence, unless corroborated by other evidence, to which I shall direct attention in the next chapter.

NOTES

1. Haatvedt & Peterson (1964).
2. Edgar (1931).
3. Christiansen (1985), p. 100 should be corrected accordingly.
4. Full publication by Milne in Boak (1933), pp. 60ff.
5. 379 is an error. The sum of the Alexandrian tetradrachms makes 320, not 322.
6. 1,419 is an obvious misprint.

CHAPTER IV

OTHER HOARDS OF TETRADRACHMS

In Egitto i ritrovi di monete se fanno sempre pui rari e non astante che bene poco sfugga dalle mie mani, cio nondimeno no ho potate raccogliere che poca roba.

Thus Dattari wrote in a letter of 9th August 1920, when he finally was able to fulfil his promise of donating a complete collection of Alexandrian coins to the Coin Cabinet in Rome.[1] Actually, the donation of 1,739 coins[2] makes up much more than a *poca roba* ('a small assemblage'), yet is not quite as magnificent as the selections of coins he had previously been able to acquire. Dattari seems to have lost the firm grip on the Egyptian market for ancient coins that he had enjoyed for decades.

For obvious reasons, the 'Dattari Hoards', presented in the second section of this chapter, form a coherent group, whereas there is not always a clearcut distinction between the other two groups ('other excavation hoards' and 'other supposed hoards') presented in the other two sections. Thus, for example, A28 (the 'Miser's Hoard') is reported to have been acquired in the wine-amphora now on display in the Royal Ontario Museum (see *fig. 2*), but we do not know when, where, or by whom it was found.[3] On the other hand, A92, also contained in a *terra cotta* vase, was dug out from a hole in the sandstone during construction works in Alexandria in 1916, but there are no traces of the original context. Furthermore, Breccia (publishing the hoard) found reason to suspect that some of the construction workers or onlookers had stolen some of the coins before the hoard came to the Museum in Alexandria.[4]

For each of the three groups the hoards will be presented in the same order and on the same lines as in the preceding chapter, ending with conclusions concerning their general value as evidence. The final section will delineate the possibilities and scope for analysing the hoard evidence as a whole.

Other excavation hoards

By an 'excavation hoard' is meant a hoard for which we have sufficient, certain knowledge about circumstances of find. This is the case for the following (for a summary, see table II, listing the hoards by name in alphabetical order).

Hoard **A25**,[5] end date Galba year 1 (= AD 68), 230 coins: 172 Alexandrian tetradrachms Nero to Galba and 57 illegible (mostly Nero).

The French Institute of Cairo found the hoard in a jar during the excavation of a house in El-Madâmûd (ancient Madit), probably in 1928. Unfortunately, the site was soon demolished and the other evidence 'bouleversé'.

Hoard **A36**,[6] end date Hadrian year 12 (= AD 127/128), 62 coins: Alexandrian tetradrachms Claudius to Hadrian.

The hoard ('Kôm el-Asl Hoard II') was found during excavations by B.P. Grenfell, A.S. Hunt, and D.G. Hogarth in Kôm el-Asl (ancient Bacchias) in 1895-96,[7] when **A60** was also found. There is no further information about the circumstances of the find.

Hoard **A37**,[8] end date Hadrian year 13 (= AD 128/129), 216 coins: Alexandrian tetradrachms Claudius to Hadrian.

The hoard was found – together with 'un blocco di bronzi agglomerati e ossidato' – under floor level in a late Roman house, during excavations by the 'Società Italiana per la ricerca dei papiri greci e latino in Egitto' in El-Hîba (ancient Ancyronpolis) in 1934-35. In the house itself some Ptolemaic bronze coins and late Alexandrian tetradrachms were also found, but the description does not make it clear if they were found together.

Hoard **A47**,[9] 14 coins: 13 Alexandrian tetradrachms Nero to Hadrian with end date Hadrian year 19? (= AD 134/135) and one undescribed Alexandrian bronze coin of Antoninus Pius year?

The hoard ('Umm el-Breigat 4') was marked as 'found together' during excavations in 1900 in Tell Umm el-Breigât (ancient Tebtunis), where **A42** and **A52** were also found and two Ptolemaic hoards (140 'base-silver tetradrachms, respectively 107 small bronze coins).

Hoard **A42**,[10] end date Antoninus Pius year 2 (= AD 138/139), 28 coins: Alexandrian tetradrachms Claudius to Antoninus Pius.

The coins were 'all stuck together' and therefore probably the 'equivalent of a hoard' ('Umm el-Breigât 5'). It was found during excavations in 1900 in Tell Umm el-Breigât (ancient Tebtunis), where **A47** and **A52** were also found and two Ptolemaic hoards (140 'base-silver tetradrachms', 107 small bronze coins, respectively).

Hoard **A43**,[11] end date Antoninus Pius year 7 (= AD 143/144), 237 coins: Alexandrian tetradrachms Claudius to Antoninus Pius.

The hoard was found in a house during the German excavations in El-Hîba (ancient Ancyronpolis) in 1913-14. It was contained in two bags, which got mixed up during later transport. Uxkull-Gyllenband, the editor, suggested that 173 coins from Claudius to Titus were contained in one of the bags, whilst 64 coins were in the other bag, but he does not make clear if the bags were found together or at different places. The group will be treated here as one hoard.

Hoard A45,[12] end date Antoninus Pius year 13 (= AD 149/150), 102 coins: Alexandrian tetradrachms Claudius to Antoninus Pius.

The hoard was found in the foundation of a house during Egyptian excavations in El-Manshâh (ancient Ptolemais Hermiou) in 1968.

Hoard A52,[13] end date Antoninus Pius year 19 (= AD 155/156), 119 coins: Alexandrian tetradrachms Nero to Antoninus Pius.

The hoard ('Umm el-Breigât 3') was found during excavations in 1900 in Tell Umm el-Breigât (ancient Tebtunis), where A42 and 47 were also found and two Ptolemaic hoards (140 'base-silver tetradrachms', and 107 small bronze coins, respectively).

Hoard A60,[14] end date Marcus Aurelius year 5 (= AD 164/165), 4,426 coins: two Ptolemaic bronze coins, one Alexandrian bronze drachm of Antoninus Pius, and 4,423 Alexandrian tetradrachms Claudius to Marcus Aurelius.

The hoard ('Kôm el-Asl 1') was found in three large amphorae dug out of the cellar of a house during excavations by B.P. Grenfell, A.S. Hunt, and D.G. Hogarth in Kôm el-Asl (ancient Bacchias) in 1895-96[15] when A36 was also found.

Hoard A62,[16] end date Marcus Aurelius year 7 (= AD 166/167), 160 coins: three Ptolemaic bronze coins, seven Alexandrian bronze coins (one of Hadrian, size III and six undescribed), 86 Alexandrian tetradrachms Nero to Marcus Aurelius, 64 illegible coins, and one ring.

The hoard (Mallawi 'K') is reported to have been found in an alabaster container dated to ca. 300 BC (sic!) during excavations in 1977 in Mallawi (ancient?) by the Egypt Exploration Society, at which time A128 was also found. It was mixed up with another hoard of some 130 coins, which have not been identified. There is no further information about their circumstances of find.

Hoard A63,[17] end date Marcus Aurelius year 10 (= AD 169/170), 98 coins: Alexandrian tetradrachms Claudius to Marcus Aurelius.

The hoard[18] was found in a small pot in a house, during excavations by B.P. Grenfell, A.S. Hunt, and D.G. Hogarth in Kôm Aushîm (ancient Karanis) in 1895/1896. In the same house many 'broken scraps of papyrus' were found and a number of small objects.[19]

Hoard **AX1**,[20] end date Philip I year 4 (= AD 246/247), 229 Alexandrian tetradrachms Nero to Philip and four illegible.

The hoard was found during construction work in Abu el-Gud (near Luxor) 'als Korrosionsklumpen geborgene Schatz' in 1968 and came to The Greco-Roman Museum in the same year. A preliminary publication in Arabic from 1995 will be superseded by a forthcoming publication in German.

Hoard **A92**,[21] end date AD Gallienus year 9 (= 260/261), ca. 1,300 coins: 1,184 Alexandrian tetradrachms Vespasian to Gallienus and some 100 illegible.

The hoard was found in 'un ordinario vaso di terra cotta' in a fairly deep hole, dug out in the sandstone, during construction work in Alexandria in 1916. There were no traces of the original context. As stated above, Breccia suspected that some of the coins had been picked out before the hoard came to the museum.

Hoard **A132**,[22] end date Diocletian year 9 (= AD 292/293), 1,199 Alexandrian tetradrachms Claudius II to the Tetrarchy and an uncertain number of illegible coins.[23]

The hoard was found in 1972 in two small pots, 'lying flat on their side next to a big decorated jar' in an underground room of a house, during Egyptian excavations at the northwestern central part of Kôm Aushîm (ancient Karanis). There were no 'traces of any accommodities that could help in assessing the social status of its owner', but the absence of stucco decorations and limestones made the excavators suggest that it was 'an ordinary house of an ordinary peasant'.

Hoard **A128**,[24] end date Diocletian year 9 (= AD 292/293), 98 coins: 97 Alexandrian tetradrachms Probus to the Tetrarchy and one illegible.

The hoard (Mallawi 'A') is reported to have been found in a pot during excavations by the Egypt Exploration Society in Mallawi (ancient?) in 1977, when **A62** was also found. There is no further information about circumstances of find.

Hoard **A130**,[25] end date Diocletian year 9 (= AD 292/293), 33 coins: 26 Alexandrian tetradrachms Aurelian to the Tetrarchy and seven illegible; and a fragment of a bronze ring.

The hoard[26] was found in a wooden jar in a courtyard, just in front of a door to a house, during the German excavations in Bathn Ihrît (ancient Theadelphia) in 1902. It was found at the same place as No. **A84** (pottery jar, containing 20 bronze coins with end date AD 230/231; cf. above chap. 2, p. 50) and a bronze jar, containing 172 imperial 'folles' Diocletian to Constantine/Licinius.

The house itself was found completely empty, which made Regling, the editor, suppose that the inhabitants had left the house, taking all their belongings apart from the three jars with the coins.

Hoard A135,[27] end date Maximian year 9 (= AD 294/295), 22 coins: Alexandrian tetradrachms Numerianus to the Tetrarchy.

   The hoard was found in a little hole in a wall of a house during excavations in 1927-32 in Baqaria (ancient?), a Roman village, which the excavators, based on the coin evidence (stray finds in addition to the hoard), dated to have been founded during the Tetrarchy, although they would not exclude a somewhat earlier or later date.

Taken together, these seventeen hoards with a total of 8,313 identifiable Alexandrian tetradrachms make up the best evidence we have, due not only to their different size and range, but also due to the fact that they have been found at ten different localities during eleven different excavations. The flaw is that the reports on the circumstances of find – and other objects found – are not always as detailed as we would like, and a more exact date of burial than the latest datable coin in each hoard may therefore remain unsettled or disputed.

The Dattari Hoards

In 1905 Currelly made a deal with Dattari on behalf of Milne and Currelly himself.[28] Dattari would offer groups of coins to Milne, who – if he accepted the offer – would pay a fixed price per coin. The deal took effect from 1905 to 1914, during which period Milne bought, among other groups of coins, eleven groups of billon coins, which he called 'hoards'.[29]

   Apart from the first lot, which Milne – for reasons unknown to us – called 'Upper Egypt Hoard' ('Dattari A'o6' = A97), there is no information about the professed site of these hoards, nor in any case about any find circumstances. Milne's own words should be quoted in full:[30]

   in each case the appearance of the coins was homogeneous, so that there was no reason to suppose that anything had been added: but there was no guarantee that the hoards had not been picked over, and some of the more attractive pieces taken out, by the dealers through whose hands they had passed: still, when considered in conjunction with the figures obtained under more rigidly scientific conditions, the statistics of these hoards are of some use for purposes of comparison.

It is clear from Dattari's letters to Milne that he made a brief inspection of the coins, before offering and selling them to Milne, during which he picked out the specimens he wanted for his own collection, far the best of the day. This will probably mean some rare coins, e.g. from the reign of Septimius Severus, or interesting variations of reverse types and obverse legends, although some of them may have escaped his attention.

We may also suspect that Dattari – or his dealers – added some coins of ordinary occurrence or types, e.g. from the reigns of Nero or Diocletian, since the price agreed on was per coin.

Yet, we should not overlook that Milne explicitly remarked of the first six lots he received that – apart from one ('Dattari B'07' = **A103**), which he considered 'to be made up from two distinct lots' – there was no 'internal evidence of confusion: the coins were, in each instance, in generally similar conditions of preservation, and ran in fairly even distribution'.[31] These five hoards are 'Dattari A'06' (**A97**), 'A'07' (**A109**), 'C'07' (**A104**), 'B'09' (**A110**), and 'C'09' (**A140**).

In his handwritten notes on three other lots, Milne made remarks about coins which he suspected did not belong to the original lot. I take this to mean that he had no suspicions about the rest of the lots nor the other lots, but considered them, generally, to be original hoards, although of less scientific value. For such reasons, I will list the 'Dattari Hoards' in the same way as done for the other three groups, only excluding the coins also excluded by Milne.

A14 ('Dattari D'09') stands apart. It is the only hoard Milne published in full.[32] It contained 65 late Ptolemaic silver tetradrachms and 136 Alexandrian tetradrachms, all Tiberius year 7. It is useful for the discussion in the following chapter, but due to its special composition will not be included in the tables.

For the contents of the other hoards, we can only rely on Milne's handwritten lists (done with his usual meticulous care), since attempts to verify the original lots among the vast remains of them in the present Toronto Collection have proved to be unsuccessful.[33]

The hoards are as follows (summary in Table III, listing the hoards by 'Dattari' numbers):

A54, end date AD Antoninus Pius year 20? (=156/157),[34] 883 coins: two Ptolemaic bronze, 874 Alexandrian tetradrachms Claudius to Antoninus Pius, and seven illegible.

'Dattari A'13' was offered and bought in 1913, together with **A65** (bronze hoard). The lot also comprised four late coins, which Milne condemned as intrusive: three Alexandrian tetradrachms Maximinus to Valerianus and 1 'follis' of Maximian. Accordingly, they will not be included here.

A114, end date Marcus Aurelius year 10 (= AD 169/170), 2,394 coins: 2,302 Alexandrian tetradrachms Claudius to Marcus Aurelius and 92 illegible.

'Dattari A'09' was offered and bought in 1909 together with **A14** (bronze hoard), **A64**, **A110** and **A140**. The lot also comprised 32 Alexandrian tetradrachms Commodus to the Tetrarchy, on which Milne noted: 'Stray coins mixed up with A'09 probably not belonging to it.' Accordingly, they are not included here.

A103 ('Dattari B'07') was offered in 1906 and bought in 1907, together with **A104** and **A109**.

Milne explicitly remarked that it 'appeared to have been made up from two distinct lots' and gave the following reason: 'there were many instances in which coins from Claudius to Commodus were corroded together; but I did not find any third-century coins united to any of an earlier date'.[35] Accordingly, the group will be listed here and treated as two hoards:

B'07A, end date Commodus year 30 (= AD 189/190), 25 coins: two Ptolemaic bronze and 23 Alexandrian tetradrachms Nero to Commodus.

B'07B, end date Aurelian year 5 (= AD 273/274), 1,103 coins: 1,066 Alexandrian tetradrachms Septimius Severus to Aurelian and 37 illegible.

A69, end date Commodus year 31 (= AD 190/191), 2,275 coins: two Ptolemaic bronze, two Alexandrian bronze (size II, one of Trajan and one of Hadrian), and 2,271 Alexandrian tetradrachms Tiberius to Commodus.

'Dattari A'11' was offered in 1910 and bought in 1911, together with **A159**. The lot also contained seven Alexandrian tetradrachms Elagabalus to Probus. In his notes, however, Milne remarked 'Probably mixed up from B'11' (i.e. **A159**). Accordingly, they will not be included here.

A97, end date Gallienus year 13 (= AD 262/263), 950 coins: Alexandrian tetradrachms Elagabalus to Gallienus.

'Dattari A'06', the 'Upper Egypt Hoard', was offered in 1905 and bought in 1906.

A104, end date Aurelian year 3 (= AD 272[36]), 1,839 coins: five Ptolemaic bronze, 1,803 Alexandrian tetradrachms Nero to Aurelian, and 31 illegible.

'Dattari C'07' was offered in 1906 and bought in 1907, together with **A104** and **A109**.

A109, end date Probus year 2 (= AD 276/277), 2,232 coins: two late Ptolemaic silver tetradrachms, one Alexandrian bronze (Claudius, size III), 2,167 Alexandrian tetradrachms
Claudius to Probus, and 62 illegible.

'Dattari A'07' was offered in 1906 and bought in 1907, together with **A103-104**.

A110, end date Probus year 4 (= AD 278/279), 2.005 coins: 1,955 Alexandrian tetradrachms Nero to Probus and 50 illegible.

'Dattari B'09' was offered and bought in 1909, together with **A64** (bronze hoard).

A140, end date Diocletian year 12 (= AD 295/296), 4,122 coins: two Ptolemaic bronze,
4,116 Alexandrian tetradrachms Marcus Aurelius to the Tetrarchy, and four illegible
coins.

'Dattari C'09' was offered and bought in 1909, together with **A64** (bronze hoard),
A110, and **A114**.

A159, end date Diocletian year 12 (=AD 295/296), 12,582 coins: 12,434 Alexandrian tetradrachms Nero to the Tetrarchy and 48 illegible.

'Dattari B'11' was offered in 1910 and bought in 1911, together with **A69**. The lot
also contained the following bronze coins: four Ptolemaic, three Alexandrian, six late
Roman, one Ummayad, and two illegible. Milne listed them apart, probably considering them as intrusive. Accordingly, they have not been included here.

According to W.E. Metcalf,[37] the whole lot 'must represent the combination of two
or more lots of material', since it 'extends (uniquely)' back to the reign of Nero. This
may be true, of course, but the fact remains that Milne, who had the coins in his hand,
nourished no such suspicion about the composition of the group apart from the bronze
coins (of a predominantly late date). I shall return to that question later (see Chap. 8
below, p. 132.).

The Dattari Hoards form our largest group, and due to their different size, range, and
composition, these eleven hoards with a total of 30,062 identifiable Alexandrian tetradrachms are valuable from a statistical point of view, especially offering clues for trac-
ing the original variations in the output of the mint – such as Milne did. For other
purposes their evidence is too flawed for allowing tenable conclusions unless corroborated by other – more certain – evidence. The worst defect is that there is no way of
reconstructing which – or how many – coins may have been picked out, nor which
– or how many – may have been added before Milne got them in his hands. We rely
on his judgments and identifications, of course, because no one before him – and few
after him – had his profound knowledge of the Alexandrian coinage. His meticulous
care is proverbial.

Other supposed hoards

By 'other supposed hoards' I mean groups of coins, which are claimed to be – or have been acquired as – original hoards, but about which we have no certain evidence of find circumstances. Some of them may actually be as certain as some of the 'excavation hoards', whereas others are more similar to 'the Dattari Hoards', meaning that we cannot know if – and if so, how many – coins may have been picked out or added before publication.

The hoards are as follows (for a summary, see Table IV, listing the hoards by names in alphabetical order):

Hoard CHVII **sine numero**,[38] end date Nero year 12 (= AD 65/66): 15 Alexandrian tetradrachms, Claudius to Nero.

The hoard was received in 1902 by the Museum of Art in Detroit (now the Detroit Institute of Art) among other Egyptian antiquities deriving from excavations by the Egypt Exploration Fund at Abydos and in the Faiyûm, probably those done by Grenfell and Hunt. There are no explicit records, but the 'uniform dark brown patination and encrustations of soil' make it plausible that the coins belong to a single find. The 'noticeable wear' on two-fifths of the coins made Visonà, the editor, suggest that they had 'witnessed a great deal of circulation before being consigned to the earth'.

Hoard **A22**, end date Nero year 13 (= AD 66/67): 108[39] Alexandrian tetradrachms, all Nero.

The coins, 'apparently from one find, the surface poor', were part of the Jungfleisch Collection, most probably acquired in Egypt, and offered for sale at Sotheby's 9th March 1972 (Item No. 286).

Hoard **A26**,[40] end date Galba year 2 (=AD 68/69): 481 Alexandrian tetradrachms Tiberius to Galba and 46 illegible.

The coins are stated to have formed one hoard, acquired by Daira Sanieh under unknown circumstances and presented to the Egyptian Antiquities Service in 1889. Not all the coins are described.

Hoard **A27**,[41] end date Vespasian year 2 (= AD 69/70): 1,175 Alexandrian tetradrachms Claudius to Vespasian.

The coins are reported to have been found as one hoard by the Egypt Exploration Fund somewhere in Egypt ca. 1900. Only the Neronian coins have been described.

Hoard **A28**,[42] end date Vespasian year 2 (= AD 69/70): 197 Alexandrian tetradrachms Claudius to Vespasian.

The coins (the 'Miser's Hoard') were contained in an amphora, acquired by Currelly 1910 somewhere in Egypt.

Hoard **A29**,[43] end date Vespasian year 2 (= AD 69/70): 1,293 Alexandrian tetradrachms Nero to Vespasian, two silver ingots and eight silver bracelets (on these items, see Chap. 2 above, p. 39).

The police had confiscated the hoard from a native silver- and goldsmith in El-Manshâh (ancient Ptolemais Hermiou) in 1925. The coins had 'not suffered much wear', but only a brief summary of them was given.

Hoard **A48**,[44] end date Antoninus Pius year?[45] (= mid-2nd century AD): 45 Alexandrian tetradrachms Claudius to Antoninus Pius.

Tony Hackens examined and photographed the coins in 1962 at an antiquities dealer in Athens. From the appearance of the coins he declared them to be a hoard – or at least part of a hoard, which was said to have been found near Aswân (ancient Syene).

Hoard **A58**,[46] end date Marcus Aurelius year 2 (= AD 161/162), 427 Alexandrian tetradrachms Claudius to Marcus Aurelius.

Newell acquired the coins in 1913 from an antiquities dealer in Cairo, and from their appearance, he declared them to have been found together.

Hoards **A61**, **A78**, **A86-87**, and **A89** were purchased 1905 by Currelly and Frost from 'native finders, without the intervention of dealers' in Tell el-Maskhûta (ancient Heroonpolis), and from 'the conditions of the coins' Milne declared[47] that 'those in each lot had been found together', although 'any one of the lots may only be part of an original hoard'.

Hoard **A61**, end date Lucius Verus year 7 (= AD 166/167): 89 Alexandrian tetradrachms Nero to Lucius Verus.

Hoard **A78**, end date Geta year 20 (= AD 211/212): 313 Alexandrian tetradrachms Claudius to Geta.

Hoard **A86**, end date Trebonianus Gallus year 3 (= AD 251/252): 162 Alexandrian tetradrachms Claudius to Trebonianus Gallus.

Hoard **A87**, end date Valerian year 3 (= AD 254/255): 39 Alexandrian tetradrachms Claudius to Valerian.

Hoard **A89**, end date Valerian year 6 (= AD 257/258): 131 Alexandrian tetradrachms Nero to Valerian.

Hoard A113,[48] end date Carinus year 1 (= AD 282/283): 1,058 Alexandrian tetradrachms Claudius to Carus.

The coins were reported to have been found as a hoard in the region of Girga in Upper Egypt and were examined by Jacques Schwartz in 1947 at an antiquities dealer.

Hoard A138,[49] end date Diocletian year 12 (= AD 295/296): 822 Alexandrian tetradrachms Marcus Aurelius to the Tetrarchy.

In 1895 Milne bought the coins as two hoards from two Arab dealers in Cairo who had declared their provenance to be Zagagzig and Giza respectively. Milne doubted this, but from the condition of the coins, he considered them to form two original hoards. They got mixed on their way to England, however, and since then have been treated as one hoard (the 'Cairo Hoard').

Hoard A142,[50] end date Galerius year 4 (= AD 295/296): 237 Alexandrian tetradrachms Probus to the Tetrarchy.

The coins were presented to Rijksmuseum van Oudheden in Leyden in 1929 by J.H. Insinger, according to whose notes they formed an original hoard found in the Faiyûm.

With a total of 6,590 identifiable coins, these 16 supposed hoards form the smallest of the four groups. It goes without saying that suspicions must adhere to the original composition of each lot. Their value lies in their – professed – different provenances from 11 different places and 12 different years. They may therefore serve to corroborate or moderate the picture given by the other groups.

The scope of the investigation

The overall picture of the hoard evidence can be summarized in the following way (cf. Tables V-IX and *Figs* 10-13):

HOARDS DEPOSITED DURING THE TETRARCHY

Totals	24 hoards	40,133 coins = 58.85%
Karanis group	16 hoards	21,086 coins = 90.8%
Excavation group	4 hoards	1,344 coins = 16.16%
Dattari group	2 hoards	16,650 coins = 55.38%
Other groups	2 hoards	959 coins = 14.55%

Hoards deposited before the Tetrarchy

Total	48 hoards	28,054 coins = 41.14%
Other groups	14 hoards	5,531 coins = 83.93%
Excavation group	13 hoards	6,969 coins = 83.83 %
Karanis group	12 hoards	2,142 coins = 9.22%
Dattari group	9 hoards	13,412 coins = 44.61%

Hoards deposited after Gallienus' debasement

Total	40 hoards	51,229 coins = 75.13%
Karanis group	26 hoards	23,176 coins = 99.8%
Dattari group	7 hoards	24,529 coins = 81.59%
Excavation group	5 hoards	2,528 coins = 30.41%
Other groups	3 hoards	2,117 coins = 32.12%

Hoards deposited before Gallienus' debasement

Total	32 hoards	16,958 coins = 24.86%
Other groups	13 hoards	4,473 coins = 67.87%
Excavation group	12 hoards	5,785 coins = 69.58%
Dattari group	4 hoards	5,470 coins = 18.19%
Karanis group	2 hoards	46 coins = 0.19%

At first glance, end dates of the sufficiently known hoards of tetradrachms seem to cluster around certain dates/periods: eight (whereof six among 'other supposed hoards') belong to AD 65/66 – 70 (the end of Nero's reign and the 'year of the four emperors'), six to 161/162 – 169/170 (the reign of Marcus Aurelius), and the greatest number to the latter part of the 3rd century, most conspicuously the reigns of Valerian/Gallienus (6) and Aurelian (7), and especially the Tetrarchy (24, whereof 16 from the American excavations in Karanis).

If the end dates represent the actual dates of deposit, or the hoards were deposited not long thereafter, there may be some connections with unruly times caused by known events inside or affecting Egypt. The civil war following Nero's death does not seem to have raged in Egypt itself, but Egypt, and especially Alexandria, played an important part in Vespasian's *coup d'état*, and it is possible that some people participated in the warfare abroad and did not return to recover their buried fortunes. During the reign of Marcus Aurelius Egypt was ravaged by a plague, a revolt in the Delta area, and Avidius Cassius' revolt, which may explain the deposits of the next group.

Nor would it cause surprise if the disturbances during the latter part of the 3rd century caused many hoards to be deposited and not regained. To be noted especially: probable devastations during the revolts of Macrianus and Quietus, the Palmyrene occupation, the revolt of Domitius Domitianus, followed by the reconquests by Gallienus, Aurelian, and Diocletian, whereto add the attacks by the Blemmyes.

The three(?) hoards deposited during the latter years of Hadrian may be seen as an indirect effect of the revolt in nearby Judaea and its suppressing. On the other hand, the 'event theory' fails to explain why apparently no hoards apart from perhaps A35 (see Chapter 2 above, p. 42) were buried and lost during the Jewish unrest at the end of Trajan's reign, and one may wonder which events caused six(?) hoards to be deposited and not regained during the peaceful reign of Antoninus Pius.

Events may also cause a high production of coins, and if this is reflected in the hoards, it may be no coincidence that according to my survey of 1985,[51] the highest proportions of tetradrachms belonged to the reign of Nero (15.10%) and the Tetrarchy (25.19%). We may then wonder why the reign of Marcus Aurelius only constituted 0.36% and the reign of Aurelian only 1.86% (plus 0.73% from his joint rule with the Palmyrenes), whereas there seems to be no obvious reason why the reign of Probus, especially, should come in third with 12.85%.

If the coin hoards represent the contemporary circulation of coins, they may also reflect coin debasements, especially if such debasements were accompanied by attempts to collect the older coinage. Walker's investigations demonstrated debasements of silver content during the reigns of Nero[52] and Marcus Aurelius.[53] We have no such exact measurements for the later period, but it is commonly assumed – on more or less firm ground – that the silver content and weight of the Alexandrian tetradrachm were lowered again in successive turns, and the diameter of the flan reduced, during the reigns of Gallienus, Probus, and Diocletian.[54] Recently, W. Metcalf has made clear that at least a new weight standard was introduced during the reign of Aurelian.[55]

For all these reasons, together, I have selected the following periods for closer investigation: the reigns of Nero, Marcus Aurelius (or rather – for reasons stated below – Commodus), Gallienus, Aurelian, and Probus to the Tetrarchy.

For each reign I will try to ask what the hoards can tell us about fluctuations in the original production of the Alexandrian tetradrachm, whether caused by events or debasements; how far the new coins supplanted the older coinage or increased the pool; how long they continued in circulation, were supported by or supplanted by new coinage (and possible effects in turn).

In an attempt to overcome the general defects of the hoard evidence, I will pose these questions to each of the four groups presented in this chapter and discuss how far the answers support or contradict each other. By doing so, I hope to come closer to a true picture of the original production and circulation of the coins than that which would be offered by a mere examination of the evidence as a whole.

NOTES

1. See Christiansen & Easson (forthcoming) with further references.
2. See Christiansen (1983/84), p. 38.
3. Note by Easson in *CH* 7,1985, p. 33.
4. Breccia (1919), p. 230.
5. Baratte (1974).
6. The promised 'full account' in *The Numismatic Chronicle* never appeared. Details to be published in Christiansen & Easson (forthcoming).
7. Milne in Grenfell, Hunt & Hogarth (1900), p. 65.
8. Botti (1955).
9. Milne (1935), p. 212.
10. Milne (1935), p. 213.
11. Uxkull-Gyllenband (1926).
12. El Khafif (1981).
13. Milne (1935), p. 212.
14. The promised 'full account' in *The Numismatic Chronicle* never appeared. Details to be published in Christiansen & Eassson (forthcoming).
15. Milne (1900), p. 65.
16. Unpublished. I rely on the late Martin Price's handwritten list.
17. The promised 'full account' in *The Numismatic Chronicle* never appeared. Details to be published in Christiansen & Easson (forthcoming).
18. Milne in Grenfell, Hunt & Hogarth (1900), p. 65.
19. Grenfell, Hunt & Hogarth (1900), p. 28.
20. I am grateful to Professor Hans-Christoph Noeske (Frankfurt am Main) for information and detailed list.
21. Breccia (1919).
22. El-Nassery & Wagner (1975).
23. Exactly 1,500, on p. 186, whereof 65 'entirely corroded'. 294 pieces with their obverse 'defaced' and the reverse 'hardly identifiable', and 1,141 in a 'satisfactory state' do not correspond with the total of 1,558 coins listed in the 'catalogue', pp. 189ff.
24. Unpublished. I rely on the late Martin Price's handwritten list.
25. Regling (1912), pp. 117ff.
26. Cf. also Rubensohn (1905), pp. 1 and 15ff.
27. Mond & Myers (1934), pp. 115ff.
28. For the following, see Christiansen & Easson (forthcoming); summary in Christiansen & Easson (1997/2000).
29. Milne 1933(1971), note to tables.
30. As preceding note.
31. Milne (1911), p. 31.
32. Milne (1910).
33. Christiansen & Easson (forthcoming); cf. Christiansen & Easson (1997/2000).

34. Year 20 of the latest coin is not certain; the preceding two coins are dated Antoninus Pius year 17 (= AD 153/154).
35. Milne (1911), p.31.
36. For this date see Price (1973), esp. p. 85.
37. Metcalf (1998), p. 272, note 6.
38. Visonà (1983).
39. '107' must be an error.
40. Dutilh (1891) and (1900).
41. Note by Martin Price in *CH* 5, 1979, p. 17. For details (and different totals) I rely on the late Martin Price's handwritten notes, of which he offered me a copy in 1978.
42. Note by Easson in *CH* 7, 1985, p.33.
43. Wainwright (1925).
44. Hackens (1965).
45. The latest datable coin is Hadrian year 15 (= AD 130/131).
46. Metcalf (1976), pp. 70ff., based on Newell's notes.
47. Milne (1911), p. 31.
48. Schwartz (1948).
49. Milne (1903).
50. Evers (1968).
51. Christiansen (1985), p. 81.
52. Walker I (1976), pp. 139ff., for which see below next chapter.
53. Walker II (1977), pp. 114ff. On this, see below, next chapter.
54. Thus, see Savio 3 (1997), p.21, mainly based on West & Johnson (1944), p. 172.
55. Metcalf (1998), pp. 272f.

CHAPTER V

NERO AND A STABLE CURRENCY

> Although at first his acts of wantonness, lust, extravagance, avarice and cruelty were
> gradual and secret, and might be condoned as follies of youth, yet even then their na-
> ture was such that no one doubted that they were defects of his character and not due
> to his time of life.
>
> (SUETONIUS, *Nero* XXVI)

Nero has been left with a bad reputation by the ancient authors. Modern scholarship
has not rehabilitated him, but generally today we are less interested in the fate of indi-
vidual senators and would rather like to ask questions concerning matters that in our
view are of more importance, such as the 'financial state' of the Empire.

To such questions Suetonius provides us with easy answers: Nero was guided by
nothing but extravagance and prodigality, having 'confidence in the resources of the
empire', hoping for 'a hidden treasure',[1] but actually bankrupting and ruining the provinces by his demands.[2] In the end (i.e. after the fire of Rome in AD 64), Suetonius tells
us that Nero became 'so utterly impoverished that he was obliged to postpone and
defer even the pay of the soldiers and the rewards due to the veterans'.[3]

However profligate he may have been, the emperor would soon realize – or have
been told to recognize – how dangerous such a situation was. Rebellious legions could
easily mean loss of power.

Incidentally, Suetonius also mentions, among other accusations against Nero, that he
demanded 'newly minted coin' (*nummum asperum*).[4] We do not know what Suetonius
exactly means by this remark nor, of course, how he knew. Pliny the Elder, however,
reports that the weight of the denarius was reduced,[5] and modern measurements have
made clear that the silver content was reduced as well.

Walker's exact figures for the reduction of the mean weight of silver from 3.47 to
2.97 gram (compared to a reduction of mean weight of the coin from 3.57 to 3.18 gram)[6]
are no longer as generally accepted as they were at the time of publication, since it has
become clear that his method could not deal with the problem of surface enrichment.[7]
But no one has disputed that the Roman denarius underwent a debasement of its silver
standard in AD 64.

Normally, such a reduction would be explained as an attempt to collect older coinage for new coins, in order to reap a profit or at least to amass bullion for striking more coins.[8]

With this sketchy background we may now turn to Egypt.

The Alexandrian tetradrachms of Nero

It has been known for at least a century that Nero's Alexandrian tetradrachms have survived in large numbers for posterity. Dutilh made explicit comments on this in 1896,[9] and Dattari likewise in 1900.[10] According to my survey of 1985, Nero's tetradrachms made up 11,116 coins or 15.1% of the billon hoard evidence sufficiently known and described,[11] and the total will further increase if we add some large hoards which are less sufficiently known or described, such as A19-20 (two hoards with probably almost 1,400 coins),[12] and A85 (great numbers).[13]

The evidence, as presented here, is quite consistent with such a picture (cf. Tables I-IV): although there are only three hoards with a total of 33 Neronian tetradrachms (= 0.14%) in the Karanis group, they make up 51.71% (3.408 coins, 13 hoards) in 'other supposed hoards', 43.01% (3,576 coins, 12 hoards) in 'other excavation hoards', and 13.71% (4,122 coins, eight hoards) in the Dattari group.

Milne, however, made clear that according to his evidence, this dominance is mainly effected by coins from years 10-14 (AD 63/64 – 67/68) with year 12 (AD 65/66) as 'the peak of the curve, probably the highest ever reached'.[14]

This is consistent with the hoards of ancient forgeries, the 'Neronian coins', all of which imitate well-known coins from years 10-14: A21 and 23,[15] A41,[16] and – less sufficiently described – A38.[17] Whereas a modern forger will try to create 'new' – and rare coins,[18] an ancient forger could only succeed if the pieces could be hidden among common coins.

Actually, coin production during Nero's reign began in a somewhat staggering way on a less extensive scale, and rather late (see *fig. 5*).

Year 6 (AD 45/46) was the last year for the mint of Alexandria to coin tetradrachms for Claudius (375 specimens, two(?) types recorded by the hoard evidence).[19] After a pause of ten years the production was re-opened in Nero's third year (AD 56/57) with 'a larger issue... than in any year of Claudius', according to Milne,[20] but witnessed by a somewhat lower total in the hoard evidence (322 specimens, 11 types).[21]

From the same year – and year 4 – we also have a few silver coins, never found in the hoards, of a smaller size and weight.[22] Similar – rare – pieces are also found from the third year of Claudius (although neither are these coins found in hoards). Milne, who only knew the specimens from Claudius' reign, suggested that they were meant

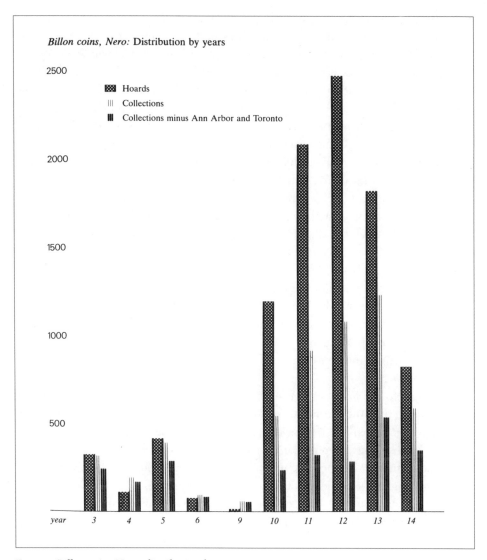

FIG. 5. *Billon coins Nero; distribution by years.*

as silver didrachms and silver drachms,[23] but I still find it tempting to ask if actually they represent a short-lived experiment with creating a new coin to replace the tetra-drachm.

Nevertheless, we may wonder why the Roman government still bothered to produce silver tetradrachms of approximately the same size (ca. 25 mm.) and weight (around 13 gram) as their Ptolemaic predecessors. Was it pure tradition or deliberate deceit to make the – new – Roman coin look like just as fine a silver coin? Hazzard has claimed that the debased tetradrachms looked brownish, so that 'anyone could tell coins of fine silver from those of base content'.[24] This is true today when copper works its way through the surface, but not in antiquity when the billon coins probably still had a shiny surface around the copper core.[25] Actually, the tetradrachms of Ptolemy XII and Cleopatra VII[26] look shabbier than the Roman and the previous tetradrachms.

According to Walker's measurements, the striking of Nero's tetradrachms began on a slightly improved Claudian standard with a mean weight of 13.19 gram (*versus* 13.04 gram) and a mean weight silver of 3.05 gram (*versus* 2.97 gram) until year 4 (AD 57/58), when a new standard was introduced having an average weight of 13.22 gram and mean silver weight of 2.19 gram.[27]

The coinage of year 4 can be divided into two series, one with – and one without – a stroke over the *delta*. Walker had two coins of the 'delta-stroke' series for analysis (with an average weight of 3.07 gram) and eight for the 'delta' series (with an average weight of 2.67 gram), and if I am right in claiming the 'delta' series to have preceded the other,[28] we have oscillations of the existing standard within year 4 rather than the introduction of a new standard.

As mentioned above, Walker's method had defects, and although A. Savio and M. Oddone had less coins for analysis[29] (which therefore was less firmly based), their conclusion of variations in silver contents during year 4 may give further support to this modification.

According to the hoard evidence, the first series was produced in less numbers (34 specimens) than the second (63 specimens), followed by a remarkable increase in year 5 (418 specimens) and a likewise remarkable decrease in year 6 (77 specimens) (see *fig. 5.*).[30] This may support the view taken by Savio[31] that the Alexandrian mint barely had sufficient silver to keep up the necessary production of tetradrachms during the first part of Nero's reign. Then a radical change set in.

From the observations above on the oscillating standards during year 4, it may follow that year 9 (AD 62/63) meant the introduction of a new and a more lasting standard with a mean weight silver of perhaps 2.09 gram.[32] In the following year there was a radical change on the obverse, from the hitherto laureate head to a radiate crown,[33] perhaps signaling the coins as belonging to a new coinage. In the same year 10 (AD 63/64) the production of tetradrachms in Alexandria began on the vast scale (1,198 specimens, according to the hoard evidence)[34] it had for the rest of Nero's reign.

By way of die studies and probability calculations I tried in 1988 to quantify the original production of this coinage by offering some comparable figures. Since, however, present scholarship seems to mistake 'qualified estimates' and 'reasonable guesses'[35] for professed knowledge,[36] I shall not enter this game again but instead restrain myself to two basic sets of notions:

1. Admittedly, my die studies of the 759 specimens in Toronto with reverse Alexandria relied on an unsatisfactory method.[37] The fact remains that although I have seen thousands of Alexandrian coins in my life, I have never found such an extraordinarily high number of crudely cut dies and carelessly struck coins,[38] which in itself is clear evidence of a hectic activity.

2. The 273 specimens (reverse Alexandria) found in the other collections differ so much that they almost represent different types more than variants of the same type, and I actually found no more than five pairs of dies among them, in other words a total of 268 different dies among 273 coins, whereas 58 specimens of reverse eagle provided as many as 55 different dies.[39] The discovery of so many different dies among so many coins increases the probability for an even higher number of original dies in use. Regardless of the actual number of coins struck by each die, both results are clear indications of a coin production on an unprecedented and unparalleled scale.

Judging from the hoard evidence, year 12 (AD 65/66) was the most prolific year (2,478 coins; two reverse types), but according to the same evidence, the other years were prolific as well (see also *fig. 5*):[40] Year 10 (AD 63/64) = 1,198 coins; three reverse types; year 11 (AD 64/65) = 2,085 coins; three (four) reverse types; year 13 (AD 66/67) = 1,595 coins; nine reverse types; year 14 (AD 67/9th January 68) = 824 coins; two series, each of six reverse types.

Part of this coin production may of course be explained by actual or planned events, especially the renewal of the Parthian war in AD 62,[41] including reinforcements sent from Egypt during spring AD 63,[42] the emperor's planned visit to Egypt,[43] the projected expeditions into Ethiopia and Caucasus,[44] a large concentration of troops in Alexandria in AD 66 for unknown reasons,[45] and the beginning of the Jewish Revolt during the same year.

On the other hand, the riots in Alexandria[46] do not seem to have hampered coin production. Furthermore, if the Roman government needed to strike a large amount of new coins to cover for example military expenditure, we would have to acknowledge a level of cost for such demands to have been at an extremely high scale, and if the large volume of coinage struck is directly related to necessary payments, Egypt would have been seething with military preparations. Even if this may be accepted from about AD 66 onwards, it remains to be explained how the sudden outburst of the coin production in year 10 (AD 63/64) is compatible with Tacitus' account that the Romans concluded peace with the Parthian king in the latter part of AD 63, and that the following year was 'most peaceful'.[47]

If the present hoard evidence represents or reflects the coin circulation at the time, there can be no doubt that a vast amount of the new coins was sent into immediate circulation within Egypt. We have eight hoards with end dates during or immediately following Nero's reign:

Karanis Hoards

Hoard 12; end date AD 65/66: total 40; Nero = 23 (57.5 %), whereof 18 belonging to years 10-12.[48]

Other excavation hoards

El Madamûd 1928; end date AD 68: total 173; Nero = 172 (99.99%), all belonging to years 10-14.[49]

Other supposed hoards

Faiyûm 1902?; end date AD 65/66: total 15; Nero = 14 (93.33%), all belonging to years 11-12.[50]

Jungfleisch 1972; end date AD 66/67: total 107; all belonging to Nero years 11-13.[51]

Sanieh 1889; end date AD 68/69: total 481; Nero = 328 (68.19%), distribution unknown.[52]

Currelly 1910; end date AD 69/70: total 197; Nero = 51 (25.88%), all belonging to year 13.[53]

EEF c.1900; end date AD 69/70: total 1,175; Nero = 1,128 (95.99%), whereof 1,043 belonging to years 10-14.[54]

El Manshâh 1925; end date AD 69/70: total 1,293; Nero 1,292 (= 99,9%), with a preponderance of years 11-13. [55]

The large percentages of coins from years 10-14 can be no coincidence, and whatever the actual size of the original production, a large invasion of new coins added to the existing pool would have caused two effects: a suddenly increased monetization or an economic crisis.

The first explanation cannot be rejected out of hand, and an economic crisis has been asserted,[56] mainly based on the edict issued by Tiberius Julius Alexander as prefect of Egypt in AD 68 after Nero's death.[57]

In the edict the prefect declares an end to the abuses referred to him, and among other things states the following (l.45-51; French translation) 'car les cultivateurs de tout le "pays" ont souvent adressé des pétitions et représenté qu'ils se sont vu imposer, sans précédents, beaucoup […] d'impôts en blé et en argent bien qu'il ne soit pas permis à qui bon semble introduire à son gré une innovation à caractère général.'

If this is a true description of the economic situation, it is similar to the plight of the provinces, as claimed by Suetonius (quoted above, p. 89). This would have been felt seriously enough by those complaining, but implies no effects on the economy caused by an excess of currency, such as unsteady price conditions or the like.

New coins for old?

In 1984 I was able to list[58] 58 instances of 'Ptolemaic' (silver coins) in the papyri, whereof at least 19 are mentioned together with 'the emperor's silver coins', in the period from 22 BC to AD 64, when the term disappears at a stroke, not to reappear until mid 3rd century (whereto see below, Chap. 7, p. 119.).

This made me suggest that the main aim of the heavy production of silver tetradrachms during the latter part of Nero's reign was to replace the Ptolemaic – partly also the Tiberian – tetradrachms still in circulation, and that the aim was successful.[59]

I had to admit, though, that the hoard evidence offered little support for this view. In a letter to Milne of 14th January 1904,[60] Dattari says that coins of Ptolemy Auletes are often found together with Tiberian tetradrachms, but he may have been generalizing from insufficient evidence, and apart from a few scattered coins in late hoards, we actually have only one hoard, deposited in the Roman period, containing Ptolemaic silver.

The hoard is 'Dattari D'09', bought by Milne from Dattari in 1909 and published by himself the following year.[61] It contained 65 Ptolemaic tetradrachms (of which 61 were Cleopatra VII[62]) and 136 Tiberian tetradrachms, all belonging to year 7.

Among the other reliable hoards one Tiberian tetradrachm is found in 'Sanieh 1889' and two in hoard 'Dattari A'11', which counts for nothing, but according to the less reliable evidence, Tiberian tetradrachms are found in substantial numbers during the reign of Nero (A18) and even as late as mid-3rd century (A100).

The main problem is that there is a gap in the reliable hoard evidence between 'Dattari D'09' (A14, end date AD 20/21) and the hoards with Nero's last years as end dates, which makes it impossible to say with any certainty how long – and to what extent – the Ptolemaic and the Tiberian silver coins remained available for circulation and hoarding. One may just wonder what was meant by the term 'Ptolemaic' in the papyri if not actual Ptolemaic coins, especially considering the 19 cases where they are mentioned alongside the 'emperor's' coins.

Among the coins of Tiberius year 7 in 'Dattari D'09' Milne found several sets deriving from the same dies,[63] but he generally concluded that it was 'difficult to compare the extent of the output with that of later years',[64] exactly due to the insufficient hoard evidence. He furthermore suggested that the Tiberian tetradrachms had been called in and melted down during the reign of Claudius, which may be an obvious explanation for their rare occurrence in the hoard evidence as a whole (139 specimens or 0.19% out of totals).[65]

We are much better off with the Claudian tetradrachms. Milne found a few die links among the coins from year 3,[66] which yet, according to him, represented the 'highest figure' in output.[67] Based on the hoard evidence, I have suggested a total production of the whole reign to be in the same range as years 3-6 of Nero's reign.[68]

A central point, however, is that the Claudian tetradrachms stayed to some extent with the Neronian coins in the hoards as presented here.

Karanis Hoards
Hoard No. 12; end date AD 65/66: 17 coins (42.5%)

Other excavation hoards
Kôm el-Asl 2; end date AD 127/128: five coins (8.06%)
El Hîba 1935; end date AD 128/129: seven coins (3.24%)
Umm el-Breigat 5; end date AD 138/139: one coin (3.57%)
El Hîba 1914; end date AD 143/144: 12 coins (5.08%)
El Manshâh 1968; end date AD 149/150: two coins (1.96%)
Kôm el-Asl 1; end date AD 164/165: 361 coins (7.22%)
Kôm Aushîm 1896; end date AD 169/170: three coins (3.06%)

Dattari Hoards
'A'13'; end date AD 156/157: eight coins (0.92%)
'A'09'; end date AD 169/170: 73 coins (3.17%)
'A'11'; end date AD 190/191: 189 coins (8.32%)
'A'07'; end date AD 276/277: 19 coins (0.87%)

Other supposed hoards
Faiyûm 1902?; end date AD 65/66: one coin (6.66%)
Sanieh 1889; end date AD 68/69: 151 coins (31.39%)
Currelly 1910; end date AD 69/70: 144 coins (73%)
EEF c. 1900; end date AD 69/70: 24 coins (2.04%)
Aswan 1962?; end date AD 130/131: three coins (6.66%)
Newell 1913; end date AD 161/162: 15 coins (3.51%)
Tell el-Maskhûta 5; end date AD 211/212: three coins (0.96%)
Tell el-Maskhûta 4; end date AD 252/253: one coin (0.61%)
Tell el-Maskhûta 1; end date AD 255/256: one coin (2.56%)

Although some numbers are small, the general picture of a certain survival is clear among all four groups, which makes it rather improbable that the Claudian coins were forced out (or called in) by the coins from Nero's reign.[69]

To this may be added the observation made by A. Burnett[70] that the occurrence of Augustus and Tiberius on Nero's Alexandrian reverses of year 13 may mean a replacement of the emperors, which would have disappeared from circulation by the demonetization of the Tiberian tetradrachms (always carrying a portrait of Augustus on the reverse).

Walker's measurements gave a mean weight silver of 5.76 grams for Cleopatra's tetradrachms and 4.01 grams for the coins of Tiberius, *versus* 2.97 grams after the debasement under Nero[71]. Hazzard's objection that Walker's method – i.e. testing only the thin layer of surface – will overestimate the percentage of silver,[72] will also apply to the late Ptolemaic and the early Roman billon coins[73] and will not eliminate the comparable estimates, apart from the possibility that the Roman coins may have had a higher intentional enrichment of silver of the blanks before striking.[74]

A mere count of the numbers in the hoards gave a sum of 8,406 coins from years 10-14 of Nero's reign.[75] If, for every new coin produced the Roman government got one old coin back, the silver gain from Cleopatra's coinage would have been ca. 48 kilograms (8,406 x 5.76 grams) and ca. 33 kilograms from Tiberius' coinage (8,406 x 4.01 grams), sufficient for striking ca. 22,000 and 15,000 new coins, respectively, with a mean silver weight of 2.19 grams. Loss of silver during the re-melting should, however, be deducted from this theoretical increase in coin production. Yet the calculation is a clear illustration of the possible profit from such re-coining, and furthermore shows that the process will continue unassisted when first started.

No one can deny that the hoard evidence we have only represents a small – perhaps tiny – part of the original number of coins. I shall venture on no further calculations, just point out that the actual profit must have been much higher, and therefore maintain my original conclusion:[76] at least part of this profit was meant for Nero's empty chest in Rome.

A stable currency

Considering the few ruling months of each emperor, the hoard evidence indicates a continued rather high production of Alexandrian tetradrachms during the ensuing civil war: Galba 485 coins (0.67% out of total), Otho 131 (0.18%), Vitellius 54 (0.07%).[77] This is even true for Vespasian, whose tetradrachms (563 in hoards = 0.76%) scarcely go beyond his second Egyptian year (AD 69/70).[78] According to Dio Cassius (LXV.8.3-4), he increased his income by levying additional contributions and taxes from the Alexandrians, and during his reign the Alexandrian mint seems also to have cut dies (and struck coins?) meant for Syria.[79] It is tempting to suggest that the preceding hectic activity had left an over-capacity of idle men. It may be even more tempting to see some of the reverse types of the Alexandrian tetradrachms from these reigns (such as Eleutheria, Kratesis, Roma, Nike) as representing new coinage spent on expenses caused by the warfare, whereas the Neronian coins remained in use for more daily payments, such as taxes and exchange at the border.

Tetradrachms from Titus' reign are rare in hoards (61 specimens = 0.08%) and from Domitian's reign almost nil.[80] Accordingly, the increase of the legionary pay during Domitian's reign[81] is not reflected in the production of tetradrachms in Alexandria, but the production of bronze coinage may have been rather plentiful.[82] The spasmodic production of tetradrachms during years 2, 6, and 8[83] seems to have no connection with Domitian's general management of the finances.[84] It may have had connections with events which have left no traces in the records, but – as ably concluded by Carradice: 'some minting is in any case to be explained by the need to produce coinage for a closed currency area'.[85]

This verdict may be valid for the whole following period.

Events might have caused the production of new coins, although the need could just as well have been defrayed by existing coinage, if available in sufficient numbers. We would expect a wish for advertising a new emperor and his most remarkable exploits. Such messages would have been understood by soldiers, veterans, and well-educated Alexandrians, whose opinion would have rated more than the ordinary fellahîn, who probably were less interested. The silver might anyway be reaped – at least to some extent – by re-melting a stock of old, perhaps even worn coins. The amount of circulating coins will then remain at the same level.

If nothing else, the hoard evidence tells us that a considerable amount of tetradrachms left circulation. We do not know if – and how much – the Roman government cared about a general supply of coins for Egypt. I suspect that they did not care very much. On the other hand, there can be no doubt that the prefect – or the person who decided on such matters – would have reacted if the tax collectors reported a lack of coinage for the population to pay their coin taxes, and if the customs stations reported an insufficient amount for effecting the obligatory exchange of coinage.

On the supposition that the existing hoard evidence represents the actual circulation of coins, Nero's tetradrachms dominated the use of coins in Egypt for at least a century. They constitute 47.3 – 86.11% of all 14 hoards with end dates Hadrian – Marcus Aurelius with an additional amount of coins from Hadrian's reign (up to 24.71%) and to a lesser extent coins from the reign of Trajan (4.44% or less, and often less amounts than coins from Claudius' reign). Even in the three hoards with end dates of Hadrian, his tetradrachms are merely represented by 0.46 – 7.69%, and Trajan's coinage hardly at all.

This phenomenon is not witnessed by the Karanis group (cf. *fig. 14*), where there is a gap between one hoard of end date Nero and the later hoards. This gap, however, may be due to which layers were accessible for the American expedition to Kôm Aushîm

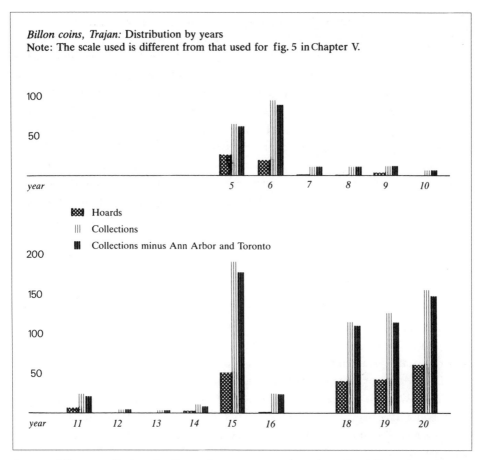

FIG. 6. *Billon coins Trajan; distribution by years. Note: The scale used is different from that used for fig. 5.*

(see above, Chap. 3, p. 66), and the gap seems to be closed by Kôm Aushîm 1896, excavated by Grenfell and Hunt, probably in the area which later became depleted by the *sebabkîn*.

Accordingly, Nero's coinage seems only slowly to have been supplanted by later coins, and according to my survey of 1985, all hoards together have a total of 2,131 (= 2.89%) coins from Hadrian's reign, but only 261 (= 0.35%) from the reign of Trajan and 699 (= 0.95%) from the reign of Antoninus Pius.[86]

The low production of tetradrachms during Trajan's reign may partly be explained by the Egyptian famine reported by the younger Pliny[87] (which may be dated to AD 99/100),[88] partly by the revolt ravaging Egypt during the last part of his reign. But exactly years 18-20 (AD 114-117) are represented by relatively high numbers in the hoards (39-61 specimens)[89] (cf. *fig. 6*).

It cannot be excluded that the relatively high production of tetradrachms during year 5 (AD 101/102: 27 coins; three types in hoards) and year 6 (AD 102/103: 20 coins; two types in hoards) may be connected with the first Dacian war (AD 101-102). Likewise, the probable increase during years 18 (AD 114/115: 39 coins; four types in hoards), 19 (AD 115/116: 43 coins; four types in hoards), and 20 (AD 116/117: 61 coins; four types in hoards) may have been caused by the Parthian war.

My die studies of coins of especially years 5 and 20 gave no definite conclusions but indicated a slower production than during the first part of Nero's reign, not to speak of the latter part.[90] Anyway, the available stock of existing coins may not have been sufficient for the required expenses, which accordingly were met by a combination of existing and a small amount of new coins.

Even then, the rather low production during these years must make us wonder if actual or planned warfare is the explanation of the vast production during Nero's last years.

The Roman government may have felt a need for advertising the triumphal events by issuing new coins and might have got the necessary silver from re-melting older coinage, but the reverse types offer little to support such views. In year 5 we do find Nike (only one specimen found in the hoards) and trophy (no specimens found in the hoards), and in year 6 emperor in quadriga (three specimens in hoards). However, if these coins were meant for special donations, for example to the soldiers, such donations cannot have been a conspicuous part of the coinage. Also, the dominant type for both years is a standing eagle, which is a recurrent reverse type for the whole Alexandrian series.

No specific types exist from years 18-20, and it will scarcely be possible to look for any special advertising among the types of Zeus, Dikaiosyne, Sarapis, and Nilus.

Furthermore, if the varied production of Alexandrian tetradrachms is to be explained by military events during Trajan's reign, it remains to be explained why the production seems very low at the time of the second Dacian war (AD 105/106 = years 8-9: one coin, one type, respectively three coins and two types in hoards), whereas year 15 (AD 111/112) – for which no particular events are recorded – is the peak of the curve (51 coins, 7-8 types in hoards).

Walker may be right in explaining that the debasement of the denarius in AD 104-107 and a subsequent increase in its production was caused by the increased expenses during the Dacian wars,[91] and the parsimonious striking of silver tetradrachms in Egypt may in the same way be explained as a parsimony caused by lack of available silver.

The Alexandrian coinage may add another point to this conclusion. Whereas the mint in Alexandria struck no tetradrachms during Trajan's first four ruling years in

Egypt, it commenced already in the first year an apparently rather large production of bronze coins of size I, which continued throughout the reign.[92] If I am right in explaining this coin to represent a drachm, and four bronze drachms to be the equivalent of one silver tetradrachm,[93] then this bronze coinage would have been a valuable addition to the circulating currency. The Roman government might advertise the emperor thrice as much without spending silver.

In the long run, Trajan's coin politics and the gold mines in the newly captured Dacia[94] may have alleviated the financial situation, but according to the Scriptores, Hadrian on his accession gave a grandiloquent and detailed statement on the 'straits of the public treasury'[95].

Such declarations on an emperor's accession are almost a *topos* among ancient authors on imperial history, and as always we do not know the source of this quotation. Anyhow, it is contradicted by the information given by the same author that the new emperor was able to give a double donation to the soldiers[96] and a double *congiarium* to the populace of Rome (in addition to the three *aurei* already distributed in his absence).[97] Hadrian's cessation of the eastern war may have lessened the financial distress, and Dio Cassius lauds his generosity towards individuals and communities.[98]

His plentiful supply of silver coinage in the East may be explained by his travels there,[99] implying expenditure on new cities, erecting or refurbishing public buildings and the like.[100] Direct expenses for his needs during such trips, and the needs of his entourage, may have been defrayed more by requisitions and other local contributions than by payments in cash.[101]

Whereas the silver coinage in Caesarea underwent a debasement during the 130's,[102] the Egyptian tetradrachm kept the Neronian standard until the reign of Marcus Aurelius (see next chapter), and according to the hoard evidence was produced at an even level during the whole reign of Hadrian,[103] apart from year 1 (AD 116/117) and year 7 (AD 122/123).

If the riot in Alexandria, caused by the discovery of a new Apis-bull,[104] can be dated to AD 122/123, we may have a direct connection between this event and disruption of the minting, and in fact the riot is stated to have occurred just after Hadrian's visit to Britain and Gaul, which can be dated to AD 121/122.[105]

Similarly, the lack of coinage from year 1 may be explained by the riots in Egypt upon Hadrian's accession to power,[106] but could also have been due to the fact that the Egyptian regnal year consisted of only a few days.

More decisive is that the revolt in Judaea in AD 133-135 (= years 18-20) does not seem to be reflected by the Alexandrian tetradrachms, either with regard to an increase in the production or in choice of types.

The imperial visit to Egypt can be dated to AD 130-131 (the Egyptian year 15),[107] and is no doubt reflected in the reverse type (in billon as well as in bronze) showing the emperor standing together with Alexandria, perhaps also the occurrence of Sabina on the reverse. If, however, a concentration of few types as a general rule implies a vast increase in the coin production, it is but meagerly supported by the hoard evidence in this particular case.[108]

In the Scriptores we find the remarkable statement that Hadrian had 'as complete a knowledge of the state-budget (*omnes publicas rationes*)' as 'any careful householder (*paterfamilias*) has of his own household'.[109] If this is a true description of Hadrian's financial politics, he would not have squandered a possible surplus on empty purposes. His vast coinage in the East may reflect his benevolence towards, and interest in the eastern provinces, including Egypt.

In Egypt, however, at least part of the silver needed for minting new coins may have been gained by re-melting older coinage rather than producing an increased amount of totally new coinage.

This may have lessened the circulating amount of Nero's tetradrachms, but did not cause them to disappear. The pool of coins seems to have remained constant, and since the new coins kept to the same standard, it will cause no surprise to find a stable level of prices in the papyrus documents for such staple commodities as wine, donkeys, and wheat.[110] We may be more surprised that Nero – an emperor so badly reputed – still adorned the obverse of the coins most in use, for as long as a century after his death.

NOTES

1. Suetonius, *Nero* XXXI and XXXVIII.
2. Cf. also Tacitus, *Annales* XV. 45.
3. Suetonius, *Nero* XXXII.
4. Suetonius, *Nero* XLIV.
5. Pliny, *Naturalis Historiae* XXXIII.13.
6. Walker I (1976), p.18.
7. See Butcher & Ponting (1996), pp. 75f.
8. The explanation given by Walker III (1978), p.111.
9. Dutilh (1896), p. 60.
10. Dattari (1900), p. 386.
11. Christiansen (1985), p. 81.
12. Caron (1894), p. 155.
13. Dattari (1900), p. 270.
14. Milne (1933/1970), p. xx.
15. El-Khachab (1951), pp. 31ff.
16. Metcalf (1976), pp. 65ff.

17. Mentioned by Dattari in a letter to Milne (See Christiansen & Easson (forthcoming)).
18. Examples in Christiansen (1988) I, p. 88.
19. Christiansen (1992b), p. 102.
20. Milne (1933/1971), p.xx.
21. Christiansen (1988) I, pp. 61f.
22. Christiansen (1988) I, pp. 36, 39, and 100.
23. Milne (1933/1971), p. xvii.
24. Hazzard (1990/1993), p. 97.
25. Christiansen (1988) I, p. 13 (with references II, p. 29, note 48).
26. Cf. SNGCop. Egypt: The Ptolemies 40 (1974), Nos. 376ff., esp. 413ff.
27. Walker I (1976), pp. 146f. and 154.
28. Christiansen (1988) I, p. 90; cf. p. 104.
29. Oddone & Savio (1989) and Savio & Oddone (1990).
30. Christiansen (1988) I, pp. 62ff.
31. Savio (1988).
32. Christiansen (1988) I, p.104.
33. Christiansen (1988) I, p. 12; cf. p. 104 and Baratte (1974), pp. 86f.
34. Christiansen (1988) I, p. 68.
35. Christiansen (1988) I, p. 307.
36. See esp. Howgego (1990) and Metcalf (1989) and (1990b), pp. 467ff.
37. Christiansen (1996), p. 93.
38. Christiansen (1988) I, p. 94.
39. Christiansen (1988) II, pp. 106f.
40. Christiansen (1988) I, pp.68ff,
41. Tacitus, *Annales* XV.1ff.
42. Tacitus, *Annales* XV.26.
43. Suetonius, *Nero* XXXV.5 and Dio Cassius LXIII(LXII).18.1; but cf. also Tacitus, *Annales* XV.36 and Suetonius, *Nero* XIX.1 on the postponement of the visit.
44. Seneca, *Questiones Naturales* VI.8.3f. and Pliny, *Naturalis Historiae* VI.181; but cf. also Dio Cassius LXIII(LXII).8.1 on the cancellation of these expeditions.
45. Tacitus, *Historiae* I.31 and 70; Josephus, *Bellum Judaicum* II.18.8 (494).
46. Josefus, *Bellum Judaicum* II.18.7 (487).
47. Tacitus, *Annales* XV.46: 'quippe haud alias tam immota pax'.
48. Haatvedt & Peterson (1964), p. 19.
49. Baratte (1974). Almost 57 illegible coins also belong to Nero's reign.
50. Visonà (1983).
51. Sotheby Sale 9th March 1972, No. 286.
52. Dutilh (1891).
53. *CH* 7 (1985), p. 33, note 150 (A. Easson).
54. See above, Chap. 4, p. x, note 40.
55. Wainwright (1925).
56. Most prominently Bell (1938), but see now Bowman in *CAH²* X, 1996, p. 691.

57. Edition with comments and translation into French by Chalon (1964).
58. Christiansen (1984), pp. 292ff. I have made no systematic examination of later publications.
59. Christiansen (1988), I, p. 104.
60. See Christiansen & Easson (forthcoming).
61. Milne (1910).
62. Ptolemy XIII according to Milne, but see *IGCH*, p. 242, No. 1732.
63. Milne (1910), p. 337.
64. Milne (1933/1971), p. xx.
65. Christiansen (1985), p. 81.
66. Milne (1933/1971), p. 3.
67. Milne (1933/1971), p. xx.
68. Christiansen (1992b), p. 109.
69. *Pace* Bruun (1991), pp. 75f.
70. In *RPC* I.1 (1992), p. 705.
71. Walker I (1976), p. 142ff.
72. Hazzard (1990/1993), p. 97.
73. Cf. Christiansen (1996), p. 96.
74. For which see Butcher & Ponting (1996), p. 66.
75. Christiansen (1988) I, pp. 68ff.
76. Christiansen (1988) I, p. 105.
77. Christiansen (1985), p. 81. For a probable estimate of the actual production of tetradrachms during Otho's reign, see Savio (1991), esp. pp. 122f.
78. For which see *RPC* II (1999), pp. 319ff.
79. RPC II (1999), pp. 270 and 276.
80. Christiansen (1985), p. 81.
81. Speidel (1992), p. 88, Table 1.
82. Milne (1933/1971), p. xxi.
83. See now RPC II (1999), pp. 328ff.
84. As presented by Caradice (1983), pp. 153ff.
85. In *RPC* II (1999), p. 12.
86. Christiansen (1985), p.81.
87. Pliny, *Panegyricus*, 30ff.
88. Christiansen (1988) I, p. 250.
89. Christiansen (1988) I, pp. 129ff.
90. Christiansen (1988) I, pp. 239f.
91. Walker III (1978), pp. 121f. For conflicting views and discussion see Christiansen (1988) I, pp. 252f.
92. Christiansen (1988) II, pp. 118ff.
93. Christiansen (1988) I, p. 254.
94. Mrozek (1977).
95. Scriptores, *Hadrian* VI.5: 'difficultatibus aerarii ambitiose ac diligenter expositis'.

96. Scriptores, *Hadrian* V.7.
97. Scriptores, *Hadrian* VII.3.
98. Dio Cassius LXIX.5.1.
99. Cf. Walker III (1978), p. 124.
100. As explicitly mentioned by Dio Cassius LXIX.5.3.
101. See Halfmann (1986), pp. 70ff.
102. Walker II (1977), p. 83.
103. Milne (1933/1971), p. xxi; cf. also Christiansen (1973/1976). There is no detailed study of this question.
104. Scriptores, *Hadrian* XII.1.
105. See Halfmann (1986), p. 190.
106. Scriptores, *Hadrian* V.2.
107. See now Halfmann (1986), pp. 193f.
108. Cf. Christiansen (1973/1976), p. 247.
109. Scriptores, *Hadrian* XX.11.
110. Rathbone (1993/1996), pp. 329ff. and (1997), pp. 213ff., with precautions taken, pp. 183ff., for probable windfalls etc.

CHAPTER VI

COMMODUS AND A DORMANT CRISIS?

Now this 'Golden One', this 'Hercules', this 'god' (for he was given even this name, too) suddenly drove into Rome one afternoon from his suburb and conducted thirty horse races in the space of two hours. These proceedings had much to do with his running short of funds. He was also fond, it is true, of bestowing gifts, and frequently gave largesses to the populace at the rate of one hundred and forty denarii per man; but most of his expenditures were for the objects I have mentioned.

DIO CASSIUS LXXIII.16.1

Financial distress

Although the biographer of Commodus in the same vein claims that the expenses for Commodus' luxurious living had drained the treasury,[1] Dio's verdict on Commodus' finances does not seem quite fair. Walker even declared:

if a date must be given for the origins of the decline of the Roman world, it would not be that of the death of Marcus Aurelius but his accession.[2]

Expenditure, especially wars in the West as well as in the East, seems to have caused serious financial problems for Marcus Aurelius. When he returned from the Marcomanic war, the treasury was so empty that, according to the favourable description given by his biographer in the Scriptores, Marcus was obliged to have a great auction of imperial property, since he did not want to increase the taxation of the provinces.[3] Added to continuous warfare were barbarian invasions, the revolt of Avidius Cassius, and outbreak of the plague. The income of the Empire could scarcely cover expenditure, and the emperor was forced to debase the coinage.[4] The first debasement in AD 161 has an evident connection with the vast donatives[5] that a new emperor was expected to offer upon his accession to the praetorians, the legions, and the populace of Rome just at the outbreak of the Parthian war. Peace and triumph in AD 166 seem to have been followed by a slight improvement of the denarius standard, but a new debasement took place in the period AD 170-179, and it would be interesting to have more precise information about the discussion the emperor then had with the senate concerning the treasury, according to Dio Cassius.[6]

Debasements of the denarius were no novelty. It had recently occurred in AD 148 during the reign of Antoninus Pius.[7] They now began to take place at shorter intervals than before, and yet Marcus probably left an empty treasury to his son – in spite of Eutropius' claim to the opposite.[8]

Whatever the truth of this, recent scholarship has added an even more serious problem regarding the financial administration of the Roman Empire. During the 170's the mining activities at Rio Tinto in Spain were disrupted.[9] This disruption of what apparently had formed the 'largest single minting site of antiquity',[10] originally 'making the largest bullion contribution from the Western Empire',[11]will have meant a serious loss of reserves.

Regardless of the extravagance, or otherwise, of Commodus, any emperor – even a prudent one – would have had difficulties in making ends meet. Yet, according to the unfavourable description given by Herodian, Commodus after his acclamation not only gave generous donatives in cash to the soldiers in the West,[12] but even bought an (ignominious) peace with the barbarians by offering them 'an exorbitant sum of money'.[13]

Be that as it may, he did, however, enact a new debasement of the denarius, lowering not only the silver content, but this time the weight as well (down to 3 grams).[14] The imperial denarius had entered a vicious decline, from which it never really revived.

The Alexandrian tetradrachms of Commodus

In Marcus Aurelius' 10th regnal year in Egypt (AD 169/170) the mint of Alexandria stopped producing tetradrachms. During the preceding years the production had been low,[15] and the silver fineness had begun to decline.[16] The emperor's visit to Egypt in AD 175/176[17] may dimly be reflected in the – meagre – production of bronze coins, but otherwise Vogt's interpretation of the types[18] may serve as an example of his farfetched conclusions. Based on a few – rarely represented – reverse types, he claims this 'Vermehrung der ägyptisch-griechischen Göttertypen' to show the emperor's interest in 'Religion des Landes', whereas one of the thirteen types, depicting Eirene and Euthenia (which is not uncommon among the Alexandrian series), proclaims that the Egyptians after the restored peace following the revolt of Avidius Cassius can return to their usual work in the fields 'im Dienste Roms'.

When the striking of tetradrachms re-opened the following year, a new standard was introduced. Notwithstanding the debasements of the denarius, the tetradrachm had previously kept the Neronian standard. Now, according to Walker's measurements, mean weight of silver fell to 0.92 grams and the mean weight of the coin to 11.90 grams (cf. *fig. 1*).[19]

The last point – which is not in dispute – is the most important. Whereas doubts may be raised regarding how much contemporaries knew and cared about the actual silver value of the previous tetradrachms, a weight reduction of almost two grams would be quite evident for everyone.

The production of tetradrachms ceased again, and when it was re-opened during Commodus' reign, in AD 180/181 (reckoned as year 21 of Marcus Aurelius), all the coins were produced to this new standard and with a thinner flan than before. Anyone who has had some hundreds of these coins between his fingers can tell the difference!

We would expect such coinage to have been followed by an increased production of the new coins with the aim of calling back the older and better coinage. Nero had done so – with great success as it seems (cf. Chap. 5 above, p. 97), and whether or not Commodus was aware of this precedent, he – or his prefect of Egypt – seems to have tried a similar attempt.

According to my survey of 1985,[20] the tetradrachms of Commodus – with a total of 920 – make up 1.24% of totals in the hoards. Milne found a few die links among the obverses,[21] but we have no other die studies to serve as a possible clue to the original production. According to Milne's survey, the issue 'soon developed to a larger output than had been made at Alexandria for over a century'.[22] According to the same evidence, the distribution across years 21 to year 30 (AD 189/190) is very uneven, and specimens from the last three years are rare.

According to the hoard-evidence as presented here, Commodus' tetradrachms never dominated the circulation of coins to the same extent as Nero's coinage (cf. *fig. 18*).

Two Dattari Hoards have an end date during Commodus' reign. In one of them (Dattari B'07A) 15 tetradrachms of Commodus make 65.21% (*versus* 5 = 21.73% of Nero), whereas the other (Dattari A'11) contains only 17 or 0.74% (*versus* 1,330 = 58.56% of Nero). Nor does Commodus' coinage figure largely in the later hoards (regardless of groups). The only exceptions seem to be 'Alexandria 1916' (end date Gallienus year 9), where 256 specimens are found (= 20.48%), surpassed by 341 of Severus Alexander (27.28%), and Dattari A'07, end date Probus year 2, with 352 specimens or 16.24% (*versus* 707 of Nero or 32.62%). Among the other Dattari Hoards (cf. *fig. 16*) Commodus' coinage is only represented in three hoards (with percentages between 2.7 and 6.6), among the Karanis Hoards (cf. *fig. 14*) in only five (with percentages between 0.33 and 1.94), and among 'other supposed hoards' (cf. *fig. 17*) only in four hoards (with percentages between 0.12 and 6.1).

The conclusion seems to be that the Roman government during the first part of Commodus' rule did try to bring in the older coins, but failed in the attempt, and the explanation may be that too little silver was available for initiating or at least completing it, although continued warfare might have caused a need for striking new coins. Another reason may be that Egypt still suffered from a decline in population and production, caused by the plague,[23] meaning fewer possibilities for effecting the change in practice.

A look at the bronze coinage is also revealing. The striking of bronze coins, especially the 'drachms', continued during the reigns of Hadrian and Antoninus Pius on a comparatively large scale, but diminished rapidly during Marcus Aurelius,[24] whereas the reign of Commodus only produced bronze coins of size III to any large extent.[25]

From now on, copper was probably needed for striking the highly debased silver coins in Alexandria as well as in Rome. Yet it is tempting to ask if the imperial government was even running out of reserves of copper.

It has been claimed[26] that the based silver tetradrachm meant no need for the lesser denominations in bronze. We do not seem to know, however, if the tetradrachm lost in nominal value, whereas the need for minor exchange may from now on have been met by continuous use of the older bronze coins (see Chap. 2 above, p. 51), furthermore by leaden tokens,[27] although we cannot date their appearance in circulation with sufficient certainty.[28]

Commodus may have been extravagant, but the financial administration was met with even more serious problems. The time seems past when an emperor might expect sufficient income to cover expenditure. Reserves were dwindling and expenses growing. Previous debasements had cured similar symptoms with success. Now they must have seemed the only way to save the monetary system, unless the burden of taxation could be increased or the soldiers be content with less than their due.

A dormant crisis?

In a way, the story now repeats itself. The new standard of the Alexandrian tetradrachm was kept during the rule of subsequent emperors, although this time, apparently only for a period of some fifty years (see Chap. 7 below, p. 117). The coin production during these years may again be explained by 'the need to produce coinage for a closed currency area' (see Chap. 5 above, p. 98), although it cannot be excluded that, to some extent at least, it was stimulated by events, whether causing minting of totally new coins or replacement by re-melting older coinage.

According to my survey of 1985, tetradrachms from the reign of Septimius Severus hardly ever occur in the hoards (20 specimens = 0.03% of totals),[29] and – if nothing else – my die studies of 1988 proved that the original production of billon as well as bronze coins must have been very low.[30] Among the few coins known I found many identical dies and die links, even overlapping the two metals, from which follows a decreasing probability for discovering new dies among other coins and an increasing probability for a very low number of dies in actual use.

This may seem surprising since we know of several conspicuous events which might have caused a need for striking coins in Alexandria.[31] Severus' *coup d'état* and the war in the East against Pescennius Niger AD 193/194 may be the reason behind some minting activity in Alexandria, but according to the hoard evidence, the production was low (year 2 = AD 193/194: 10 specimens, five reverse types; year 3: one specimen only),[32] especially compared with the other mints in the East,[33] and the Alexandrian mint seems even to have struck denarii (although for use outside Egypt).[34] A similar connection may be claimed between the first Parthian war, especially its end, and the minting activity in year 4 (AD 195/196), but again only to some extent (six specimens, four types in the hoards).[35] Severus' second war against Parthia AD 197/198 (year 6) seems to have had almost no effect on the production of Alexandrian tetradrachms (only one coin in the hoards),[36] which may be explained by an apparent concentration of all eastern coinage in Laodicea ad Mare in AD 196 to 202.[37]

One existing coin of year 17 (AD 208/209)[38] and three of year 19 (AD 210/211)[39] have a reverse legend running NEIKH KATABPET[ANΩN] ('victory over the Britons'). Although they are rare instances of an explicit reference to a specific war among the Alexandrian reverses, even they will not affect the conclusion that wars and planned warfare, in the East as well as in the West, had little effect on the coin production in Alexandria during Severus' reign.

It may be more surprising that the same is true for the emperor's visit to Egypt in AD 199/200 (years 8-9).[40] Although year 9 is fairly well represented among the bronze coins in the collections (13 specimens, 8-9 types),[41] there is only one tetradrachm in the hoards (of year 8),[42] and among the coins known, the visit is only directly referred to by one reverse type (of year 8), depicting the emperor standing together with Alexandria.[43] Although we have a papyrus (PSI 683) testifying to expenditure for this visit being met by local requisitions in kind, the same text also mentions 'silver (money) sent in advance from the treasury'[44] for the same purpose. Of course, we do not know which coins were meant, but on the whole, the explanation that coin production was mainly caused by public expenditure is vanishing, at least regarding the Alexandrian mint during this period. Neither Severus' doubling of the legionary pay,[45] nor his other expenses,[46] are reflected in the production of Alexandrian coins. All this ought to be a warning against putting too much emphasis on the wish to advertise the emperor and his exploits.

On the whole, the coin production in Alexandria was very parsimonious during the reign of Septimius Severus. That this parsimony was a deliberate choice may be implied by a decree in which the emperor strictly forbade *adaeratio* (i.e. converting levies of produces into equivalences of coinage).[47] If enforced, this would have meant less need for ready coinage. On the other hand, I am still inclined to believe that he – or his prefects of Egypt – tried to conceal this parsimony by striking new coins every year,[48] avoiding the impression of a scarce availability of coins.

Earlier scholarship has claimed a *replacement* of the Alexandrian tetradrachm by the imperial denarius during the reign of Septimius Severus.[49] The papyrological evidence does not vindicate this view,[50] nor does the hoard evidence. Even if Dattari was right in claiming that the majority of imperial denarii found in Egypt belong to the Severan period,[51] 142 Severan denarii in one hoard = A80 (or 20.67% of totals)[52] and 118 imperial silver coins belonging to the Maspero Collection (and probably being a hoard found in Egypt)[53] may be an interesting indication that some denarii crept in across the border, but not to any substantial degree, compared with the other evidence. Interestingly enough, the same may have been the case during Trajan's reign, from which are attested 115 imperial silver coins in three hoards or 21.83% of totals.[54]

During the first years of Caracalla's reign there was a brief revival of striking large bronze coins (the 'drachms'),[55] after which the Alexandrian mint was closed, quite unaffected by the new increase in the legionary pay.[56] At least no coins are known with a later date than year 23 of Septimius Severus (= AD 214/215). This has been explained as part of Caracalla's revenge on the Alexandrians,[57] following his furious massacre in the city itself.[58]

The explanation has a clear modernist flavour: coins were meant for the benefit of the population, and especially for promoting trade. There is no cogent reason why the Roman emperors should have had such motives behind their coin politics. It does seem rather strange, though – even for an emperor like Caracalla – to take revenge by lessening the amount of coins available for paying taxes! Another explanation may be found in the contemporaneous debasement of the Syrian tetradrachm,[59] followed by a vast increase in the coin production by the eastern mints.[60] Large amounts of silver and copper will have been used for this purpose, no metal was left for striking other coinage in the East, where we know of other towns of military importance which did not strike coins during Caracalla's Parthian war.[61]

At least we should not forget that a temporary closure had happened in Alexandria before, e.g. during the reign of Marcus Aurelius. Caracalla's short reign ended before a later revival could have taken place.

The revival came during the reigns of his successors, apart from Macrinus, whose rare Alexandrian coins are never found in the hoards. According to my survey of 1985,[62] 510 tetradrachms from the reign of Elagabalus constitute 0.69% of totals in hoards and 1,569 from the reign of Severus Alexander 2.13%. A look at the collections may give the impression of a more equal proportion between these two reigns,[63] but obverses of five imperial women (*versus* two of Alexander) have caused a disproportionately high amount of coins from the reign of Elagabalus to be represented in the collections.

The revival of the Alexandrian mint during the reign of Elagabalus began at a low rate in year 1, covering a period of only about two months, but rose considerably in year 2 (AD 218/219),[64] coinciding with an apparent concentration of the other silver issues in Antiochia.[65] Alexandria seems to have rejoined Antiochia as a central mint for the eastern silver coinage, and the production rose steadily during the following years, but the time seems past when the Roman government could afford or allow several busy mints in the East. If right, this explanation will imply a central control of the silver stock available for minting coins within the whole empire. Another explanation may of course be that the prefect of Egypt (or whoever it was) was free to dispose of the silver available within his own province or even entitled to ask for additional supplies.

It may be tempting to conclude that the centre for meeting expenses for warfare and planned warfare in the East had been moved back to Alexandria and therefore – again – consider public expenditure as a determining factor behind the Alexandrian coinage. The question remains, which expenditure was spent in Egypt, and if the conclusion is tenable, it will be interesting to note not only the great variations in the output of Alexandrian tetradrachms during Severus Alexander's reign,[66] but also that the amount of coins was supplemented by tetradrachms (of 'Roman' style and Alexandrian standard), produced in and apparently sent from Rome, as convincingly demonstrated by Burnett and Craddock on metrological grounds.[67] Was Alexandria unable to regain enough silver from melting in older coins? Is the reason that the production during Commodus' reign had been insufficient to refill the pool necessary for needs within the Egyptian province and the coin exchange at the borders? Had the pool even decreased during the meagre years in between?

Fewer circulating coins might have caused – at least a partial – demonetization, which will be difficult to trace. If, on the other hand, the level of production remained the same, the effect would have been a fall in prices.

According to the papyrological evidence, however, the price of staple goods seems to have doubled at the end of the 2nd century, followed by a long period of broad stability.[68]

The leap in prices may have been provoked by the coin debasement at the end of Marcus Aurelius' reign, but another – more serious – cause may have been the devastating effects of the plague that hit Egypt in AD 166/167, as explained by D. Rathbone.[69] I cannot share his view, however, that the debasement of the coinage was a reaction to the rise in price levels. He asks why the government should issue double the amount of silver to buy, for example, the same amount of wheat. Actually, the silver content was more than halved, and yet the nominal value may have remained the same. The subsequent stabilization of prices may find its counterpart in the continued use of the older bronze coins, especially the 'drachms', as testified by – admittedly meagre – evidence of the bronze hoards until the time of Severus Alexander.[70]

The bronze coinage may have compensated for the decreasing number of tetra-drachms, at least for use inside Egypt, or replaced them to some extent, at least for paying amounts higher than the smallest. If true, it is interesting to note the sudden revival of the production of bronze 'drachms' in the 10th year of Severus Alexander (AD 230/231),[71] although the specimens known today rarely seem very worn. The Roman government may have repeated Trajan's attempt – whether they knew of it or not – to remedy a shortage of silver bullion (see Chap. 5 above, p. 101). The palm, always represented on the reverses of these coins, testifies to the emperor's *decenalia* as the formal occasion for this – almost last – striking of Alexandrian bronze coins. The two purposes may not be mutually exclusive.

NOTES

1. Scriptores, *Commodus* XVI.8: 'Luxuriae sumptibus aerarium minuerat'.
2. Walker III (1978), p. 125.
3. Scriptores, *Marcus Antoninus* XVII.4: 'he held a public sale.. of the imperial furnishings' (The story is repeated in XXI.8).
4. For this and the following, see Walker III (1978), pp. 125f.
5. 20,000 sesterces apiece to 'the common soldier and to the others money in proportion' (Scriptores, *Marcus Antoninus* VII.9).
6. Dio Cassius LXXII.33.2.
7. See Walker III (1978), p. 124.
8. Eutropius VIII.8; but see Walker III (1978), p. 125.
9. Jones (1980), pp. 161ff.
10. Jones (1980), p. 146.
11. Jones (1980), p. 161.
12. Herodian I.5.1.
13. Herodian I.6.9.
14. Walker II (1977), p. 47 and III (1978), p. 126.
15. Cf. Milne (1933/1971), p. xxii.
16. Walker II (1977), pp. 114f.
17. Halfmann (1986), p. 213.
18. Vogt (1924), I, p. 144.
19. Walker II (1977), p. 115.
20. Christiansen (1985), p. 81.

21. Milne (1933/1971), nos. 2639 and 2646 (year 23); 2660 and 2661 (year 26, the reverse date of both has been recut from an E to a Σ); 2685 and 2688 (year 30).
22. Milne (1933/1971), p. xxii.
23. Cf. Rathbone (1993/1996), p. 334 on the evidence of the papyri.
24. This is evident from table 4 in Bland (1996), p. 121. Although based on number of types in Vogt (1924), the picture is confirmed by Milne (1933/1971), pp. xxif.
25. See Milne (1933/1971), p. xxii.
26. Thus see recently, Savio 3 (1997), p. 22.
27. Milne (1908) and (1922), p. 159.
28. See also Christiansen (2002).
29. Christiansen (1985), p. 81.
30. Christiansen (1988) I, pp. 287ff., cf. also Metcalf (1979).
31. Further discussion and full references in Christiansen (1988) I, p. 297.
32. Christiansen (1988) I, p. 276.
33. Cf. e.g. Walker III (1978), pp. 79 and 97.
34. See, most recently, Savio (1985) and Bland (1996), p. 124.
35. Christiansen (1988) I, pp. 276f.
36. Christiansen (1988) I, p. 277.
37. Cf. *BMCRE* V, intr., pp. XIVf (Mattingly) and Mattingly (1932), pp. 180f.
38. Milne (1933/1971), no. 2726.
39. See Metcalf (1979), p. 180.
40. Halfmann (1986), p. 218.
41. Christiansen (1988) I, pp. 280f.
42. Christiansen (1988) I, p. 277.
43. Milne (1933/1971), no. 2723. For a similar specimen in Athens – from a different die – see Christiansen (1988) I, p. 271.
44. Lines 15-16.
45. Speidel (1922), p. 88, table 1.
46. Cf. Crawford (1975), p. 565.
47. P. Col. 123a; further discussion in Christiansen (1988) I, p. 299.
48. Christiansen (1988) I, p. 301.
49. Further discussion and references in Christiansen (1988) I, p.296.
50. See Christiansen (1984), pp. 272ff., esp. p. 282.
51. See chap. two above, p. 42.
52. Christiansen (1985), p. 88.
53. Callu (1969), p. 181.
54. See Christiansen (1985), p. 88 and chap. two above, p. 42.
55. Milne (1933/1971), p. xxiii.
56. Speidel (1992), p. 88, table 1.
57. Vogt (1924), I, p. 173.
58. Dio Cassius LXXVIII (LXXVII), 22f.
59. Walker III (1978), pp. 131f.

60. Bellinger (1940), pp. 6f.
61. Bellinger (1940), p. 11.
62. Christiansen (1985), p. 81.
63. Cf. Bland (1996), table 5 at p. 121, based on Vogt (1924).
64. Milne (1933/1971), p. xxiii.
65. Bellinger (1940), p. 7.
66. As shown by Milne (1933/1971), p. xxiii.
67. Burnett & Craddock (1983).
68. Rathbone (1993/1996), p.333 and (1997), p. 215.
69. Rathbone (1993/1996), p. 334.
70. See Chap. 2 above, p. 51.
71. Milne (1933/1971), p. xxiii.

CHAPTER VII

GALLIENUS and AURELIAN

I am ashamed to relate what Gallienus used often to say at this time, when such things were happening, as though jesting amid the ills of mankind. For when he was told of the revolt of Egypt, he is said to have exclaimed: 'What! We cannot do without Egyptian linen!'

SCRIPTORES, *The Two Gallieni* VI.3-4

Whereas the biographer of Gallienus in the Scriptores describes Gallienus in most vilifying terms, the biography of Aurelian rates Aurelian among the 'good emperors', although with some reservations,[1] and explicitly mentions his care for supplies from Egypt to the city of Rome.[2]

This may have an evident connection with political events. During Gallienus' sole reign after Valerian's captivity by the Sassanid emperor in AD 260, revolts flared up all over the Roman Empire, which was still being ravaged by hostile warfare almost everywhere, and even was threatened by dissolution with an independent 'Gallic empire' in the West and a *de facto* Palmyrene rule over the East. Aurelian, on the other hand, not only re-united the Empire but also seems – to some extent at least – to have re-established peace and order within, and at, the borders.

The Alexandrian tetradrachms of Gallienus

In AD 260 the strategos of the Oxyrhynchite nome ordered the bankers to re-open their banks and to accept 'the emperors' coins'.[3] It remains a matter of dispute whether this reflects a general distrust of the coinage or reflects momentary lack of confidence in the rule of Macrianus and Quietus,[4] who just had usurped power over Egypt.[5]

Whereas Quietus held his stand in Upper Egypt, Alexandria – or at least its mint – was soon regained by troops loyal to Gallienus, and Alexandrian tetradrachms were struck in his name during the 9th year of Valerian (AD 260/261).

Some of these coins have HA for date,[6] and Alföldy explained the *alpha* to be a declaration of a new era (year 1) initiated by Gallienus in the 8th year of his father (the *η̄ta*).[7]

On some of these coins, however, the *ῆta* (H) is clearly cut over an orginal *theta* (θ) on the die,[8] and another – evident – explanation is that the mint of Alexandria originally had struck tetradrachms with a *theta* for year 9, but soon recut the date on the die as H (plus) A (8+1 = 9), in order to erase the ominous letter of death (θανατος) just when the captured Valerian's fate still was at stake.[9] There are, however, other indications that a new coinage had been introduced in year 8 (AD 259/260).

During the reign of Valerian the Alexandrian mint had struck coins for Gallienus as co-ruler. All the obverses portray a laureate bust of Gallienus, wearing cloak and cuirass, and the legend has a ου (= for Valerian) in addition to Gallienus' own name. In year 8 this part of the legend was omitted.[10] Furthermore, the tetradrachm was now struck on a new standard of a somewhat lower weight and an almost halving of the silver content.[11] At least from now on, the Alexandrian tetradrachm was hardly more than a bronze coin covered by a silver wash, easily worn off, and it must have become obvious for everyone rather soon that this coin had far less intrinsic value than all previous billon coins.

During the preceding reign of Trebonianus Gallus, the Alexandrian mint had only struck tetradrachms in year 3 (AD 251/252). According to Alföldy, such 'decay' tells us 'how loosely the government had been holding the reins'.[12] Although he rightly claims that the coin production had otherwise been incessant since the reign of Elagabalus, similar gaps had not been uncommon before, when – as it seems – a stock of older coins had been paid out instead of striking new coins. This is what may have happened again, although for the last time before the end of the Alexandrian coinage.

In the following period, the Alexandrian mint produced tetradrachms every year, which may have an obvious connection with the continued warfare in the East, including heavy fights over the control of Egypt. The output seems to have varied considerably from year to year, but it would be useless to compare it with specific events in each case, since public expenses may still have been met with old coinage at hand or a mixture of old and new coins, unless the government for some reason or another decided to strike and spend new coins only.

According to my survey of 1985,[13] 2,459 tetradrachms from Valerian's reign make up 3.34% of totals in hoards; and 3,543 from Gallienus' reign, a percentage of 4.81. The production fluctuated 'a good deal' during both reigns,[14] was very low in year 8 – probably due to the revolt of Macrianus and Quietus (represented by a total of 83 coins in the hoards or 0.11%) – and rose again in year 9, and especially from year 11.

If the hoard evidence as presented here mirrors the actual circulation pattern, coins from Gallienus' sole rule never became a conspicuous part of the contemporaneous circulation (cf. *fig. 18*). There are five hoards with end dates from these years, being Karanis Hoards 14-15 and 32, Alexandria 1916 (A92), and Dattari A'06. The tetradrachms of Gallienus constitute only 7.78 % or less in these hoards and even less than tetradrachms from Valerian's reign.

Milne made some interesting observations among the coins in Karanis Hoard 1. It has end date Claudius II year 2 (AD 268/269), but contains only one coin from this reign and only ten (1.16%) from Gallienus' sole reign, in contrast to 93 (11.16%) from the reign of Severus Alexander and 106 (12.72%) from the reign of Gordian III. Among the coins of Severus Alexander he found 'some coins of almost every year in fine condition', and among the coins from year 6 of Gordian III he found fourteen instances of two coins deriving from the same pair of dies.[15] Accordingly, this is probably an original savings hoard with a mixture of fresh coins coming almost directly from the mint and older coins saved for later use.

Coins from Gallienus' sole reign are not frequent in hoards with later end dates, except in three out of six of the Dattari Hoards (cf. *fig. 16*). It would be unsafe, however, to put forward an argument based on these three only, but a closer view of them may be illuminating if compared with other evidence,

Dattari B'07 has end date Aurelian year 3 (AD 271/272), but contains only 17 coins (1.59%) from Aurelian's early rule (plus two coins from the joint rule with Vaballathus), compared to 133 (12.47%) from Valerian's reign, 462 (43.33%) from Gallienus' sole rule, and 319 (29.92%) from the reign of Claudius II.

Dattari C'07 has the same end date, but contains only 49 coins (2.71%) from Aurelian's reign, compared to 111 (6.15%) from Valerian's reign, 504 (27.95%) from Gallienus' sole rule, and 978 (54.24%) from the reign of Claudius II, furthermore even 38 coins from Nero's reign (2.1%) and 19 from the reign of Hadrian (1.05%).

Dattari B'09 has end date Probus year 4 (AD 278/279), but contains only one coin from this reign, compared to 451 (23.05%) from Gallienus' sole rule, 463 (23.67%) from Valerian's reign, 132 (6.74%) from the reign of Claudius II, and even 888 earlier coins (including four from Nero's reign and two from the reign of Hadrian).

In other words, all three hoards have low percentages of contemporary coinage and relatively high percentages of not only coins from the sole reign of Gallienus, but from previous periods as well.

Dattari B'09 is even more revealing by the high number of identical obverse dies Milne found among the coins of Gordianus III, Philippus, and Valerian:[16] in other words, probably an accumulation of coins which was hoarded soon after issue and saved for later use.

The composition pattern of these three hoards receives confirmation from yet another Dattari hoard, Dattari A'07, although it contains only 61 coins (2.81%) from Gallienus' sole rule. In spite of an end date Probus year 2 (AD 276/277), it contains only four of his coins (whereto Chap. 8 below, p. 128), compared to 352 coins (16.24%) from the reign of Commodus and 413 (19.05%) from the reign of Severus Alexander, furthermore 707 (32.62%) from the reign of Nero, 151 (6.96%) from the reign of Hadrian, and even two Ptolemaic silver tetradrachms.

The other hoard evidence may seem less clear-cut, but several hoards confirm the existence of older coinage in later hoards, although not as late as the preceding four Dattari Hoards.

Karanis 14 has end date Gallienus year 11 (AD 263/264) and yet contains only four coins from his reign, compared to nine from the reign of Valerian, another nine from the reign of Nero, and ten from Hadrian's reign. 'Alexandria 1916' (A 92) has end date Gallienus year 9 (AD 261/262), but contains merely one coin from his reign, in contrast to 265 (20.48%) from the reign of Commodus, 341 (27.28%) from Severus Alexander's reign, and even six coins of Hadrian. Tell el-Maskhûta Hoard 4 (A86) with end date Trebonianus Gallus year 3 (AD 252/253) contains 58 coins from Nero's reign (35.8%) and 34 from the reign of Hadrian (20.98%). Rather high percentages of these coins are also found in Tell el-Maskhûta 1 (A87) and 3 (A89), both with end dates of Valerian's reign.

All in all, much of the hoard evidence we have from the period from Gallienus to Probus seems to indicate a preference for hoarding older coins, which probably were withdrawn from circulation.

It would have been evident for everyone that tetradrachms from before the debasement during Gallienus' sole rule were better silver coins, and, as time went on, that even tetradrachms from his reign had a higher weight than the coins from Aurelian's reign and a larger size than the coins from the reign of Probus (see Chap. 8 below, p. 126). Even the coins of Gallienus seem now to have been preferred for hoarding. A fundamental question will then be if such older coinage represented a better value in daily practice.

The papyrological evidence is very illuminating on this point. In 1984 I noted the re-appearance of 'Ptolemaic' coins in the papyri from AD 267 to 291,[17] even including one instance of 'Ptolemaic silver denarii',[18] which is an absurd term. My findings should be corrected by the revised list given by D. Rathbone,[19] according to which there are nine instances of 'old Ptolemaic' (coins), of which one was mentioned together with 'new imperial' (coins), another six of 'old imperial' (coins), and 12 or 13 of 'new imperial' (coins), in addition to the papyrus mentioning the 'Ptolemaic denarii'. All instances refer to private transactions (sale or loan), and it would have been interesting if the 'old' coinage had represented a higher value than the 'new'.

This is not the case, however. On the contrary, one papyrus is an agreement of a loan in 'Ptolemaic silver drachms' to be repaid by the same amount of 1,000 drachms in 'new silver drachms'.[20] The editor's interpretation that the repayment only represented an installment of the original loan is tempting but difficult to maintain,[21] and thus 'new coins' seem to represent the same value as the 'old (Ptolemaic)'.

This is puzzling and raises some important questions. We may generally ask if the 'old coins' in the hoards were preferred, (a) for fear of further debasements to come,

(b) if they merely had an air of being better coinage from the 'good old days', or (c) if they implied invisible favours. The only certain conclusion seems to be that their presence in hoards as well as the papyri reflects distrust in the actual coinage.

The Alexandrian tetradrachms of Aurelian

Some 25 years ago, Martin Price drew attention to the fact that there is not enough room in our calendar for Aurelian's reign to have lasted seven years, as found on the Alexandrian coins as well as in the papyri.[22] He furthermore argued for the convincing solution that the coins from Aurelian's 2nd and 3rd year should be combined as the product of the year that began 29th August AD 271 and ended in August the following year.[23]

After his re-conquest of Egypt, Aurelian enacted a change in the coinage, described by Zosimus (writing around AD 600?) in the following way:

> Now he officially issued new money after arranging for the state to buy in the debased coinage to avoid confusion in financial decline.[24]

It is very unclear what Zosimus actually meant by this passage and – of course – uncertain how he knew. There has been common agreement that it – in some way or another – should be combined with the curious occurrence of XX and XXI on some imperial coins,[25] but as Watson recently remarked: 'there the agreement ends'.[26]

There seems though to be agreement among scholars today that the existing coins testify to a better control of the weight standard and a slight increase of the silver value.[27]

Neither the XX nor the XXI (or its equivalent KA on the 'Greek' coins) occur on the Alexandrian tetradrachms, and yet Aurelian's coin enactment may have had effects in Egypt as well.

Recently, W. Metcalf observed an interesting pattern in the composition of the late hoards. Generally, there is a clear distinction around Aurelian's year 4 (AD 272/273) or 5 (AD 273/274): some hoards contain few, or no later coins than that, and many other hoards contain predominantly, or exclusively, coins of a later date.[28]

In five cases, the explanation of this disruption may be that the hoards have end dates Aurelian year 3 (Dattari B'07 and C'07), year 4 (Karanis 5), or year 6 (Karanis Nos. 6-7) and therefore may have been deposited as 'emergency hoards' during the unruly events connected with the re-conquest of Egypt. Another explanation may be that the government had forcibly retracted coins from Vaballathus' independent rule over Egypt (being represented by only eight coins in all hoards (0.01%) or the coins from his joint rule with Aurelian, which is represented in the hoards by 534 specimens (or 0.73%),[29] but almost only in two hoards (Dattari C'09 and B'11).

From measuring the weights, however, W. Metcalf concluded that a lower, but more stable standard was introduced during year 5 (AD 273/274) with full effects from the following year.[30] Furthermore, since the coins of year 5 'show a much-improved portrait of the emperor along with a neater epigraphy',[31] it is evident that a new coinage was introduced.

My survey of 1984 gave a total of 1,369 tetradrachms (1.86%) from Aurelian's reign,[32] but Milne made clear that the coin production was much higher during years 5-6 than before.[33]

Whatever the connection may have been with the imperial coinage, the conclusion seems to be that Aurelian's coin enactment comprised a vast production of new Alexandrian tetradrachms at a lower, but more regular weight, that the intention was to collect the older coins, and that the attempt succeeded to a large extent.

On the other hand, pre-Gallienus tetradrachms do not totally disappear from the hoards before Diocletian's currency reform, but their percentages fall remarkably. They are only found in one of the hoards with an end date during Aurelian's reign and therefore perhaps deposited at that period. The hoard is Dattari C'07, and the amounts are small: 38 (2.1%) of Nero, five (0.27%) of Trajan, and 19 (1.05%) of Hadrian.

This is a remarkable fall from the percentages in hoards with end dates of Valerian's reign and Gallienus' sole rule (as demonstrated above, p. 119), and may mean that Aurelian's new coinage and recall of older coins resulted in some – although not very high – gain of silver. It may have been enough, however, for giving a considerable amount of new coins their silver wash.

In substance, the gain from calling in later tetradrachms can hardly have been anything but copper. If that was the aim, the Roman government seems now to be in serious want of metals for striking even the heavily debased 'silver' coins.

The Alexandrian mint had ceased to strike bronze coins. Milne may be right though in explaining some coins from the joint rule of Aurelian (year 1) and Vaballathus (year 4)[34] to represent 'an isolated issue of bronze ... which does not correspond with anything else in the regular Alexandrian series'.[35] But although the type is distinctly different from the other issues, neither size (21.5 – 25 mm.) nor weight (4.27 – 8.69 gram) mark them as a specific coinage compared to the billon issues, and their original silver coat may have been too thin to have left any trace. On the other hand, they are roughly of the same weight and size as the asses struck in Rome (21-28 mm.; 6.5-10.5 gram).[36]

These apart, the last Alexandrian bronze coins were struck in years 5-6 of Philippus,[37] year 12 of Gallienus,[38] and years 1-2 of Claudius II.[39] The size (falling from 34 to 28.5 mm.) and – less so – their weight (falling from 23.57 to 9.81 grams) make them look like 'drachms'. The symbol of a palm on most of the reverses probably indicates 'commemorative pieces', which may not have been part of the ordinary currency.[40] They are never found in the known hoards and are rarely found even in the collections.[41] Otherwise, bronze coins of an earlier date may still have been in use and perhaps even as late as in the 280's, if the billon coin of Carinus reported for hoard A53 is no 'intruder', but actually belongs to the original hoard of at least 15 bronze drachms (Hadrian – Antoninus Pius).

The doubling of prices of staple goods which took place in Egypt at the end of the 2nd century according to the papyri (cf. Chap. 6 above, p. 112) was followed by 'another long period of broad stability' until around AD 274/275, when a tenfold leap suddenly sets in, followed by a new period of stabilization until the end of the century.[42]

Dominic Rathbone, to whom I owe these observations, explains the sudden price leap to have been caused by Aurelian's coin enactment. According to his 'hypothesis', this enactment involved a retariffing of the tetradrachm in relation to the *aureus* – supposedly the governmental standard for aggregate payments of cash taxes – and evoked a general fear of new retariffings, which destroyed the credibility of the token 'silver' coinage.[43] He considers the occurrence of 'new' and 'old' coins in the papyri to reflect such distrust. Actually, we have no evidence of such a gold standard.

Regardless of the 'hypothesis', a recall of debased coins – as implied by Zosimus – by other debased coins might anyway have caused a general distrust in the nominal value of the new coins. The result could have been that people tried to spend the new coins on immediate purposes, such as tax payments, and reserve the older coins for 'better' use, in the fictitious or factual belief that they represented a higher value. If this is true, we would expect to find the old coins even after Aurelian's reign, and so we do.

The large Dattari Hoard B'11 has end date Diocletian's year 12 (AD 295/296) and yet contains only 676 coins (5.39%) from the Tetrarchy and 431 (3.43%) of Aurelian's post-reform coinage. It is dominated by coins from Probus' reign (3,633 coins = 28.98%), but contains a total of 1,911 (15.24%) pre-Gallienus tetradrachms, which even includes seven coins from the reign of Nero, one of Trajan, and three of Hadrian. And although its authenticity has been disputed,[44] we have other evidence in this regard (see Chap. 8 below, p. 132).

It may be doubtful how much control the government in Rome (or wherever it resided) actually had over Egypt and the Alexandrian mint during the sole rule of Gallienus. Aurelian regained control and restored unity in the Empire. His coin enactment was probably part of this and may have aimed at restoring confidence in the coinage, but failed. In Egypt at least it seems rather to have inadvertently caused a loss of its credibility.

Inflation?

'Inflation' has been a common expression for the economic state of the Roman Empire during the latter part of the 3rd century. In a recent book on Aurelian the author makes the following comment to the attempt at a coin reform:

> Financial stability was not restored. Inflation galloped ahead with renewed vigour, and it was running at a level virtually unknown before the modern world.[45]

'Inflation' is derived from Latin *inflare* (= flare up, blow up) and has the following meaning today according to The *Oxford English Dictionary* (2nd ed., Oxford 1989), p. 237:

> Great or undue expansion or enlargement; increase beyond proper limits; esp. of prices, the issue of paper money, etc. *spec.* An undue increase in the quantity of money in relation to the goods available for purchase; (in lay use) an inordinate rise in prices.

A tenfold leap in prices of staple wares, as apparently shown by the papyri around AD 274/275, would have been 'beyond proper limits' and 'inordinate' according to ancient as well as modern notions. But according to Rathbone's observations, the leap came with 'an unprecedented suddeness' and was followed by a 'rapid restabilization' and a long period of stability.[46] If tenable, this does not warrant descriptions like 'inflation galloping ahead with renewed vigour'.

A mere look at the hoard evidence (cf. Table V and *fig. 18*) may give the impression of 'an undue increase in the quantity of money' (*read* coins), which may have been caused by an increase of public expenditure due to continuous warfare. If, however, Aurelian's coin enactment actually succeeded to a large extent in recalling previous coinage, the result would have been a replacement of coins rather than an increase in the circulating number.

If there was an increased coin production, followed by an increased number of coins in circulation, this may have been absorbed by a still-spreading monetization of the economy, which is actually the 'general impression' given by the 3rd century documents, at least according to Rathbone,[47] and apparently the evidence of the stray finds.[48] In a period of unstable coinage any credit system will lose its underlying basis of confidence in forthcoming fulfilments and people will demand immediate cash instead.

Another consequence of lost confidence in the existing currency may be that surviving remains of older coinage will be preferred for savings and therefore withdrawn from actual circulation, as the case seems to have been.

It is generally assumed that – apart from the donations – 3rd century soldiers were remunerated to an increasing degree more in goods than in coins,[49] which may have resulted in an excess of coins 'in relation to the goods available for purchase'. The effect, however, would have been less if ordinary payments to the soldiers played a less determinant role for the production of new coins than hitherto claimed.

Fighting for control of Egypt may have devastated production and caused a high death toll among the population, meaning an 'excess of money in relation to the goods available'. As argued in Chapter 6 above, (p. 112), this is what may have happened during the reign of Commodus and caused the sudden leap in prices. A subsequent stabilization of prices – if true – might then be the companion to a subsequent revival of production and population.

The Alexandrian coinage never turned into paper money, but even when the 'silver' coins became so debased that they were mere tokens or even purely fiduciary, their notional value may not have been utterly destroyed as long as the government accepted them at nominal value for payments of taxes.

If, however, Aurelian's coin enactment meant that only the new coinage would be accepted for such purposes, the effect could have been confusion and bewilderment regarding the use of the existing currency and its future validity. The proper word for such a situation is 'coin crisis', showing symptoms of inflation without being inflation in the proper sense of the word.

It could be argued that such a diagnosis is based only on Egypt, which after all was only a part of the whole empire. But before Diocletian's price edict, the papyrus documents from Egypt offer the only reliable evidence of prices.

NOTES

1. See esp. Scriptores, *The Deified Aurelian* XLII.
2. Scriptores, *The Deified Aurelian* XLV and XLVII.
3. P.Oxy XII, 1411, explicitly stating: 'των Σεβαστων νομισμα'.
4. MacLennan (1968), pp. 31f.
5. For these events see *CAH* XI (1956), pp. 171ff. (Alföldy).
6. E.g. Milne (1933/1971), Nos. 4062-4064.
7. Alföldy (1938), p. 72, repeated by the same author in *CAH* XI (1956), p. 183.
8. As, e.g., Milne (1933/1971), Nos. 4063-4064.
9. Christiansen (1986), p. 236.
10. Milne (1933/1971), pp. 93ff.
11. See West & Johnson (1944), p. 173.
12. Alföldy in *CAH* XI (1956), p. 170.
13. Christiansen (1985), p. 81.

14. Milne (1933/1971), p. xxiv.
15. Milne in Boak (1933), p. 60.
16. See briefly Milne (1933/1971), pp. 81ff. For details see Christiansen & Easson (forthcoming).
17. Christiansen (1984), p. 295.
18. P.Oxy XLI,2951: 'ἀργυρίου δηναρίων Πτολεμαικων'.
19. Rathbone (1993/1996), p. 336.
20. P.Oxy XXXI, 2587.
21. See Christiansen (1984), p. 297, note 155.
22. Price (1973), esp. p. 78.
23. Price (1973), pp. 82 and 88.
24. Zosimus, New History I.61.3.
25. See, e.g., Carson (1965), pp. 231ff. and Crawford (1975), p. 575.
26. Watson (1999), p. 129. For similar doubts, see Webb in *RIC* V,1 (1927), pp. 8ff.
27. As also concluded by Watson (1999), p. 129.
28. Metcalf (1998), pp. 270f.
29. Christiansen (1984) p. 81.
30. Metcalf (1998), pp. 272f.; cf. Lafaurie (1974) and (1975), pp. 85ff.
31. Metcalf (1998), p. 276.
32. Christiansen (1984), p. 81.
33. Milne (1933/1971), p. xxiv.
34. Milne (1933/1971), Nos. 4327-4329.
35. Milne (1933/1974), p. xvii. The classification of these coins as bronze denominations is also found in Geissen/Weiser (1983), No. 3057; cf. Savio 3 (1997), Nos. 2101-02, the sizes(?) and weights of which are remarkably higher.
36. *RIC* V, 1, pp. 274f., Nos. 79-85.
37. Milne (1933/1971), Nos. 3742-3744, 3778-3781, 3744a, and 3749a.
38. Milne (1933/1971), No. 4112 and 4112a.
39. Not in Milne (1933/1971), but see Geissen/Weiser (1983), No. 3026 (year 1) and Savio 3 (1997), No. 2088 (year 2).
40. Milne (1933/1971), p. xvii.
41. Christiansen (1983/1984), Table II at p. 15.
42. Rathbone (1993/1996), p. 333 and (1997), p. 215.
43. Rathbone (1993/1996), pp. 337f.
44. Metcalf (1998), p. 272, note 6.
45. Watson (1999), p. 142.
46. Rathbone (1993/1996), p. 142.
47. Rathbone (1993/1996), p. 338.
48. Christiansen (2002).
49. Thus see Crawford (1975), pp. 570f. and Speidel (1992), p. 105.

CHAPTER VIII

PROBUS AND THE TETRARCHY

> As for myself when I compare Probus as a ruler with other emperors, in whatever way almost all Roman leaders have stood out as courageous, as merciful, as wise, or as admirable, I perceive that he was the equal of any, or indeed, if no insane jealousy stands in the way, better than all.
>
> (SCRIPTORES, *Probus* XXII.1)

Probus is one of the few heroes in the Scriptores, but apart from such praise his biography – how little reliable as it may be – relates almost nothing but incessant warfare from his accession to power in AD 276 to his assassination in 282. If this is true, we may wonder how much time and energy he was able to spend on other responsibilities during these seven years, and considering the many different theaters of war, we may wonder how close and well-functioning communications were to subordinates all over the Empire, as for example the prefect of Egypt, or how much was left – and had to be left – to their own discretion.

The Alexandrian tetradrachms of Probus

'Imperator Caesar Marcus Aurelius Probus Pius Felix Augustus Gothicus Maximus Persicus Maximus Germanicus Maximus Medicus Maximus Parthicus Maximus' was the full nomenclature. But on the obverses of the Alexandrian tetradrachms is only found 'ΑΚΜΑΥΡΠΡΟΒΟCCΕΒ'.[1] There was no more space on the flan. On average, the diameter was reduced to ca. 20-18 mm. from previously ca. 21-20 mm., and we even have a coin from the reign of Aurelian re-coined with the portrait and inscription of Probus, but still showing the legend of Aurelian in an outer circle, which the moneyer forgot to cut off (*fig. 7* = Paris Inv. No. 3673 (unpublished); rev. Eirene standing, year 3). The average weight of the coins was reduced as well to as low as ca. 8 grams, and the silver content to 0.27%.[2] If not before, at least from then on, the tetradrachms were covered by only a thin layer of silver wash. Everyone would have been aware that they

FIG. 7. *Billon coin of Probus, year 3.*

had no intrinsic value and were useless, unless accepted by others – including the tax authorities – at a formal value.

In my 1985 survey of hoards,[3] Probus' tetradrachms numbered 9,449 or 12.83% of totals. Only the Tetrarchy and the reign of Nero have higher percentages. According to Milne's survey,[4] the Alexandrian mint had a high activity especially in years 2-4 and years 6-8, and the underlying reason may of course have been expenditure on incessant warfare, as may often have been the case previously. It does seem, however, that another attempt was made to force older and better coins out of circulation by yet another large issue of new coins.

The hoard evidence offers no clear-cut picture. The tetradrachms of Probus derive predominantly from hoards with end dates of the Tetrarchy and may be the result of Diocletian's currency reform – resulting in a high number of 'debasement' and even 'waste' hoards of Alexandrian tetradrachms in circulation at the time. This evidence therefore offers no certain clue to the original amount of coins produced or in circulation. Nor are Milne's die-studies conclusive: He found three pairs of coins from years 2-3 deriving from the same obverse die (one of them even struck by the same reverse die).[5]

Two of the Dattari Hoards have end dates during the reign of Probus and may therefore have been deposited in that period: A'07 contains only four of his coins or 0.18%. B'09 contains only one of his coins or 0.05%. Both have a dominance of older tetradrachms. A'07 contains 707 coins from Nero's reign, 352 from the reign of Commodus, 61 from the reign of Gallienus, and even two Ptolemaic silver tetradrachms. B'09 contains four coins from Nero's reign, 38 from the reign of Commodus, and 451 from the reign of Gallienus. The impression from these two hoards is that the older coinage was kept for hoarding, whereas the tetradrachms of Probus were the coins spent for daily use.

The Girga Hoard 1947 and two of the Karanis Hoards have end dates during the reign of Carus, and they offer quite another picture. The 886 tetradrachms of Probus dominate the Girga Hoard with 83.74%. This hoard contains no coinage older than Claudius II (seven coins or 0.66%). A similar pattern is visible in Karanis 20: 31 coins from the reign of Probus (56.42%) and 15 from the reign of Claudius II (27.3%). In Karanis 31, 104 coins are found from the reign of Probus (27.04%) and no coinage older than Gordianus III. If these three hoards are taken as representative, the impression will be that, in the end, the tetradrachms of Probus actually forced in and supplanted the previous coinage to a large extent.

It does not seem advisable to draw firm conclusions on such feeble ground, and instead I will turn to the Tetrarchy and the end of the Alexandrian coinage.

The Alexandrian tetradrachms of the Tetrarchy

According to my survey of 1985, the tetradrachms of the Tetrarchy made up 18,551 coins and the largest proportion (25.19%) of the hoard evidence.[6] According to Milne, the coin production had a steady increase during years 1-3 – especially compared to a very low issue during the last part of the preceding short reign of Carus' sons. It then had a slight fall in years 4-6, a considerable decrease in year 7, a recovery in year 8, followed by a steady decline until the end in Diocletian's year 12.[7] It might be tempting, but not very useful, to connect these oscillations with events inside or outside Egypt and the uncertain increase in army numbers.[8]

According to W.E. Metcalf, the issues of Diocletian's year 12 may after all have been 'substantial' in spite of the meagre representation in the hoards. He based this assumption on the existence of 36 substantive reverse types, 'more than for any other year in the whole history of the Alexandrian coinage'.[9] As stated earlier, however, a higher number of types will normally be an indication of a low production, whereas years with a prolific production were characterized by a concentration on few types.

This may not always be true, of course. Milne found two pairs of coins of year 12 deriving from the same obverse dies and one pair deriving from the same reverse die.[10] This allows no firm conclusions, however. More die studies might offer further clues, but may not be necessary, since Milne also concluded that the number of workshops (*officinae*) seems to have been reduced from two(?) to one(?),[11] which certainly will indicate a slowing down of the coin production.

Hoards, which according to the latest datable coin were deposited after Diocletian's currency reform, rarely contain any coinage from the previous period.[12] There are no such coins in the two late Karanis Hoards (Nos. 2-3),[13] and with the exception of two Alexandrian tetradrachms (late 3rd century AD) in A160, we only find a few Alexandrian bronze coins in the other hoards: one and two late imitations in A154, one in A155, one in A157, and one in A160. The only real exceptions are Dattari B'11 and the still unpublished A158, both containing later coinage in addition to a large number of late Alexandrian tetradrachms. The archaeological context of either hoard is unknown, however, and the later coins may be intrusive or we may have two 'encapsulated' hoards here, perhaps even deposited as late as the Omayyad period.

The 26+ late tetradrachms in the Batn Ihrît Hoard are of more significance since the hoard was found in a wooden jar in the same place (the courtyard of a house) as a pottery jar, containing 30 bronze drachms (A84; Cleopatra – Severus Alexander), and a bronze pot, containing 172 late bronze coins, dated AD 296-315.[14] Accordingly, we seem to have a clear case here of not only tetradrachms, but also bronze coins surviving the reform for two decades.

The papyrological evidence may seem less clear on this point. It is questionable what is meant by the 3,000 drachms in 'old coins' in SB 7338 (= P.Berl.Möller 1) from AD 300, and I doubt Callu's statement[15] that the 332 drachms in 'new silver coins' in P.Lips 84 from AD 303(?) represent tetradrachms.

Taken together, however, the evidence seems to show that Diocletian's currency reform caused a significant, but not a total shift in the use of coinage. Even the fire of *insula* 33 in Karanis and the loss of the 23 hoards may have happened after the currency reform. On the other hand, none of these hoards contain later coinage and may therefore have been caused by an effective annulment of the previous coinage, i.e. the coins were worth too little to be regained. If that is true, we find an interesting proportion between contemporary coins from the Tetrarchy (almost 60%) and older tetradrachms (some 40%, whereof one-fourth from the reign of Probus).

The tetradrachms of the Tetrarchy constitute the largest proportion of billon coins in the single finds (357 or 7.72%)[16] and may therefore represent the coins in circulation at the time, whereas the hoards which according to the latest datable coin have been deposited during this period may be taken to represent the actual pattern of coinage used for hoarding in the years immediately preceding the currency reform.

Divided into the four groups, we have the following patterns:

Karanis Hoards: 21,080 coins (16 hoards)
TETRARCHY: 13,019 (16 hoards) = 61.75%
PROBUS: 4,270 (13 hoards) = 20.25%
EARLIER COINAGE: 1,374 = 10.55% (whereof Nero: 1, Commodus: 53 [two hoards], Gallienus: 11 [three hoards], and Aurelian: 219 [11 hoards]).

Other excavation hoards: 1,352 coins (four hoards)
TETRARCHY: 1,062 (four hoards) = 78.55%
PROBUS: 116 (four hoards) = 11.09%
EARLIER COINAGE: 17 = 1.25% (whereof Aurelian: 6 [two hoards]).

Dattari Hoards: 16,630 coins (two hoards)
TETRARCHY: 3,729 (two hoards) = 22.42%
PROBUS: 3,960 (two hoards) = 23.8%
EARLIER COINAGE: 8,094 = 48.67% (whereof Nero: 7 [one hoard], Commodus: 80 [one hoard], Gallienus: 1,934 [two hoards], and Aurelian: 468 [two hoards]).

Other supposed hoards: 1,059 coins (two hoards)
TETRARCHY: 758 (two hoards) = 71.5%

PROBUS: 72 (two hoards) = 6.79%
EARLIER COINAGE: 123 = 11.61 % (whereof Commodus: 1, Gallienus: 10 [one hoard],
and Aurelian: 10 [one hoard]).

Although the Dattari Hoards deviate somewhat from the other groups, the overall conclusion is that the tetradrachms of the Tetrarchy – to some extent also Probus – supplanted the earlier coinage at large.

It will be more difficult to say to what extent these new coins also added to the existing pool, but a comparison with earlier reigns of debasement may be useful.

Hoards with end dates Nero:
KARANIS (one hoard): 40 coins (whereof Nero: 23 and earlier coinage: 17 = 42.5%)
OTHER SUPPOSED HOARDS (two hoards): 122 coins (whereof Nero: 121 and earlier
coinage: 1 = 0.81%).

Hoards with end dates Commodus:
DATTARI HOARDS (two hoards): 2,294 coins (whereof Commodus: 32 and earlier
coinage: 2,262 = 98.6%).

Hoards with end dates Gallienus:
KARANIS (three hoards): 559 coins (whereof Gallienus: 13 and earlier coinage: 546 =
98.55%);
OTHER EXCAVATION HOARDS (one hoard): 1,184 coins (whereof Gallienus: one
and earlier coinage: 1,183 = 99.9%);
DATTARI HOARDS (one hoard): 950 coins (whereof Gallienus: 74 and earlier coinage: 876 = 92.21%).

Hoards with end dates Aurelian:
KARANIS (three hoards): 220 coins (whereof Aurelian post-reform: 189 and earlier
coinage: 13 = 5.9%);
DATTARI HOARDS (two hoards): 2,869 coins (whereof Aurelian post-reform; 0 and
earlier coinage: 2,801 = 97.62%).

This comparison does not allow firm conclusions. The impression, though, is that –
compared to earlier – the coin production during the last twenty years (except the short
reign of Carus and sons, which is only represented by a total of 3,526 coins or 4.79%
in the hoards)[17] was much larger than previously, and heavily increased the amount of
available coins. How far this caused economic repercussions of the Egyptian economy

is difficult to say, but according to D. Rathbone, the papyrological evidence testifies to a new leap of prices during the 290's.[18] This, however, may rather be connected with the currency reform.

The hoard evidence as such has little to say on that. According to the editors, El-Nassery and Wagner, the house of Kôm Aushîm 1972 belonged to 'an ordinary peasant', who 'certainly … was not a well-to-do'[19]. Whether a hoard of at least 1,199 tetradrachms may have been the fortune of an 'ordinary' man will, of course, depend on the question of the nominal versus the actual value of the late coins. It does seem, however, to be the editors' wishful thinking, caused by an eagerness to find the ordinary people among the archaeological remains.

The hoard evidence on the other hand may be valuable in telling us that some early coins were still available for hoarding. This is especially the case for the Dattari Hoards, one of which, B'11, even ranges back to the reign of Nero. Recently, W. Metcalf has denied the authenticity of this hoard, which according to him 'must represent the combination of two or more lots of material'.[20]

Of course, we must be suspicious of the Dattari group as representing original hoards, but the argument seems to run like this: since we would not expect to find older coins in late hoards, a hoard which actually contains such coins can only be a combination. Yet, even if it is a 'composite hoard', the composition may have been made at the time of, or just before, deposition.

As stated above (Chap. 4, p. 81), Milne, who had the whole lot in his hand, expressed no doubt about its composition of Alexandrian tetradrachms, as he did with other lots he received from Dattari.

Actually, the composition is not as surprising as it may seem to be. Both Dattari A'07 and B'09, which have end dates of Probus, also have rather high percentages of older coins and even some coins of Nero and Hadrian. In Karanis Hoard No. 17, the original composition of which no one will doubt, almost all the coins are pre-Gallienus tetradrachms, including (admittedly, only an insignificant number of) early coins, in spite of Maximian year 11 as its end date. To this may be added the evidence of the less sufficiently known or described hoards, among which old tetradrachms are found together with coins of the Tetrarchy in A120, 123, 126, and 129.[21] Even some Alexandrian bronze coins of an earlier date seem to have been available for hoarding, as witnessed by the 55 pieces in Karanis Hoard No. 27, which was also found in *insula* 33 and therefore may have been lost during the same fire. The high proportion of illegible coins (33) may be the result of repeated use during many years.

The end of the Alexandrian coinage

The exact date of Diocletian's currency reform has caused much discussion and little agreement. Webb concluded that the earliest date seems to be AD 293 and the latest 296,[22] and the prevalent view until recently has been AD 294.[23] As rightly stated by W. Metcalf, there is no cogent reason why the new coinage should have been introduced all over the Empire at the same time.[24]

The end of the Alexandrian coinage and the introduction of the new – Latin – coins are normally considered in connection with and dated before the revolt of Domitius Domitianus. According to Jacques Schwartz, this revolt can be dated to AD 296/97 and the currency reform therefore to August 296,[25] but J.D. Thomas has argued that the papyrological evidence rather favours 297/98 for the revolt,[26] and according to Geissen, the numismatic evidence is quite consistent with such a date.[27] Domitius minted coins in both Alexandrian and in the new style. The absence of his Alexandrian coinage from the hoard evidence will be no surprise and adds nothing to the question of the date. His rule was short and his coinage probably declared invalid immediately after his fall.

Some rare tetradrachms portray Maximian on the obverse and are dated year 12 on the reverse,[28] Unless we consider them to be hybrids with reverses actually belonging to Diocletian, they will show AD 296/297 to be the last year of the special issues from the Alexandrian mint, which is quite consistent with a few of the new coins, also dated to year 12 of Maximian, and one of Constantius Caesar, dated to year 5.[29] The few existing issues may be explained if the revolt of Domitius began in August 297, soon after the currency reform,[30] which made an end to the Alexandrian coinage and integrated the Alexandrian mint into the ordinary Imperial system.

Hereby ended the special coinage minted in – and for – Egypt only, although linked to the imperial system, and that will cause no wonder since Egypt at the same time was totally integrated into the empire and lost its previous status as a special province.

NOTES

1. See Milne (1933/1971), p. 108.
2. Cope (1975), p. 190.
3. Christiansen (1985), p. 81.
4. Milne (1933/1971), pp. xxivf.
5. Milne (1933/1971), pp. 108f.
6. Christiansen (1985), p. 81.

7. Milne (1933/1971), p. xxv.
8. See brief discussion in Demandt (1989), p. 256.
9. Metcalf (1987), p. 160.
10. Milne (1933/1971), pp. 123f.
11. Milne (1916), p. 216.
12. See also Ford (2000).
13. Haatvedt & Peterson (1964), p. 14.
14. Regling (1912); cf. Rubensohn (1905), p. 12.
15. Callu (1961/1965), p. 375.
16. Christiansen (2002).
17. Christiansen (1985), p. 81.
18. Rathbone (1993/1996), p. 338.
19. El-Nassery & Wagner (1975), p. 186.
20. Metcalf (1998), p. 272, note 6.
21. Milne (1935), p. 211, observed a similar mixture of good and debased tetradrachms in the hoards from the late Ptolemaic period.
22. Webb in *RIC* V,II (1933/1968), p. 206.
23. Thus see Crawford (1975), p. 578.
24. Metcalf (1987), esp. pp. 158f.; cf. already Bruun (1979).
25. Schwartz (1963), pp. 149f. and (1975), pp. 141f.
26. Thomas (1976), esp. p. 263.
27. Geissen (1976).
28. Huber (1871), p. 297; rev. Nike walking r. (author's own – dispersed – collection). Voetter (1911), pp. 173: rev. Elpis. Dattari (1901), No. 5857; rev. Dikaiosyne.
29. Geissen (1976), pp. 280f. with references in note 10.
30. So also Geissen (1976), p. 281 and – more hesitantly – Metcalf (1987), p. 164.

CHAPTER IX

From Corrosion to Clarity

Fig. 8.

The young Jim Hawkins in Robert Louis Stevenson's *Treasure Island* would soon have become tired, but less excited by disentangling this corroded lump of coins (Alexandrian tetradrachms?), probably found or acquired by Currelly in Egypt. As a matter of fact, it is questionable if it would add anything new to our present evidence, at least as regarding the general patterns and structures, which is my main concern in this book.

The Roman coins of Alexandria

Tourists in Egypt marvel not only at the pyramids, but also at the temples. They may not be aware that many of the best-preserved temples were actually built or refurbished during the Roman period before Christianity. In these temples we often find reliefs of Pharaohs in a disguise that is even more Pharaonic than the ancient Pharaohs. Decipherment of the accompanying hieroglyphs will tell us that he was 'ever-living, beloved of Ptah and Isis', but also disclose him as 'KAICAR CEBACTOC AYTOKRATOR', the usual titles in Greek for the Roman emperor (cf. plate III).

Among the vast number of preserved papyri we may often read long extracts from the Homeric epics, but also find fragments of Greek authors hardly otherwise known. Furthermore, we have a lot of private letters and official documents written in more or less 'proper' Greek (a few in Latin), making use of concepts and terms, which are familiar from other parts of the Roman Empire, but also concepts and terms which seem totally foreign.

The 'Roman coins of Alexandria' are part of that story. The obverses are Roman, presenting a picture of the emperor (or a member of the imperial family). The well-known names and titles in Greek are added as in other parts of the East, but the emperor's consular or tribunician dates – as normally stated on the imperial coins – are rarely added. On the reverses are found some Roman or rather Greco-Roman types (Demeter, Euthenia, Dikaiosyne, etc.), but more often designs which most properly may be called 'Alexandrian' (such as Alexandria, Nilus, Sarapis), whereas 'pure' Egyptian motives are less common and then rendered in a Greco-Roman disguise, such as the *female* – not the traditional male – sphinx (see, e.g., plate II). The vast diversity of reverse types is a typical Roman feature (different from the conformity among the Greek, including the Ptolemaic, coins) and, paradoxically, the variety of Alexandrian designs may be called a romanizing element. If the choice was made by the prefect of Egypt or another Roman official, which seems likely, we may simply call them 'Roman phantasies on Egyptian themes'.

Since Zoëga and Eckhel the Alexandrian coins have been treated as a separate part of the Greek coinage and as such included in the *Sylloge Nummorum Graecorum* together with the other Roman coins of the Greek East. Only recently have scholars become increasingly aware of them as basically a part of the Roman imperial coinage.

On the other hand, the find evidence – whether hoards or stray finds – in- and outside Egypt, corroborated by the papyrological evidence, clearly shows that Egypt as a Roman province constituted a closed currency system. All attempts to prove otherwise have been in vain! This may be no surprise since other parts of the Roman East (such as Cappadocia) normally seem to have made use of the locally struck coins. For Egypt, however, the evidence is so clear that we can suppose an official ban against importing 'foreign' coins and exporting the coinage meant for use within the borders.

Such was the case in the preceding, Ptolemaic period. The main and important difference is that, at least from the time of Vespasian, the Alexandrian tetradrachm was formally and artificially rated on a par with the Imperial denarius inside the province of Egypt and was not legal tender outside.

Ancient coins and economic history

Numismatics is a special branch of learning, and coins are often exclusively left to the numismatists. This is a pity. Although numismatists are good at their work, they rarely have an interest in economic history. As artefacts, however, the ancient coins we have today are the still-existing remains of the objects used as money in antiquity for making payments, storing wealth, and reckoning units, for which the other evidence we have is poor, even including the references in the papyri.

It does seem so easy: disentangle the coins from the corroded lumps, then clean, identify, and count them! Doing so, however, is but one necessary – and often difficult – step on our way towards understanding them as an actual part of the ancient economy. Neither the coins nor the hoards tell us about the past without being questioned. The problem may seem to be, though, that the questions need to be posed by us, living as we do in a modern and quite different world. And even if the answers are scrupulously based on the existing evidence – no more, no less! – they might produce a different picture from what the ancients themselves perceived, and yet may be true. The worst problem is that even under ideal conditions (normally never found), we can only postulate that the hoards we have for investigation sufficiently present the coinage then in circulation and available for hoarding. This claim may neither be totally true nor totally preposterous.

Dividing the hoards of the Alexandrian billon coins into four groups elucidated some peculiarities of each group, notably the vast preponderance of coins from the Tetrarchy among the Karanis hoards, but also the long survival of coins from Nero's reign witnessed by the other groups. Such peculiarities require explanation.

A mere look at publications of coin collections may leave the impression that the different types or series exist in equal numbers. Modernists will rejoice and explain this as meaning that the original production was equally even, since its purpose was to provide a steady and sufficient amount of coinage to the benefit of the population, and not least trade.

A mere look at publications of Alexandrian coin collections, however, will show that some emperors and some types are always well-represented, others barely so or not at all. Dated by the emperor's regnal year in Egypt, the coins even testify to a striking disproportion within single reigns.

The hoards make this even much clearer, and based on the assumption that this evidence represents not only the original production but also the coins then in circulation and therefore available for hoarding, I have in this book posed some questions and offered some answers.[1] I do not pretend these answers to be 'the truth and nothing but the truth', but I do think they reveal possible and important aspects of coins as money in Roman Egypt and by implication consider them to be a contribution to the scholarly debate on the economy of the Roman Empire.

Coins as money in Egypt as a Roman province

Judging from the evidence of the stray find groups, Roman Egypt enjoyed a widespread monetized economy (defined as use of coins for payments). This may seem to be contrary to the credit system testified by the papyri, but is not. The existence of a credit system requires a high amount of reliable means of payment available in cash on demand. The stray find groups also testify to the 'silver' tetradrachms as the main coinage and – contrary to the preceding Ptolemaic period – to the bronze coins being subsidiary. Both statements are corroborated by the papyrological and the hoard evidence, neither of which, however, offers sufficient clues to an understanding of any importance that gold coins may have had before Diocletian's currency reform.

The production of Alexandrian tetradrachms was extremely large during the last years of Nero's reign. This is beyond any doubt, and it is tempting to explain it by public expenditure, especially military exploits or plans. It must be asked, however, what the Roman army needed to provide and pay for in Egypt apart from possible donations to the soldiers in service or the final pay to those dismissed. Even in such cases, we furthermore have to ask why the Roman government decided to strike new coins instead of paying in older coins available, as they must have done later when the production of tetradrachms was demonstrably low during Trajan's rule and any production of Alexandrian coins was extremely parsimonious under Septimius Severus. Military exploits and plans are plentifully attested from both these reigns. To this should be added that such heavy increase in the coin pool would have provoked disastrous effects on the economy, for which there is no convincing evidence.

A large increase in coin production may of course have resulted in an increased monetization; may have been accompanied by heavy exactments of taxes in coinage (perhaps witnessed by Tiberius Julius Alexander's edict), or may have been absorbed by an increase in population or production (which can hardly be sustained by the existing evidence). Actually, we do have other clues to an explanation.

Until the last years of Nero's reign, when the term 'Ptolemaic' silver coins disappears (to return 200 years later in another context), 'Ptolemaic' silver coins are mentioned by several papyri: sometimes alone, sometimes together with 'the emperor's silver coins'. The hoard evidence from the early imperial period is too meagre, though, to confirm the time of their disappearance. A radical change in the designs of the obverse and the reverses from Nero's year 10 (AD 63/64) may, however, mark the introduction of a new coinage.

Modern measurements have shown us that the new coin had a lower content of silver than its Ptolemaic and even early imperial predecessor, and the result of calling in the earlier coins (by what means we do not know) must have been a large profit of silver.

Contemporaries would not have had that knowledge, and if they suspected a lower intrinsic value, would only have been able to verify it by melting down the coins. That would be high treason and was punished by cruel death penalties if detected. They may have had no suspicion. The new coin had approximately the same weight, size, and flan. Today many of these coins disclose themselves by a brownish surface, which, however, is the result of a later chemical process, during which the copper tries to migrate to the surroundings through the silver surface. Originally, the new coins would have had a shiny assembly of silver on the surface.

Even if contemporaries had some suspicions or came to know the facts, they did not need to care as long as the new coin was accepted at face value by others inside Egypt (it was not legal tender outside), including the tax collectors.

According to the hoard evidence, Nero's tetradrachms remained the main currency for at least some hundred years after his death. It may seem a surprise that the portrait of this hated tyrant was allowed to ornament the money paid for taxes, but perhaps it may rather be a warning against attaching too much importance to the often claimed 'message' of the imperial coin designs!

Anyway, some coins left circulation – the hoards we have are a result of that. The main alternative during Trajan's reign seems to have been an increased production of bronze coins, especially the 'one drachm' pieces (four of which equivalated one silver tetradrachm?). During Hadrian's reign there was a new increase in the production of tetradrachms, which can neither be sufficiently explained by expenditure for the Jewish War nor by the emperor's famous visit to Egypt, and may rather reflect a general improvement of the financial reserves of the Empire.

The Alexandrian tetradrachm kept its Neronian standard until the reign of Marcus Aurelius, when it was heavily debased and, furthermore, lost both size and weight. Commodus seems to have used the new currency for recalling the better coins of old, but did not succeed. This was either due to a lack of sufficient silver for striking the necessary amount of new coins, or to a reduced need for coins in an Egypt ravaged by the plague. A rise, though, in the price of staple products, witnessed by the contemporary papyri, may be a more alarming symptom of a dormant crisis.

At the same time the production of new bronze coins almost ceased, but the earlier pieces remained in continuous and repeated use (perhaps even to the end).

Such was the situation at the time of Septimius Severus, during whose reign a remarkably low coin production may have been disguised by some – rather infinitesimal – production almost every year, followed by a total standstill during the short reign of Caracalla.

Temporary cessations of coin production had previously occurred in Alexandria, but could not last too long because a closed currency system demands the availability of a sufficient number of coins at the border stations for the purpose of compulsory exchange, and a taxation system demanding some payments in coins (for political reasons?) requires the availability of a sufficient amount of coins inside the borders. This may be the obvious reason for the renewal of the Alexandrian tetradrachm during the reign of Elagabalus and especially during the reign of Severus Alexander.

During the next fifty years, the Roman Empire suffered from continuous warfare, due to civil strife and hostile attacks. The vast expenditure needed may have caused an excessive demand for the production of coins needed for payments. This may have caused a drain of reserves, resulting in successive debasements of new coins.

On the other hand, we cannot exclude that every new emperor tried to consolidate his position by striking a large number of new coins, manifesting himself on the obverse and the prospects for his reign on the reverse ('Victory', 'Peace', 'Harmony', 'Hope'). Nor can we exclude renewed attempts at calling in older coins for new.

An increase in the number of coins may have been absorbed by increased expenses or heavy exactions of taxes in coin. It may also have caused an increased monetization, due to distrust of the current or future coinage.

Anyway, the existence today of a large proportion of coins from this troublesome period probably reflects the pattern of hoards, and we would expect a large number of lost 'emergency hoards' and 'debasement hoards', perhaps also 'tax evading hoards'.

The questions are *legio*, and the only certain answer is that no certain answer can be given, but the Alexandrian coins may offer some clues.

From the sole rule of Gallienus and onwards the tetradrachm underwent frequent reductions in weight, size, and silver content. In the end, it was nothing but a small copper coin covered by a slight silver coat or mere silver wash. Its low intrinsic value would have been evident for everyone.

From this time on, payments in 'new' and 'old' (even 'Ptolemaic') coins are mentioned by the papyri, and it is tempting to compare this with the continued presence of previous tetradrachms – even from Nero's reign – in the hoards. Amazingly, the amounts stated seem to be equivalent, and we do not know which expectations coinage of the 'good old days' may have evoked.

In the meantime, worthless leaden tokens – according to the stray find groups – seem to have substituted the bronze coins for small daily change. Such *tesserae* would have had no value in themselves, and we seem to have no evidence about an assessment to the 'silver' coin, in other words, they may have constituted no more than a purely fiduciary coinage only dependent on their notional value on receipt and in the future.

Nor do we seem to have evidence about an assessment of the late tetradrachms, apart perhaps from a continued, but artificial equivalence to the denarius. If they too had become tokens, their notional value would have depended on confidence in their value in the future.

This confidence may have been utterly, but inadvertently shaken by Aurelian's currency reform, if it implied a ban on use of any other than his new coinage. The possible result was a sudden coin crisis, perhaps testified by an enormous leap of prices according to the papyrological evidence.

Anyway, the tetradrachm was further debased during the reign of Probus as well as during the Tetrarchy. The large proportion of these late coins in the hoards may be the result of a new increase in their production, but may also mean no more than that they were lost in connection with Diocletian's currency reform.

What then happened – and why – lie outside the scope of my investigations. Let me just say that it was not only the coinage, but Egypt as such, that now became fully integrated with the other provinces. Let me also remind readers of the fact that the Tetrarchy meant a transformation of the Roman Empire, but not its end.

Final remarks

Several of the questions posed, and possible answers offered by this book, may contravene prevailing opinions about the Roman coinage and the Roman economy to such an extent that some readers may reject them out of hand, or at least explain them as a possible part of Roman Egypt as a special case only.

Recent scholarship, however, has become increasingly aware that Egypt may have been no more special than other provinces, apart from being better known from the papyri – and the coinage.

The Romans often accepted local traditions as part of the imperial rule, but the administration was founded on Roman traditions and served Roman interests. Coinage was a vital part of the financial administration, and it seems unlikely that the coin politics of the province of Egypt were vastly different from other parts of the empire. The only exception may be that the closed currency system offered possibilities not usable everywhere.

Thus seen, a better understanding of the 'Alexandrian' coins as money may be a contribution to the scholarly debate on the Roman economy. A debate which is interesting, although not as exciting as Robert Louis Stevenson's *Treasure Island*.

NOTES

1. Due references and detailed arguments will be found in the preceding chapters and will not be repeated here.

BIBLIOGRAPHY

The papyrological evidence

Sel.Pap.   *Select Papyri*, with an English translation by A.S. Hunt & C.C. Edgar. Vols. I-II. *Loeb Classical Library*.

All other references are given according to John F. Oates, Roger S. Bagnall, William H. Willis & K.A. Worp, *Checklist of editions of Greek Papyri and Ostraca*, 3rd ed. (*Bulletin of the American Society of Papyrologists*. Supplement 4, 1985).

Other ancient texts

CIG   *Corpus Inscriptionum Graecaraum*, Berlin 1828-77.

Unless otherwise stated, all ancient authors are rendered from the relevant volume of the *Loeb Classical Library*. The main exceptions are:

Midrash Rabbah, translated into English with notes, glossary and indices under the editorship of Rabbi Dr. H. Freedman and Maurice Simon (1939). 2nd ed. London & Bournemouth 1951.

Zosimus, *New History*. A translation with commentary by Ronald T. Ridley. Sidney 1982.

Modern authors

Abbreviations of standard works, periodicals, etc.:

ACME   *ACME*. Annali della Facoltà di Lettere e Filosofia dell'Università degli Studi di Milano.

Actes8CIN 1973(1976) Cahn, Herbert A. & Georges Le Rider (ed.), *Actes du 8ème congrès international de numismatique, New York – Washington Septembre 1973*. Paris & Bâle 1976.

Actes9CIN 1979(1982) Hackens, Tony & Raymond Weiler (ed.), *Actes de 9ème congrès de numismatique, Berne 1979*. Louvain-La-Neuve & Luxembourg 1982.

Aegyptus   *Aegyptus*. Rivista italiana di egittologia e di papirilogia.

AfP   *Archiv für Papyrusforschung und verwandte gebiete*.

AJA   *American Journal of Archaeology*.

AktenXIIINK 1997(2000) Kluge, Bernd & Bernhard Weiser (Hg.), *XII Internationaler Numismatischer Kongress, Berlin 1997. Akten*. Berlin 2000.

AncEg   *Ancient Egypt*.

AnnLiv   (Liverpool) *Annals of Archaeology and Anthropology*.

ANOH	Aarbøger for nordisk Oldkyndighed og Historie.
ANRW	Temporini, Hildegard & Wolfgang Hase (Hg.); *Aufstieg und Niedergang der römischen Welt*. Geschichte und Kultur Roms im Spiegel der neueren Forschung, Vol. Iff., Berlin & New York 1972ff.
ANSMN	*American Numismatic Society Museum Notes*.
ArhV	*Arheoloski Vestnik* (Acta Archaeologica).
ASAE	*Annales du service des antiquités de l'Egypte*.
ASFNA	*Annuaire de la société française de numismatique et d'archéologie*.
Athenaeum	*Athenaeum*. Studi Periodici di Letteratura e Storia dell'Antichità.
AttiXVIICIP 1984	Atti del XVII congresso internazionale di papirologia. Napoli 1984.
BASP	*The Bulletin of the American Society of Papyrologists*.
BCH	*Bulletin de correspondance hellénistique*.
BIE	*Bulletin de l'Institut d'Egypte*.
BIFAO	*Bulletin de l'institut français d'archéologie orientale*.
BllMfr	*Blätter für Münzfreunde*.
BMCRE	*Coins of the Roman Empire in the British Museum*. vol. I-VI, London 1923ff.
BollItnum	*Bolletino di numismatica e di arte della medaglia*.
BSAEHistStud	*British School of Archaeology in Egypt. Historical Studies*.
BSFN	*Bulletin de la Société Française de Numismatique*.
BS[R]AA	*Bulletin de la Société [Royale] d'archéologie d'Alexandrie*.
CAH	*The Cambridge Ancient History*, Cambridge 1923-1939.
CAH²	*The Cambridge Ancient History*, 2nd ed., Cambridge 1982ff.
CdEg	*Chronique d'Egypte*.
CINRoma 1961(1965)	II *Congresso internazionale di numismatica Roma 11-16 settembre 1961*. Vol. II, Atti. Roma 1965.
CH	*Coin Hoards*
Essays Margaret Thompson	Mørkholm, Otto & Nancy Waggoner (ed.), *Greek Numismatics and Archaeology*. Essays in Honor of Margaret Thompson. Wettern 1979.
Festschrift Alföldi	*Die Münze*. Festschrift Maria R.-Alföldi. Frankfurt am Main 1991.
FMRD	*Die Fundmünzen der römischen Zeit in Deutschland*.
Hist	*Historia*. Zeitschrift für alte Geschichte.
IGCH	Thompson, Margaret, Otto Mørkholm, Colin M. Kraay (ed.), *An inventory of Greek Coin Hoards*. New York 1973.
Impero romano	*L'impero romano e le strutture economiche e sociali delle province* a cura di Michael Crawford. Como 1986.

JASB   Journal of the Asiatic Society of Bengal.
Jdi   Jahrbuch des [königlichen] deutschen archäologischen Instituts.
JEA   The Journal of Egyptian Archaeology.
JIAN   Journal international d'archéologie numismatique.
JMP   Jaarboek voer Munt- en Penningkunde.
JRA   Journal of Roman Archaeology.
JRASCeylon   Journal of the Ceylon Branch of the Royal Asiatic Society.
JRS   The Journal of Roman Studies.
JSSEA   The Journal of the Society for the Study of Egyptian Antiquities.

Kodai   Kodai. Journal of Ancient History.

Mélanges Bastien Huvelin, H., M. Christol & G. Gautier (ed.), Mélanges de numismatique offèrt
                à Pierre Bastien à l'occasion de son 75ᵉ anniversaire. Wettern 1987.

NC   The Numismatic Chronicle.
NNF-Nytt   NNF-NYTT. Meddelelser fra Norsk Numismatisk Forening.
NNM   Numismatic Notes and Monographs.
NNUM   Nordisk Numismatisk Unions Medlemsblad.
NNÅ   Nordisk Numismatisk Årsskrift (Scandinavian Numismatic Journal).
Num   Numismatist. Official Publication of the American Numismatic Associa-
                tion.
NumAntClas   Quaderni ticinesi di numismatica e antichità classiche.
NZ   Numismatische Zeitschrift.

OJA   Oxford Journal of Archaeology.

PBSR   Papers of the British School at Rome.
PCPhS   Proceedings of the Cambridge Philological Society.
Proc10INC 1986 Carradice, I.A. (ed.), Proceedings of the 10th International Congress of Numis-
                matics, London September 1986. London 1986.

Rassnum   Rassegna Numismatica.
RBN   Revue Belge de Numismatique et de Sigillographie.
RIC   Mattingly, H., E.A. Sydenham & C.H.V. Sutherland (ed.), The Roman Imper-
                ial Coinage. London 1923ff.
RIC²   Sutherland, S.H.V. & R.A.G. Carson (ed.), The Roman Imperial Coinage, rev.
                edition. London 1984ff.
RIN   Rivista Italiana di Numismatica e Scienze Affini.
RN   Revue Numismatique.
RPC   Burnett, Andrew, Michel Amandry & Pere Pan Ripollès, Roman Provincial
                Coinage. London & Paris 1992ff.

SNGCop   *Sylloge nummorum graecorum.* The Royal Collection of Coins and Medals.
                Danish National Museum.

Studia Westermark Florilegium Numismaticum. Studia in honorem U. Westermark edita. Stock-
                holm 1992.

Studies Grierson   Brooke, C.N.L. et al. (ed.), *Studies in Numismatic Method presented to Philip
                Grierson.* Cambridge 1983.

Studies Price   Hurtow, Richard & Silvia Hurter (ed.), *Studies in Greek Numismatics in Memory
                of Martin Jessop Price.* London 1998.

Studies Rudi Thomsen Studies in Ancient History and Numismatics presented to Rudi Thomsen.
                Aarhus 1988.

WZHumboldt   *Wissenschaftliche Zeitschrift der Humboldt Universität zu Berlin.*

ΧΑΡΑΚΤΗΡ   *ΧΑΡΑΚΤΗΡ. Αφιερωμα στη Μαντω Οικονοήμιδου. ΑΘΗΝΑ 1996.*

ZfN   *Zeitschrift für Numismatik.*
ZPE   *Zeitschrift für Papyrologie und Epigraphik.*

Articles and books referred to in the notes:

Alföldi, Andreas
1938   'Die römische Münzprägung und die historischen Ereignisse im Osten zwischen 260
          und 270 n. Chr., *Berytus* 5. 1938, pp. 47-91.

Amandry, Michel
1986   'Les monnaies grecques' in Depeyrot, George (ed.), *Catalogue des monnaies d'or et
          d'argent du Musée de Cognac.* Poitiers 1986, pp. 9-13.
1987   'Les trésors monétaires decouverts à Tanis' in Brissand, Ph. (ed.), *Cahiers de Tanis,*
          vol. I. Paris 1987, pp. 71-74.

Baratte, François
1974   'Un trésor de tetradrachmes Néroniens provenant de Médamoud (Égypte)', *RN* 6.
          ser. 16. 1974, pp. 81-94 + pl. VIII-X.

Beer, Leslie
1979(1980) 'Results of Coin Striking to Simulate the Mint of Aegina', *Actes9CIN 1979,* pp. 47-51
          and pls. 4-5.

Bell, H. Idris
1938   'The Economic Crisis in Egypt under Nero', *JRS* 28. 1938, pp. 1-8.

Bellinger, Alfred R.

1940 *The Syrian Tetradrachms of Caracalla and Macrinus* (American Numismatic Society. Numismatic Studies 3). New York 1940.

Benson, Margaret & Janet **Gourlay**

1899 *The Temple of Mut in Asher.* London 1899.

Bickford-Smith, Roger A.

1994/95 'The Imperial Mints in the East for Septimius Severus: it is time to begin a thorough reconsideration', *RIN* 96. 1994/95, pp. 53-71.

Blanchet, Adrien

1936 'Les rapports entre des dépots monétaires et les événements militaires, politiques et économiques', *RN* 4 ser. 39. 1936, pp. 1-70 & 205-270.

Bland, Roger

1996 'The Roman coinage of Alexandria 30 BC – AD 296: interplay between Roman and local design' in Bailey, D.M. (ed), *Archaeological Research in Roman Egypt. JRA* Suppl. 19. 1996, pp. 113-127.

Boak, A.E.R.

1933 *Karanis, the Temples, Coin Hoards, Botannical and Zoological Reports,* Seasons 1924-1931. (University of Michigan Studies, Humanistic Series, XXX). Ann Arbor 1933.

Bolin, Sture

1926 *Fynden av romerska mynt i det fria Germanien.* Lund 1926.

1938 *State and Currency in the Roman Empire to 300 A.D.* Uppsala 1958.

Botti, G.

1955 'Le monete alessandrine da El-Hibeh nel Museo Egizio di Firenze', *Aegyptus* 35. 1955, pp. 245-274 & pl. I-XII.

Bowman, Alan K. & Dominic **Rathbone**

1992 'Cities and Administration in Roman Egypt', *JRS* 82. 1992, pp. 107-127.

Breccia, Evaristo

1919 'Un ripostiglio di monete imperiali alessandrine', *BSRAA* 17. 1919, pp. 230-250.

1932 *Le Musée Gréco-Romain d'Alexandrie 1925-1931.* Bergamo 1932.

Bruun, Patrick

1979   'The Successive Monetary Reforms of Diocletian', *ANSMN* 24. 1979, pp. 129-148 &
          pl. 32-33.
1991   'The Charms of Quantitative Studies in Numismatic Research', *Festschrift Alföldi* 1991,
          pp. 65-83.

Burnett, Andrew & Paul **Craddock**

1953   'Rome and Alexandria: The minting of Egyptian tetradrachms under Severus Alex-
          ander', *ANSMN* 28. 1983. pp. 109-118.

Butcher, K. & M. **Ponting**

1996   'Rome and the East. Production of Roman Provincial Coinage for Caesarea in Cap-
          padocia under Vespasian, AD 69-79', *OJA* 14. 1996, pp. 63-77.

Buttrey, T.V.

1983   'The Roman Coinage of the Cyrenaica, first century BC to first century AD', *Studies
          Grierson*, 1983, pp. 23-46.
1993   'The President's Address: Calculating Ancient Coin Production: Facts and Fantasies'.
          NC 153. 1993, pp. 335-352.
1994   'The President's Address: Calculating Ancient Coin Production II: Why it cannot be
          done', *NC* 154. 1994, pp. 341-352.

Callataÿ, F. de

1995   'Calculating Ancient Coin Production: Seeking a Balance', *NC* 155. 1995,
          pp. 289-311.

Callu, Jean Pierre

1961(1965) 'Les monnaies de compte et le monnayage du bronze entre 253 et 295', *CINRoma
          1961*, II, pp. 363-376.
1969   *La politique monétaire des empereurs romains de 238 à 311.* Paris 1969.

Campbell, J.B.

1984   *The Emperor and the Roman Army 31 BC-AD 235.* Oxford 1984.

Caron, E.

1894   'Collection du Musée de Ghiseh (Égypte)', *ASFNA* 18. 1894, pp. 153-160.

Carradice, Ian

1983   *Coinage and finances in the Reign of Domitian* (BAR International Series 178). Oxford
          1983.

Carson, R.A.G.

1965 'The Reform of Aurelian', *RN* 6 ser. 7. 1965, pp. 225-235.

Lo **Cascio**, E.

1981 'State and Coinage in the Late Republic and Early Empire', *JRS* 71. 1981, pp. 76-86.

Casey, P.J.

1986 *Understanding Ancient Coins*. An introduction for archaeologists and historians. London 1986.

Chalon, Gérard

1964 *L'édit de Tibérius Julius Alexander* (Biblioteca Helvetica Romana 5). Lausanne 1964.

Christiansen, Erik

1973(1976) 'The Roman Coins of Alexandria. A preliminary report', *Actes8CIN 1973*, pp. 243-252.

1979 (Review of) 'A. Gara, Prosdiagraphomena e circolazione monetaria. Milano 1976', *JRS* 69. 1979, pp. 204-206.

1983-84 'The Roman Coins of Alexandria (30 B.C. to A.D. 296). A survey of collections', *NNÅ* 1983-84, pp. 5-58.

1984 'On Denarii and other Coin-Terms in the Papyri', *ZPE* 54. 1994, pp. 271-299.

1985 'The Roman Coins of Alexandria (30 B.C. to A.D. 296). An inventory of hoards', *CH* 7. 1985, pp. 77-140.

1986 'On the avoidance of *Theta* on Alexandrian Coins', *Proc10INC 1986*, pp. 231-238 + pl. 28, fig. 9.

1988 *The Roman Coins of Alexandria*. Quantitative Studies I-II. Aarhus 1988.

1988b 'From Zoëga to the Present Day. The Roman Coins of Alexandria in 200 Years of Research', *Studies Rudi Thomsen 1988*, pp. 232-242.

1991 *Coins of Alexandria and the Nomes* (British Museum Occasional Paper 77). London 1991.

1992 'The Alexandrian Coins before Zoëga', *Studia Westermark*. 1992, pp. 111-118.

1992b 'The Roman Coins of Alexandria during the Reign of Claudius', *RIN* 94. 1992, pp. 91-112.

1996 'Nero's Alexandrian Coinage Revisited', *XAPAKTHP* 1996, pp. 92-96.

2002 'Single Finds. The case of Roman Egypt', *NNÅ* 2002, pp. xx-xx.

Christiansen, Erik & Alison **Easson**,

1997(2000) 'Thousands of Alexandrian Coins on their way from Cairo to Toronto', *AktenXIIINK 1997* (2000) I, pp. 667-669.

Codrington, H.W.

1924   *Ceylon. Coins and Currency.* (Memoirs of the Colombo Museum. Series A. No. 3) Colombo 1924.

Cope, Lawrence H.

1975   'The chemical composition of a tetradrachm with a reverse type illustrating Codex Theodosianus XII,VII,1', *NC* 7th ser. 15. 1975, pp. 187-190.

Crawford, Michael H.

1969   'Coin Hoards and the Pattern of Violence in the Late Republic', *PBSR* 37. 1969, pp. 76-81.

1970   'Money and Exchange in the Roman World', *JRS* 60. 1970, pp. 40-48.

1974   *Roman Republican Coinage* I-II. Cambridge 1974.

1975   'Finance, Coinage and Money from the Severans to Constantine', *ANRW* II,2. 1975, pp. 560-593.

1990   'From Borgesi to Mommsen: The Creation of an Exact Science' in Crawford, M.H. et al. (ed.), *Medals and Coins from Budé to Mommsen.* London 1990, pp. 125-132.

Currelly, Charles Trick

1956   *I brought the Ages Home.* Toronto 1956.

Dattari, Giovanni

1900   'Appunti di numismatica Alessandrini'. I-III. *RIN* 13. 1900, pp. 267-285; IV-VII, pp. 375-393.

1903   'Appunti di numismatica Alessandrini'. XVI. *RIN* 16. 1903, pp. 11-33 & 263-327.

1906   'Piccolo ripostiglio di denari rinvenuto in Egitto', *Rassnum* 3. 1906, pp. 58-60.

Demandt, Alexander

1989   *Die Spätantikke.* Römische Geschichte von Diocletian bis Justinian 284-565 n.Chr. München 1989.

Dutilh, E.D.J.

1891   'Observations faites sur 527 médailles alexandrines parvenues au Musée de Ghiseh en 1889', *BIE* 3 ser. 2. 1891, pp. 61-65.

1896   'Des divinités et des signes astronomiques sur les monnaies alexandrines', *BIE* 3 ser. 6. 1896, pp. 57-66.

1900   'Historique des collections numismatiques du Musée Gréco-Romain d'Alexandrie', *JIAN* 3. 1900, pp. 1-36.

Eckhel, Joseph

1775   *Numi veteres anecdoti ex museis Caesareo Vindobonensi, Florentino Magni Ducis Etruriae, Granelliano nunc caesareo, Vitzaiano, Festeticisiano, Savorgnano Veneto, aliisque.* Pars I complectens numos in Europae urbibus signatos. Vindobonae 1775.

1794   *Doctrina numorum veterum conscripta.* Pars I, vol. IV. Vindobonae 1794.

Dott. Eddé

1905   'Les trouvailles des trésors monétaires en Egypte', *Bollitnum* 3. 1905, pp. 128-129 & 140-143.

Edgar, Cambell Cowan

1931   *Zenon Papyri in the University of Michigan Collection* (University of Michigan Studies. Humanistic Series 24). Ann Arbor 1931.

Evers, J.H.

1968   'Muntvondst uit Egypte', *JMP* 55. 1968, pp. 62-66.

Fink, Robert O.

1971   *Roman Military Records on Papyrus.* Case Western Reserve University Press 1971.

Foraboschi, Daniele

1993   'La tesaurizzazione o la moneta nacosta', *RIN* 95. 1993, pp. 333-336.

1986   'L'Egitto', *Impero romano* 1986, pp. 109-125.

1992(1994) 'Civiltà della moneto e politica monetaria nell'ellenismo', in Virgilo, Biagio (ed.), *Aspetti e problemi dell'ellenismo* (Atti del convegno di studi Pisa 6-7 novembre 1992). Pisa 1994, pp. 173-186.

Foraboschi Daniele & Alessandra **Gara**

1982   'L'economia dei crediti in natura (Egitto)', *Athenaeum* 60. 1982, pp. 69-84.

Ford, Michael

2000   'The coin hoards of late Roman/early Byzantine Egypt from the reform of Dicletianus to the reform of Anastasius AD 294-491', *NC* 160. 2000, pp. 335-367.

Gara, Alessandra

1975   *Prosdiagraphomena e circolazione monetaria.* Aspetti dell'organizzazione fiscale in rapporto alla politica monetaria dell'Egitto Romano. Milano 1975.

1984   'Continuità e trasformazione nella politica monetaria di Augusto', *AttiXVIICIP 1984*, pp. 1007-1014.

Geissen, Angelo

1976   'Numismatische Bemerkung zu dem Aufstand des L. Domitius Domitianus'. *ZPE* 22. 1976, pp. 280-286 & pl. XV-XVII.

Geissen, Angelo & Wolfram **Weiser**

1983   *Katalog Alexandrinischer Kaisermünzen der Sammlung des Instituts für Altertumskunde zu Köln*. Vol. 4. Claudius Gothicus – Bleimünzen (Nr. 3015-3627). Opladen 1983.

Grenfell, Bernard P., Arthur S. **Hunt** & David G. **Hogarth**

1900   *Fayûm Towns and their Papyri* (Egypt Exploration fund. Graeco-Roman Branch. Memoirs 3). London 1900.

Grierson, Philip

1965   'The President's Address: The Interpretation of Coin Finds', *NC* 7 ser. 5. 1965, pp. I-X-II.

Grinder-Hansen, Keld

1992   'Fundtyper og sammensætning af skattefund' in Jensen, Jørgen Steen et al. (ed.), *Danmarks middelalderlige skattefund c.1050-c.1550* (Denmark's mediaeval treasure-hoards c.1050-c.1550) vol. 1. København 1992, pp. 26-41 (English version, pp. 119-127).

Haatvedt, Rolfe A. & Enoch E. **Peterson**

1964   *Coins from Karanis* (The University of Michigan Excavations 1924-1935, ed. by Elinor M. Husselman). Ann Arbor 1964.

Hackens, Tony

1965   'Trésor de tétradrachmes alexandrins de l'époque impériale'. *BCH* 89. 1965, pp. 383-389 & pl. 8-9.

Halfmann, Helmut

1986   *Itinera pincipum*. Geschichte und Typologie der Kaiserreisen im Römischen Reich. Stuttgart 1986.

Harl, Kenneth W.

1996   *Coinage in the Roman Economy, 300 B.C. to A.D. 700*. Baltimore & London 1996.

Hazzard, R.A.

1990(1993) 'The composition of Ptolemaic silver', *JSSEA* 20. 1990(1993), pp. 89-107.

Holm, Arne E.

1984   'Litt om de minste alexandrinerne', *NNF-Nytt* 1. 1984, pp. 4-9 (with an English sum-
        mary).

Hopkins, Keith

1980   'Taxes and Trade in the Roman Empire (200 B.C. – A.D. 400)', *JRS* 70. 1980,
        pp. 101-125.

1995/96   'Rome, Taxes, Rents and Trade', *Kodai* 61. 1995/96, pp. 41-71.

Howgego, Christopher J.

1990   'Why did Ancient States strike coins?', *NC* 150. 1990, pp. 1-25.

1990b   '(Review of) E. Christiansen, *The Roman Coins of Alexandria*. Quantitative Studies
        I-II. 1988', *JRS* 80. 1990, pp. 231-232.

1992   'The Supply and Use of Money in the Roman World 200 B.C. to A.D. 300', *JRS* 82.
        1992, pp. 1-31.

Huber, C.W.

1871   'Alfred von Sallet's die Daten der alexandrinischen Kaisermünzen', *NZ* 3. 1871,
        pp. 277-299.

Johnson, Allan Chester

1951   *Egypt and the Roman Empire*. Ann Arbor 1951.

Jones, G.D.B.

1980   'The Roman Mines at Riotinto', *JRS* 70. 1980, pp. 146-165.

Jungfleisch, Marcel

1952-53   'Le problème des trouvailles de monnaies anciennes', *BIE* 35. 1952-53, pp. 69-75.

El-Khachab, Abd El-Mohsen

1951   'Les monnaies coulées fausses et les moules monétaires et à bijoux du cabinet des
        médailles du Musée du Caire', *ASAE* 60. 1951, pp. 29-51 & pl. I-VI.

El Khafif, Abdel Hady

1981   'A Hoard of Alexandrian Coins from el Manshâh (Ptolemais Hermiou)', *ZPE* 42. 1981,
        pp. 279-282.

Lafaurie, Jean

1974   'La date de la réforme monétaire d'Aurélien'. *BSFN* 29. 1974, pp. 517-525.

1975   'Réformes monétaires d'Aurélien et de Dioclétien', *RN* 6 ser. 17. 1975, pp. 73-138.

Lewis, Naphtali

1983   *Life in Egypt under Roman Rule.* Oxford 1983.

Lichocka, Barbara

1995   'Une trouvaille des monnaies alexandrines du haut empire dans la maison H à Kôm el-Dikka (Alexandrie)', *Études et travaux* 17. 1995, pp. 111-115.

Lockyear, Kris

1999   'Hoard Structure and Coin Production in Antiquity – an Empirical Investigation', *NC* 159. 1999, pp. 215-243.

MacLennan, Hugh

1968   *Oxyrhynchus.* An economic and social study. Amsterdam 1968.

Metcalf, William E.

1976   'Two Alexandrian Hoards', *RBN* 122. 1976, pp. 65-77 & pl. I-II.

1979   'New and Noteworthy from Roman Alexandria Pescennius Niger Diadumenian', *Essays Margaret Thompson* 1979, pp. 173-182 & pl. 19-20.

1987   'From Greek to Latin currency in third-century Egypt', *Mélanges Bastien* 1987, pp. 157-168.

1989   '(Review of) Le Monnayage des duovirs corinthiens, by Michel Amandry, Paris 1988 (and) The Roman Coins of Alexandria. Quantitative Studies I-II. Aarhus 1988, by Erik Christiansen', *AJA* 93. 1989, pp. 487-489.

1990   'Recent work on provincial coinage in the east', *JRA* 3. 1990, pp. 465-470.

1998   'Aurelian's reform at Alexandria', *Studies Price* 1998, pp. 269-276.

Milne, Joseph Grafton

1903   'Hoards of Coins found in Egypt', *AfP* 2. 1903, pp. 529-536.

1908   'The leaden token-coinage of Egypt under the Romans', *NC* 4 ser. 8. 1908, pp. 287-310 & pl. XXII.

1910   'Alexandrian tetradrachms of Tiberius', *NC* 4 ser. 10. 1910, pp. 333-339 & pl. X.

1911   'The Roman coinage of Alexandria', *BSAEHistStud* 2. 1911, pp. 30-34 & pl. XI-XII.

1914   'Graeco-Roman leaden tesserae from Abydos', *JEA* 1. 1914, pp. 93-95 & pl. XI.

1914-16   'The currency of Egypt under the Romans to the time of Diocletian', *AnnLiv* 7. 1914-16, pp. 51-66.

1915   'Leaden tokens from Memphis', *AncEg* 1915, pp. 107-121.

1916   'The organisation of the Alexandrian mint in the reign of Diocletian', *JEA* 3. 1916, pp. 207-217.

1922   'The coins from Oxyrhynchus', *JEA* 8. 1922, pp. 158-163.

1930   'Egyptian leaden tokens', *NC* 5 ser. 10. 1930, pp. 300-315 & pl. XXII.

1933(1971) *Catalogue of Alexandrian coins.* University of Oxford. Ashmolean Museum. Oxford 1933. Reprinted with a supplement by Colin M. Kraay. Oxford 1971.

1935   'Report on coins found at Tebtunis in 1900', *JEA* 21. 1935, pp. 210-216.

Mørkholm, Otto

1979   'Nogle betragtninger over klassificeringen af møntfund', *NNUM* 6. 1976, pp. 101-106.

1982   'Some Reflections on the Production and Use of Coinage in Ancient Greece', *Hist* 31. 1982, pp. 290-305.

Mond, Sir Obert & Oliver H. **Myers**

1934   The *Bucheum* vol. III (Egypt Exploration Society. Memoir 41). London 1934.

Mrozek, Stanisław

1977   'Die Goldbergwerk im römischen Dazien', *ANRW* II.6. 1977, pp. 95-109.

El-Nassery, S.A.A. & G. **Wagner**

1975   'A New Roman Hoard from Karanis (IIIrd Century A.D.)', *BIFAO* 75. 1975, pp. 183-202 & pl. XXX-XXXVI.

Nestle, W.

1896   'Funde antiker Münzen im Königreich Westfalen', *Fundberichte aus Schwaben* 4. 1896, pp. 56-64.

Newell, Edward T.

1924   'Egyptian Coin Hoards', *Num* 37. 1924, pp. 301-302.

Oddone, Massimo & Adriano **Savio**

1989   'Indagine, mediante analisi per attivazione neutronica strumentale, del contenuto di alcuni tetradrammi alessandrini di Nerone', *RIN* 91. 1989, pp. 131-150.

Parker, H.M.D.,

1935/1958   *A History of the Roman World from A.D. 138 to 337* (Methuen's History of the Greek and Roman World VII) (1935). 2nd rev. ed. by B.H. Warmington. London 1958.

Pegan, Efrem,

1969   'Najdbe novcev v slovenij. II', *ArhV* 20. 1969, pp. 257-264 & pl. 1 (Mit Zusammenfassung auf Deutsch).

Préaux, Claire,

1939   *L'économie royale des Lagides*. Bruxelles 1939.

Price, Martin Jessop,

1973   'The Lost Year: Greek Light on a Problem of Roman Chronology', *NC* 7 ser. 13. 1973, pp. 75-86.

Prinsep, J.

1832   'On the Ancient Roman Coins in the Cabinet of the Asiatic Society', *JASB* 1. 1832, pp. 392-409.

Rathbone, Dominic W.

1987(1989) 'The Ancient Economy and Graeco-Roman Egypt' in Crisculo, L. & Giovanni Geraci (ed.), *Egitto e storia antica dell'ellenismo all'età Araba* (Atti del Colloquio Internazionale Bologna 31 agosto – 2 settembre 1987). Bologna 1989, pp. 159-176.

1990   'Villages, land and population in Graeco-Roman Egypt', *PCPhS* 216. 1990, pp. 103-142.

1991   *Economic rationalism and rural society in third century A.D. Egypt.* Cambridge 1991.

1993(1996) 'Monetisation, not price-inflation in third-century AD Egypt?' in King, Cathy E. & David G. Wigg (ed.), *Coin Finds and Coin Use in the Roman World* (The Thirteenth Oxford Symposium on Coinage and Monetary History 25.-27.3.1993). Berlin 1996, pp. 322-339.

1997   'Prices and price formation in Roman Egypt', in Andreau, J., P. Briant et R. Descat (ed.), *Économie antique. Prix et formation des prix dans les économies antiques* (Entretiens d'archéologie et d'histoire). Saint-Bertrand-de-Comminges 1997, pp. 183-243.

Reece, Richard

1987   *Coinage in Roman Britain.* London 1987.

Regling, Kurt

1912   'Münzschatz aus Theadelphia', *ZfN* 29. 1912, pp. 112-138.

1931   'Der Schatz römischer Goldmünzen von Diarbekir (Mardi)', *BllMfr* 66. 1931, pp. 353-365 & 369-381.

Le **Rider**, Georges

1969   'Monnaies trouvées à Mirgissa', *RN* 6 ser. 11. 1969, pp. 28-35 & pl. III.

Rubensohn, O,

1905   'Aus griechiisch-römischen Häusern des Fayum', *JdI* 20. 1905, pp. 1-25.

Samuel, Alan S.

1984   'The Money Economy and the Ptolemaic Peasantry', *BASP* 21. 1984, pp. 187-206.

Savio, Adriano

1985   'Sui denari di Settimo Severo emessi dalla zecca di Alessandria', *ACME* 38. 1985, pp. 137-143.

1988   'Il quarto anno alessandrino di Nerone nella documentazione numismatica', *NumAntClas* 17. 1988, pp. 221-239.

1991   'Aspetti quantitative della monetazione alessandrina di Ottone', *RIN* 93. 1991, pp. 83-134.

1997   'La numismatica e i problemi quantitativi intorno al calcolo del volume delle emissioni', *RIN* 98. 1997, pp. 11-48.

3 1997   *Katalog der alexandrinischen Münzen der Sammlung Dr. Christian Friedrich August Schledehaus im Kulturgeschichtlichen Museum Osnabrück*/Catalogo delle monete alessandrine della collezione dott. Christian Friedrich August nel Kulturgeschichtliches Museum Osnabrück. Band 3/volume III. Die Münzen des 3. Jahrhunderts/Monete del III secolo (Septimius Severus – Domitius Domitianus). Bramsche 1997.

Savio, Adriano & Massimo Oddone,

1990   'Ancora sull titolo del tetradrammo alessandrino di Nerone', *NumAntClas* 19. 1990, pp. 235-240.

Schultz, Hans-Dietrich

1982   'Zur Chronologie des Lucilla-Porträts auf Münzen'. *WZHumboldt*, Ges.-Sprach w.r. 31. 1982. 2/3, pp. 283-286 & pl. 379.

Schwartz, Jacques

1948   'Note sur un trésor du IIIe siècle AP. J-C', *ASAE* 48. 1948, pp. 459-466.

1963   'L. Domitius Domitianus et l'épigraphé', *CdEg* 38. 1963, pp. 149-155.

1975   *L. Domitius Domitianus* (Étude numismatique et papyrologique). Bruxelles 1975.

Sotheby Sale

1972   *Catalogue of the Collection of Coins formed by the Late Marcel Jungfleisch*. Part II. London, 9th March 1972.

Speidel, M. Alexander

1992   'Roman Army Pay Scales', *JRS* 82. 1992, pp. 87-105.

Spufford, Peter

1988   *Money and its Use in Medieval Europe*. Cambridge 1988.

Still, John

1908   'Roman Coins Found in Ceylon', *JRASCeylon* 19,58. 1908, pp. 161-190.

Thomas, J. David

1976   'The Date of the Revolt of L. Domitius Domitianus', *ZPE* 22. 1976, pp. 253-279.

Thomsen, Rudi

1994   *Oldtidens penge*. Århus 1994.

Thordeman, Bengt

1948   'The Loke Hoard', *NC* 6 ser 8. 1948, pp. 188-204.

Turner, E.G.

1968   *Greek Papyri.* An Introduction. Oxford 1968.

Graf von **Uxkull-Gyllenband**, Valdemar

1926   'Münzen aus el Hibe', in Ranke, H., *Bericht über die badischen Gräbungen in Ägypten in der Winter 1913 und 1914.* Berlin 1926, pp. 53-57.

Visonà, Paolo

1983   'A Small Hoard of Alexandrian Tetradrachms from the Fayum in the Detroit Institute of Arts', ZPE 52. 1983, pp. 75-79.

Vogt, Joseph

1924   *Die alexandrinischen Münzen.* Grundlegung einer alexandrinischen Kaisergeschichte, I-II. Stuttgart 1924.

Wainwright, G.A.

1925   'A Hoard of Silver from Menshah Girga Mudiriah', *ASAE* 25. 1925, pp. 120-134.

Walker, D.R.

1976-1978 *The Metrology of the Roman Silver Coinage.* Part I. Oxford 1976. Part II. Oxford 1977. Part III. Oxford 1978.

Wallace, Sherman L. Roy

1938   *Taxation in Egypt from Augustus to Diocletian.* Princeton 1938.

Watson, Alaric

1999   Aurelian and the third century. London & New York 1999.

West, Louis C. & Allan Chester **Johnson**

1944   *Currency in Roman and Byzantine Egypt.* Princeton & London 1944.

Wolters, Reinhard

1999   *Nummi Signati.* Untersuchungen zur römischen Münzprägung und Geldwirtschaft. München 1999.

Zoëga, Georg

1787   *Numi Aegyptii imperatorii prostantes in museo borgiano velitris adiectis praeterea quotquot reliqua huius classis numismata ex variis museis atque libris colligere obtigit.* Roma 1787.

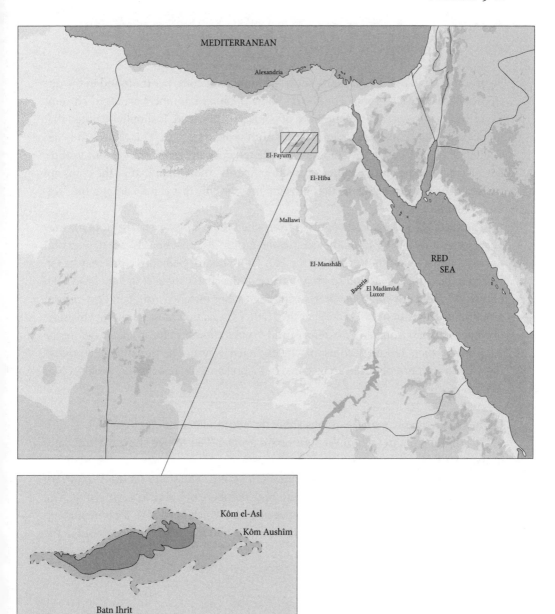

FIG. 9. *Map of sufficiently known sites of billon hoards.*

EXPLANATIONS OF FIGURES 10-18

Figures 10-13 (pillars): These charts show the number of coins per thousand in the different hoards of each group. The X-axes show the hoard numbers arranged chronologically. The Y-axes show the number of coins per thousand. It should be noted that the scales on the Y-axes vary significantly from group to group. This approach is necessitated by the fact that the coins are distributed quite differently in the four groups. For instance, in the group "Other excavation hoards" more than half of the coins are found in the A60 hoard, while the coins are more evenly distributed among the "Karanis Hoards".

The vertical lines mark the point in time when the coins of a certain emperor may be expected to show up in the hoards. In the group "Karanis hoards" we may expect to find the first Commodus coins in the 30A (A88) hoard, Gallienus coins may be expected in hoard 32 (A94) and so on. On three of the charts some emperors have been omitted to avoid crowding the charts with names. For instance, Aurelian Post-reform and Probus have not been marked on the "Other excavation hoards" chart. This simply means that no Aurelian Post-reform and Probus coins become available before the A132 hoard when Tetrarchy coins may be expected as well. The signature "Tetrarchy" therefore marks not only Tetrarchy coins but Aurelian Post-reform and Probus coins as well.

Figures 14-18 (graphs): These graphs show the accumulated number of coins of each of the six emperors in each of the four hoard groups. The X-axes show the end dates of the hoards.

The Y-axes show the accumulated number of coins. The scales on the Y-axes vary from group to group because of the different numbers of coins in each group. The graphs for each emperor show the number of coins, which have been accumulated up to a certain point in time. The information plotted into the graphs can be found in the tables 1-4 as well.

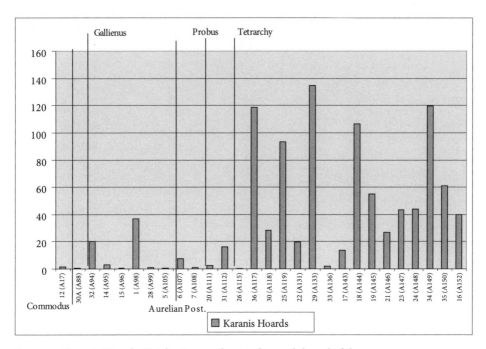

FIG. 10. *Karanis Hoards. Total coins per thousand in each hoard of the group.*

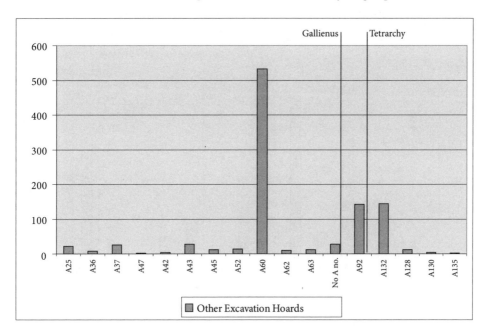

FIG. 11. *Other Excavation Hoards. Total coins per thousand in each hoard of the group.*

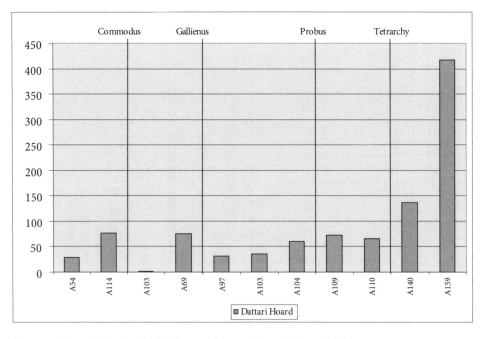

FIG. 12. *Dattari Hoards. Total coins per thousand in each hoard of the group.*

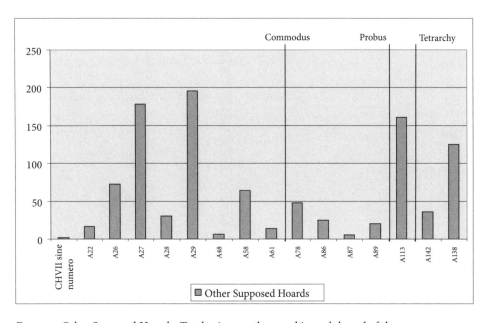

FIG. 13. *Other Supposed Hoards. Total coins per thousand in each hoard of the group.*

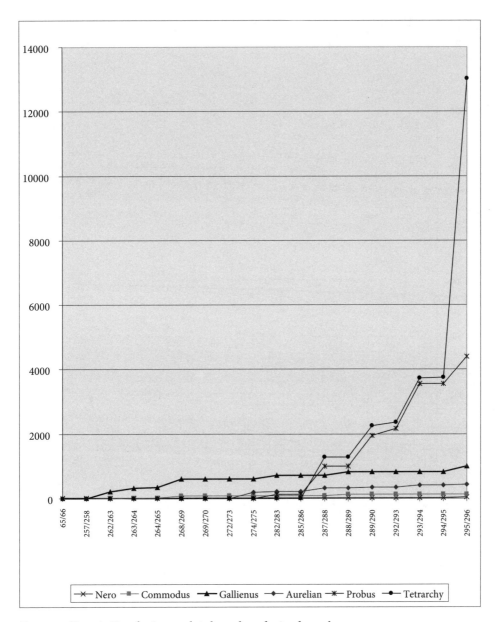

FIG. 14. *Karanis Hoards. Accumulated number of coins for each emperor.*

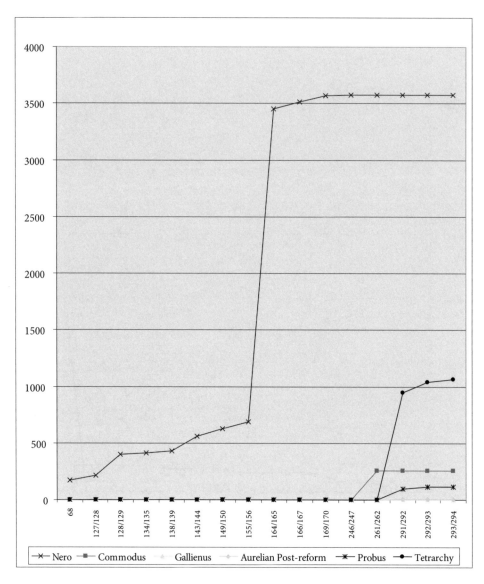

FIG. 15. *Other Excavation Hoards. Accumulated number of coins for each emperor.*

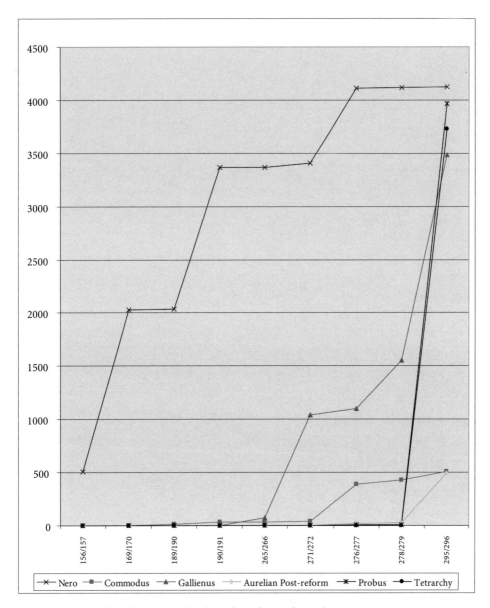

FIG. 16. *Dattari Hoards. Accumulated number of coins for each emperor.*

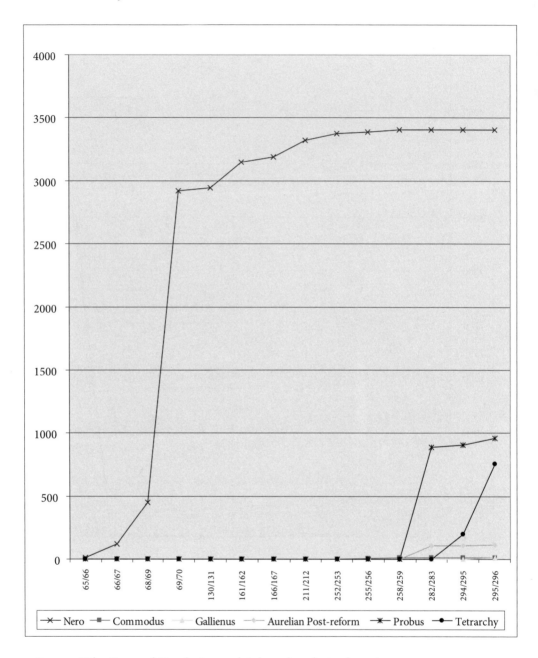

FIG. 17. *Other Supposed Hoards. Accumulated number of coins for each emperor.*

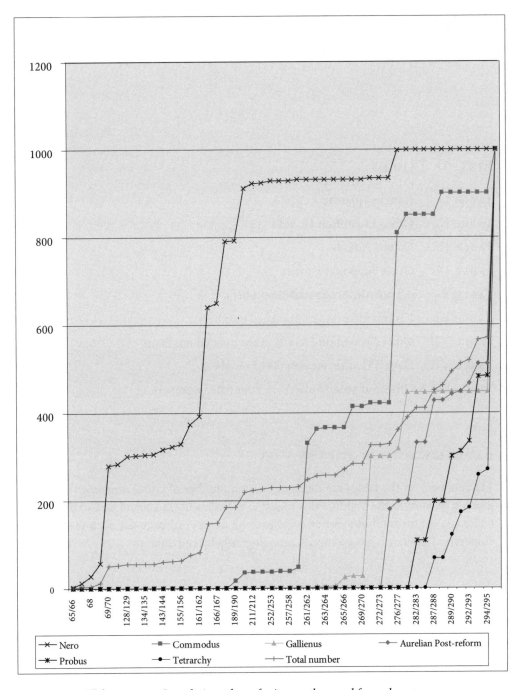

FIG. 18. *All four groups. Cumulative values of coins per thousand for each emperor.*

TABLES

LIST OF TABLES

EXPLANATION OF TABLES V-IX

The numbers on the tables are the accumulated number of coins, meaning that the number of coins in the first hoard is added to the coins of the second and so on. The tables add up the total number of coins and the number of coins for each of the six emperors. The hoards are arranged chronologically by end date.

TABLE I. KARANIS HOARDS   169

TABLE I. *Karanis Hoards*

Hoard 1 (A98). Claudius II yr 2 = AD 268/269
860
MARCUS AURELIUS pre-reform: 2 = 0.24 %
COMMODUS: 44 = 5.28 %
SEPTIMIUS SEVERUS: 1 = 0.12 %
ELAGABAL: 19 = 2.28 %
SEVERUS ALEXANDER: 93 = 11.16 %
MAXIMINUS: 49 = 5.88 %
GORDIAN I: 8 = 0.96 %
PUPIENUS & BALBINUS: 5 = 0.6 %
GORDIAN III: 106 = 12.72 %
PHILIP: 165 = 19.8 %
DECIUS: 37 = 4.44 %
TREBONIAN: 34 = 4.08 %
AEMILIAN: 4 = 0.48 %
VALERIAN: 264 = 31.68 %
MACRIAN & QUIETUS: 18 = 2.16 %
GALLIENUS: 10 = 1.16 %
CLAUDIUS II: 1 = 0.12 %

Hoards 2-3 belong to the period after Diocletian's coin-reform.

Hoard 4, deposited AD 156/57 (according to the latest datable coin), contained 60 Roman *aurei*, included in the section discussing the gold coins (chap. 2, pp. 46f.).

Hoard 5 (A105). Aurelian yr 4 = AD 272/273
17 + 14 illegible
VALERIAN: 1 = 5.88 %
CLAUDIUS II: 12 = 70.56 %
AURELIAN pre-reform: 3 = 17.64 %
AURELIAN & VABALLATH: 1 = 5.88 %

Hoard 6 (A107). Aurelian yr 6 = AD 274/275
181 + 1 undescribed, 9 illegible, and 1 bronze coin (Ptolemaic)
AURELIAN post-reform: 181 = 100 %

Hoard 7 (A108). Aurelian yr 6 = AD 274/275
22
AURELIAN & VABALLATH: 14 = 63.7 %
AURELIAN post-reform: 8 = 36.4 %

Hoards 8-9 belong to the period after Diocletian's coin-reform.

Hoards 10-11 belong to the Ptolemaic period.

Hoard 12 (A17). Nero yr 12 = AD 65/66
40 + 10 illegible
CLAUDIUS: 17 = 42.5%
NERO: 23 = 57.5%

Hoard 13 contained 32 bronze coins, apparently deposited during the reign of Claudius I and included in the section discussing that part of the Alexandrian coinage (chap. 2, p. 51).

Hoard 14 (A95). Gallienus yr 11 = AD 263/264
74 + 1 illegible
NERO: 9 = 12.15 %
GALBA: 1 = 1.35 %
VESPASIAN: 2 = 2.7 %
NERVA: 1 = 1.35 %
HADRIAN: 10 = 13.5 %
ANTONINUS PIUS: 17 = 22.95 %
MARCUS AURELIUS pre-reform: 3 = 4.05 %
COMMODUS: 2 = 2.7 %
SEVERUS ALEXANDER: 1 = 1.35 %
MAXIMINUS: 3 = 4.05 %
GORDIAN III: 4 = 5.4 %
PHILIP: 3 = 4.05 %
DECIUS: 4 = 5.4%
TREBONIAN: 1 = 1.35 %
VALERIAN: 9 = 12.15 %
GALLIENUS: 4 = 5.4 %

Hoard 15 (A96). Gallienus yr 12 = AD 264/265
13 + 20 undescribed and 24 illegible

TABLE I. KARANIS HOARDS   171

HADRIAN: 2 = 15.38 %
MAXIMINUS: 1 = 7.69 %
GORDIAN I: 1 = 7.69 %
PHILIP: 5 = 38.45 %
TREBONIAN: 1 = 7.69 %
VALERIAN: 2 = 15.38 %
GALLIENUS: 1 = 7.69 %

Hoard 16 (A152). Diocletian yr 12 = AD 295/296
931 + 172 illegible
VALERIAN: 1 = 0.11 %
GALLIENUS: 1 = 0.11 %
TACITUS: 4 = 0.44 %
PROBUS: 67 = 7.37 %
CARUS and sons: 109 = 11.99 %
TETRARCHY: 749 = 82.39 %

Hoard 17 (A143). Maximian yr 11 = AD 295/296
320 + 50 undescribed and 7 illegible
NERO: 1 = 0.31 %
HADRIAN: 1 = 0.31 %
ANTONINUS PIUS: 1 = 0.31 %
MARCUS AURELIUS pre-reform: 2 = 0.62 %
COMMODUS: 9 = 2.79 %
SEPTIMIUS SEVERUS: 1 = 0.31 %
ELAGABAL: 7 = 2.17 %
SEVERUS ALEXANDER: 18 = 5.58 %
MAXIMINUS: 18 = 5.58 %
GORDIAN I: 2 = 0.62 %
PUPIENUS & BALBINUS: 2 = 0.62 %
GORDIAN III: 35 = 10.85 %
PHILIP: 57 = 17.67 %
DECIUS: 10 = 3.1 %
TREBONIAN: 22 = 6.82 %
VALERIAN: 119 = 36.89 %
MACRIAN & QUIETUS: 5 = 1.55 %
GALLIENUS: 6 = 1.86 %
CARUS and sons: 1 = 0.31 %
TETRARCHY: 3 = 0.93 %

Hoard 18 (A144). Diocletian yr 12 = AD 295/296
2,472 + 12 illegible
AURELIAN post-reform: 6 = 0.24 %
TACITUS: 3 = 0.12 %
PROBUS: 164 = 6.56 %
CARUS and sons; 231 = 9.34 %
TETRARCHY: 2,068 = 82.72 %

Hoard 19 (A145). Diocletian yr 12 = AD 295/296
1,279 + 160 illegible
CLAUDIUS II: 3 = 0.24 %
AURELIAN post-reform: 9 = 0.72 %
TACITUS: 8 = 0.64 %
PROBUS: 114 = 9.12 %
CARUS and sons: 148 = 11.84 %
TETRARCHY: 997 = 79.76 %

Hoard 20 (A111). Carus yr 1 = AD 282/283
55 + 25 undescribed and 47 illegible
CLAUDIUS II: 15 = 27.3 %
AURELIAN pre-reform: 1 = 1.82 %
AURELIAN post-reform: 4 = 7.28 %
TACITUS: 1 = 1.82 %
PROBUS: 31 = 56.42 %
CARUS and sons: 3 = 5.46 %

Hoard 21 (A146). Diocletian yr 12 = 295/296
617 + 145 illegible
AURELIAN post-reform: 3 = 0.48 %
TACITUS: 1 = 0.16 %
PROBUS: 58 = 9.28 %
CARUS and sons: 79 = 12.64 %
TETRARCHY: 476 = 76.16 %

Hoard 22 (A131). Diocletian yr 9 = AD 292/293
462 + 16 undescribed and 45 illegible
AURELIAN pre-reform: 5 = 1.1 %
AURELIAN post-reform: 18 = 3.96 %
TACITUS: 9 = 1.98%

TABLE I. KARANIS HOARDS   173

PROBUS: 208 = 45.76 %
CARUS and sons: 110 = 24.2 %
TETRARCHY: 112 = 24.64 %

Hoard 23 (A147). Diocletian yr 12 = 295/296
1,010 + 476 illegible
AURELIAN pre-reform: 1 = 0.1 %
AURELIAN post-reform: 2 = 0.2 %
PROBUS: 61 = 6.1 %
CARUS and sons: 131 = 13.1 %
TETRARCHY: 815 = 81.5 %

Hoard 24 (A148). Diocletian yr 12 = AD 295/296
1,021 + 468 illegible
AURELIAN post-reform: 2 = 0,2 %
TACITUS: 1 = 0.1 %
PROBUS: 105 = 10.5 %
CARUS and sons: 147 = 14.7 %
TETRARCHY: 766 = 76.6 %

Hoard 25 (A119). Diocletian yr 6 = AD 289/290
2,168 + 161 illegible
AURELIAN pre-reform: 2 = 0.1 %
AURELIAN post-reform: 15 = 0.75 %
TACITUS: 16 = 0.8 %
PROBUS: 967 = 48.35 %
CARUS and sons: 195 = 9.75 %
TETRARCHY: 973 = 48.65 %

Hoard 26 (A115). Diocletian yr 2 = AD 285/286
4 + 98 illegible
AURELIAN & VABALLATH: 1 = 25 %
TETRARCHY: 3 = 75 %

Hoard 27 contained 55 bronze coins, apparently deposited during the reign of Antoni-nus Pius and included in the section discussing that part of the Alexandrian coinage (chap. 2, p. 51).

Hoard 28 (A99). Claudius II yr 3 = AD 269/270
23 + 4 undescribed and 9 illegible

PUPIENUS & BALBINUS: 1 = 4.35 %
CLAUDIUS II: 22 = 95.7 %

Hoard 29 (A133). Diocletian yr 10 = AD 293/294
3,133 + 1,367 illegible
CLAUDIUS II: 1 = 0.03 %
QUINTILLUS: 1 = 0.03 %
AURELIAN pre-reform: 4 = 0.12 %
AURELIAN post-reform: 47 = 1.41 %
TACITUS: 50 = 1.5 %
PROBUS: 1,383 = 41.49 %
CARUS and sons: 285 = 8.55 %
TETRARCHY: 1,362 = 40.86 %

Hoard 30 (A118). Diocletian yr 5 = AD 288/289
659 + 6 undescribed and 336 illegible
MARCUS AURELIUS pre-reform: 3 = 0.45 %
COMMODUS: 44 = 6.6 %
SEPTIMIUS SEVERUS: 1 = 0.15 %
ELAGABAL: 20 = 3 %
SEVERUS ALEXANDER: 69 = 10.35 %
MAXIMINUS: 34 = 5.1 %
GORDIAN I: 4 = 0.6 %
PUPIENUS & BALBINUS: 4 = 0.6 %
GORDIAN III: 68 = 10.2 %
PHILIP: 168 = 25.2 %
DECIUS: 23 = 3.45 %
TREBONIAN: 24 = 3.6 %
VALERIAN: 183 = 27.45 %
MACRIAN & QUIETUS: 8 = 1.2 %
GALLIENUS: 4 = 0.6 %
CLAUDIUS II: 1 = 0.15 %
TETRARCHY: 1 = 0.15 %

HOARD 30A (A88). Valerian yr 5 = AD 257/258
6 + 6 undescribed and 28 illegible
HADRIAN: 1 = 16.67 %
ANTONINUS PIUS: 1 = 16.67 %
SEVERUS ALEXANDER: 1 = 16.67 %

TABLE I. KARANIS HOARDS   175

GORDIAN III: 1 = 16.67 %
PHILIP: 1 = 16.67 %
VALERIAN: 1 = 16.67 %

Hoard 31 (A112). Carus yr 1 = AD 282/283
379 + 37 illegible
GORDIAN III: 2 = 0.52 %
VALERIAN: 1 = 0.26 %
GALLIENUS: 4 = 1.04 %
CLAUDIUS II: 219 = 56.94 %
AURELIAN pre-reform: 12 = 3.12 %
AURELIAN post-reform: 26 = 6.76 %
TACITUS: 8 = 2.08 %
PROBUS: 104 = 27.04 %
CARUS and sons: 3 = 0.78 %

Hoard 32 (A94). Gallienus yr 10 = AD 262/263
472 + 3 undescribed, 271 illegible, and 1 bronze coin (Vespasian)
ANTONINUS PIUS: 1 = 0.21 %
MARCUS AURELIUS post-reform: 2 = 0.42 %
COMMODUS: 30 = 6.3 %
SEPTIMIUS SEVERUS: 2 = 0.42 %
ELAGABAL: 19 = 3.99 %
SEVERUS ALEXANDER: 41 = 8.61 %
MAXIMINUS: 27 = 5.67 %
GORDIAN I: 2 = 0.42 %
PUPIENUS & BALBINUS: 3 = 0.63 %
GORDIAN III: 55 = 11.55 %
PHILIP: 110 = 23.1 %
DECIUS: 23 = 4.83 %
TREBONIAN: 14 = 2.94 %
AEMILIAN: 1 = 0.21 %
VALERIAN: 130 = 27.3 %
MACRIAN & QUIETUS: 4 = 0.84 %
GALLIENUS: 8 = 1.68 %

Hoard 33 (A136). Constantius yr 3 = AD 294/295
47 + 2 undescribed, 9 illegible, and 1 bronze coin (Vespasian)
PROBUS: 5 = 10.65 %

CARUS and sons: 4 = 8.52 %
TETRARCHY: 38 = 80.94 %

Hoard 34 (A149). Maximian yr 11 = AD 295/296
2,782 + 162 undescribed ("duplicates")
AURELIAN pre-reform: 3 = 0.12 %
AURELIAN post-reform: 9 = 0.36 %
TACITUS: 4 = 0.16 %
PROBUS: 179 = 7.16 %
CARUS and sons: 351 = 14.04 %
TETRARCHY: 2,236 = 89.44 %

Hoard 35 (A150). Diocletian yr 12 = AD 295/296
1,418 + 98 illegible
AURELIAN post-reform: 6 = 0.42 %
TACITUS: 7 = 0.49 %
PROBUS: 107 = 7.49 %
CARUS and sons: 148 = 10.36 %
TETRARCHY: 1,150 = 80.5 %

Hoard 36 (A117). Diocletian yr 4 = AD 287/288
2,757 + 134 illegible (3rd century coins)
CLAUDIUS II: 3 = 0.12 %
AURELIAN pre-reform: 11 = 0.44 %
AURELIAN & VABALLATH: 2 = 0.08 %
AURELIAN post-reform: 102 = 4.08 %
TACITUS: 39 = 1.56 %
PROBUS: 852 = 34.08 %
CARUS and sons: 478 = 19.12 %
TETRARCHY: 1,270 = 50.8 %

Hoard 37 contained 7 bronze coins, apparently deposited during the reign of Antoninus Pius and included in the section discussing that part of the Alexandrian coinage (chap. 2, p. 48).

Totals Alexandrian tetradrachms: 23,222 (28 hoards)
CLAUDIUS: 17 (1 hoard) = 0.07 % [85]
NERO: 33 (3 hoards) = 0.14% [97]
GALBA: 1 = 0.004 % [12]

TABLE I. KARANIS HOARDS   177

OTHO: 0 [4]
VITELLIUS: 0 [5]
VESPASIAN: 2 (1 hoard) = 0.008 % [84]
TITUS: 0 [1]
DOMITIAN: 0 [43]
NERVA: 1 = 0.004 % [1]
TRAJAN: 0 [41]
HADRIAN: 14 (4 hoards) = 0.06 % [112]
ANTONINUS PIUS: 20 (4 hoards) = 0.08 % [99]
MARCUS AURELIUS pre-reform: 10 (4 hoards) = 0.04 % [?]
MARCUS AURELIUS post-reform: 2 (1 hoard) = 0.008 % [?]
COMMODUS: 129 (5 hoards) = 0.55 % [124]
SEPTIMIUS SEVERUS: 5 (4 hoards) = 0.02 % [5]
ELAGABAL: 65 (4 hoards) = 0.27 % [67]
SEVERUS ALEXANDER: 223 (6 hoards) = 0.96 % [225]
MAXIMINUS: 132 (6 hoards) = 0.56 % [133]
GORDIAN I: 17 (5 hoards) = 0.07 % [18]
PUPIENUS & BALBINUS: 15 (5 hoards) = 0.06 % [10]
GORDIAN III: 271 (7 hoards) = 1.16 % [280]
PHILIP: 509 (7 hoards) = 2.19 % [511]
DECIUS: 97 (5 hoards) = 0.41 % [98]
TREBONIAN: 96 (6 hoards) = 0.41 % [97]
AEMILIAN: 5 (2 hoards) = 0.02 % [5]
VALERIAN: 711 (10 hoards) = 3.06 % [?]
MACRIAN & QUIETUS: 35 (4 hoards) = 0.15 % [37]
GALLIENUS: 38 (8 hoards) = 0.16 % [?]
CLAUDIUS II: 277 (9 hoards) = 1.19 % [248]
QUINTILLUS: 1 = 0.004 % [1]
AURELIAN pre-reform: 42 (9 hoards) = 0.18 % [?]
AURELIAN & VABALLATH: 18 (4 hoards) = 0.07 % [?]
AURELIAN post-reform: 438 (15 hoards) = 1.88 % [?]
TACITUS: 151 (13 hoards) = 0.65 % [155]
PROBUS: 4,405 (15 hoards) = 18.96 % [4,469]
CARUS and sons: 2,423 (16 hoards) = 10.47 % [2,531]
TETRARCHY: 13,019 (16 hoards) = 56.06 % [13,318]

Grand totals: 27,641
Alexandrian tetradrachms: 23,222 = 84.01 %
Bronze coins (in the hoards of billon coins): 3 (3 hoards) = 0.01 %

Undescribed coins: 295 (11 hoards) = 1.06 %
Illegible coins: 4,121 (25 hoards) = 14.9 %

NOTE 1: Numbers in square brackets are totals according to the survey in Haatvedt & Peterson (1964), pp. 5f. Higher totals may be due to straily found coins (and the few hoards of Alexandrian bronze coins). I can offer no explanation of the cases with lower totals.

NOTE 2: Several subtotals and totals in Haatvedt & Peterson (1964) are wrong. The reason may be wrong entries of actual numbers of specific coins. Such cases cannot be verified, and instead I have simply taken the additions to be wrong and corrected accordingly without further notice.

TABLE II. *Other Excavation Hoards*

Abu el-Gud 1968 (no A x1). Philip yr 4 = AD 246/247
229 + 4 illegible
NERO: 8 = 3.49 %
TRAJAN: 4 = 1.74 %
HADRIAN: 103 = 44.97 %
ANTONINUS PIUS: 100 = 43.66 %
MARCUS AURELIUS pre-reforn: 11 = 4.8 %
SEPTIMIUS SEVERUS: 2 = 0.87 %
PHILIP: 1 = 0.43 %

Alexandria 1916 (A92). Gallienus yr 9 = AD 261/262
1,184 + 116 illegible
VESPASIAN: 2 = 0.16 %
HADRIAN: 6 = 0.48 %
ANTONINUS PIUS: 91 = 7.28 %
MARCUS AURELIUS pre-reform: 152 = 12.16 %
MARCUS AURELIUS post-reform: 6 = 0.48 %
COMMODUS: 256 = 20.48 %
SEPTIMIUS SEVERUS: 9 = 0.72 %
ELAGABAL: 119 = 9.52 %
SEVERUS ALEXANDER: 341 = 27.28 %
MAXIMINUS: 34 = 2.72 %
GORDIAN I: 1 = 0.08 %
PUPIENUS & BALBINUS: 3 = 0.24 %

TABLE II. OTHER EXCAVATION HOARDS   179

GORDIAN III: 78 = 6.24 %
PHILIP: 60 = 4.8 %
DECIUS: 9 = 0.72 %
TREBONIAN: 2 = 0.16 %
VALERIAN: 14 = 1.12 %
GALLIENUS: 1 = 0.08 %

Baqaria 1932 (A135). Maximian yr 9 = AD 293/294
22
CARUS and sons: 1 = 4.55 %
TETRARCHY: 21 = 95.55 %

Batn Ihrît 1902 (A130). Diocletian yr 9 = AD 292/293
26 + 7 illegible and 1 fragment of a bronze ring
AURELIAN post-reform: 2 (+1?) = 7.7% (11.55%?)
PROBUS: 4 = 15.4 %
CARUS and sons: 3 = 11.55 %
TETRARCHY: 16 = 61.6 %

El-Hîba 1914 (A43). Antoninus Pius yr 7 = AD 143/144
236
CLAUDIUS: 12 = 5.08 %
NERO: 133 = 56.36 %
GALBA: 11 = 4.66 %
VESPASIAN: 14 = 5.93 %
TITUS: 2 = 0.85 %
NERVA: 1 = 0.42 %
TRAJAN: 6 = 2.54 %
HADRIAN: 49 = 20.76 %
ANTONINUS PIUS: 8 = 3.39 %

El-Hîba 1935 (A37). Hadrian yr 13 = AD 128/129
216
CLAUDIUS: 7 = 3.24 %
NERO: 186 = 86.11 %
GALBA: 7 = 3.24 %
OTHO: 2 = 0.92 %
VESPASIAN: 11 = 5.09 %
TITUS: 2 = 0.92 %

HADRIAN: 1 = 0.46 %

Kôm el-Asl 1 (A60). Marcus Aurelius yr 5 = AD 164/165
4,423 + 3 bronze coins (2 Ptolemaic and 1 Antoninus Pius)
CLAUDIUS: 361 = 7.22 %
NERO: 2,762 = 55.24 %
GALBA: 191 = 3.82 %
OTHO: 58 = 1.16 %
VITELLIUS: 19 = 0.38 %
VESPASIAN: 235 = 4.7 %
TITUS: 31 = 0.62 %
DOMITIAN: 1 = 0.02 %
NERVA: 22 = 0.44 %
TRAJAN: 89 = 1.78 %
HADRIAN: 572 = 11.44 %
ANTONINUS PIUS: 77 = 1.54 %
MARCUS AURELIUS pre-reform: 5 = 0.1 %

Kôm el-Asl 2 (A36). Hadrian yr 12 = AD 127/128
62
CLAUDIUS: 5 = 8.06 %
NERO: 44 = 70.96 %
GALBA: 2 = 3.22 %
OTHO: 1 = 1.61 %
VESPASIAN: 6 = 9.67 %
TRAJAN: 1 = 1.61 %
HADRIAN: 3 = 4,83 %

Kôm Aushîm 1896 (A63). Marcus Aurelius yr 10 = AD 169/170
98
CLAUDIUS: 3 = 3.06 %
NERO: 56 = 57.12 %
GALBA: 2 = 2.04 %
VESPASIAN: 4 = 4.08 %
TRAJAN: 4 = 4.08 %
HADRIAN: 18 = 18.36 %
ANTONINUS PIUS: 8 = 8.16 %
MARCUS AURELIUS pre-reform: 3 = 3.06 %

TABLE II. OTHER EXCAVATION HOARDS   181

Kôm Aushîm 1972 (A132). Diocletian yr 8 = AD 291/292
1,199 + 359? illegible
CLAUDIUS II: 1 = 0.08 %
QUINTILLUS: 1 = 0.08 %
AURELIAN pre-reform: 1 = 0.08 %
AURELIAN & VABALLATH: 1 = 0.08 %
AURELIAN post-reform: 5 = 0.4 %
TACITUS: 4 = 0.32 %
PROBUS: 101 = 8.08 %
CARUS and sons: 139 = 11.12 %
TETRARCHY: 946 = 75.68 %

El Madamûd 1928 (A25). Galba yr 1 = AD 68
173 + 57 illegible (mostly Nero)
NERO: 172 = 99.99 %
GALBA: 1 = 0.58 %

Mallawi "A" 1977 (A128). Diocletian yr 9 = AD 292/293
97 + 1 illegible
PROBUS: 11 = 11.33 %
CARUS and sons: 7 = 7.21 %
TETRARCHY: 79 = 81.37 %

Mallawi "K" 1977 (A62). Marcus Aurelius yr 7 = AD 166/167
86 + 64 illegible, 10 bronze coins (3 Ptolemaic and 7 Alexandrian), and 1 ring
NERO: 58 = 67.28 %
GALBA: 1 = 1.16%
VITELLIUS: 1 = 1.16%
VESPASIAN: 2 = 2.32 %
TRAJAN: 3 = 3.48 %
HADRIAN: 16 = 18.56 %
ANTONINUS PIUS: 4 = 4.64 %
MARCUS AURELIUS pre-reform: 1 = 1.16 %

El Manshâh 1968 (A45). Antoninus Pius yr 13 = AD 149/150
102
CLAUDIUS: 2 = 1.96 %
NERO: 66 = 64.68 %
GALBA: 3 = 2.94 %

OTHO: 2 = 1.96 %
VESPASIAN: 7 = 6.86 %
NERVA: 2 = 1.96 %
TRAJAN: 4 = 3.92 %
HADRIAN: 14 = 13.72 %
ANTONINUS PIUS: 2 = 1.96 %

Umm el-Breigat 3 (A52). Antoninus Pius yr 19 = AD 155/156
119
NERO: 64 = 53.76 %
GALBA: 7 = 5.88 %
VITELLIUS: 1 = 0.84 %
VESPASIAN: 6 = 5.04 %
TITUS: 1 = 0.84 %
TRAJAN: 4 = 3.36 %
HADRIAN: 29 = 24.36 %
ANTONINUS PIUS: 7 = 5.88 %

Umm el-Breigat 4 (A47). Hadrian yr 19? = AD 134/135
13 + 1 bronze coin (Antoninus Pius yr?)
NERO: 10 = 76.92 %
GALBA: 1 = 7.69 %
TITUS: 1 = 7.69 %
HADRIAN: 1 = 7.69 %

Umm el-Breigat 5 (A42). Antoninus Pius yr 2 = AD 138/139
28
CLAUDIUS: 1 = 3.57 %
NERO: 17 = 60.71 %
GALBA: 1 = 3.57 %
DOMITIAN: 1 = 3.57 %
TRAJAN: 1 = 3.57 %
HADRIAN: 6 = 21.42 %
ANTONINUS PIUS: 1 = 3.57 %

Totals Alexandrian tetradrachms: 8,313 (17 hoards)
CLAUDIUS: 391 (7 hoards) = 4.7 %
NERO: 3,576 (12 hoards) = 43.01 %
GALBA: 227 (11 hoards) = 2.73 %

TABLE II. OTHER EXCAVATION HOARDS   183

OTHO: 63 (4 hoards) = 0.75 %
VITELLIUS: 21 (3 hoards) = 0.25 %
VESPASIAN: 287 (9 hoards) = 3.45 %
TITUS: 37 (5 hoards) = 0.44 %
DOMITIAN: 2 (2 hoards) = 0.02 %
NERVA: 25 (3 hoards) = 0.3 %
TRAJAN: 116 (9 hoards) = 1.39 %
HADRIAN: 818 (12 hoards) = 9.84 %
ANTONINUS PIUS: 298 (9 hoards) = 3.58 %
MARCUS AURELIUS pre-reform: 172 (5 hoards) = 2.06 %
MARCUS AURELIUS post-reform: 6 (1 hoard) = 0.07 %
COMMODUS: 256 (1 hoard) = 3.07 %
SEPTIMIUS SEVERUS: 11 (2 hoards) = 0.131 %
ELAGABAL: 119 (1 hoard) = 1.43 %
SEVERUS ALEXANDER: 341 (1 hoard) = 4.1 %
MAXIMINUS: 34 (1 hoard) = 0.4 %
GORDIAN I: 1 = 0.01 %
PUPIENUS & BALBINUS: 3 (1 hoard) = 0.03 %
GORDIAN III: 78 (1 hoard) = 0.96 %
PHILIP: 61 (2 hoards) = 0.73 %
DECIUS: 9 (1 hoard) = 0.1 %
TREBONIAN: 2 (1 hoard) = 0.02 %
VALERIAN: 14 (1 hoard) = 0.16 %
GALLIENUS: 1 = 0.01 %
CLAUDIUS II: 1 = 0.01 %
QUINTILLUS: 1 = 0.01 %
AURELIAN pre-reform: 1 = 0.01 %
AURELIAN & VABALLATH: 1= 0.01 %
AURELIAN post-reform: 8 (7?) (2 hoards) = 0.09%
TACITUS: 4 (1 hoard) = 0.04 %
PROBUS: 116 (3 hoards) = 1.39 %
CARUS and sons: 150 (4 hoards) = 1.8 %
TETRARCHY: 1,062 (4 hoards) = 12.77 %

Grand totals: 8,933
Alexandrian tetradrachms: 8,313 = 93.05 %
Bronze coins: 14 (3 hoards) = 0.15 %
Illegible coins: 608 (7 hoards) = 6.8 %
Other objects: 2 (2 hoards) = 0.02 %

TABLE III. *Dattari Hoards*

A'06 (A97). Gallienus yr 13 = AD 265/266
950
ELAGABAL: 15 = 1.57 %
SEVERUS ALEXANDER: 61 = 6.42 %
MAXIMINUS: 24 = 2.52 %
GORDIAN I: 1 = 0.1 %
GORDIAN III: 65 = 6.84 %
PHILIP: 235 = 24.73 %
DECIUS: 28 = 2.94 %
TREBONIAN: 13 = 1.36 %
VALERIAN: 429 = 45.15 %
MACRIAN & QUIETUS: 5 = 0.52 %
GALLIENUS: 74 = 7.78 %

A'07 (A109). Probus yr 2 = AD 276/277
2,167 + 2 Ptolemaic silver tetradrachms, 1 bronze coin (Alexandrian), and 62 illegible
CLAUDIUS: 19 = 0.87 %
NERO: 707 = 32.62 %
GALBA: 27 = 1.24 %
OTHO: 8 = 0.36 %
VITELLIUS: 2 = 0.09 %
VESPASIAN: 34 = 1.56 %
TITUS: 7 = 0.32 %
NERVA: 3 = 0.13 %
TRAJAN: 16 = 0.73 %
HADRIAN: 151 = 6.96 %
ANTONINUS PIUS: 62 = 2.86 %
MARCUS AURELIUS pre-reform: 18 = 0.83 %
MARCUS AURELIUS post-reform: 1 = 0.04%
COMMODUS: 352 = 16.24 %
SEPTIMIUS SEVERUS: 4 = 0.18 %
ELAGABAL: 144 = 6.64 %
SEVERUS ALEXANDER: 413 = 19.05 %
MAXIMINUS: 5 = 0.23 %
GORDIAN III: 16 = 0.73 %
PHILIP: 21 = 0.96 %

TABLE III. DATTARI HOARDS   185

DECIUS: 5 = 0.23 %
TREBONIAN: 3 = 0.13 %
VALERIAN: 30 = 1.38 %
MACRIAN & QUIETUS: 2 = 0.09 %
GALLIENUS: 61 = 2.81 %
CLAUDIUS II: 17 = 0.78 %
AURELIAN pre-reform: 9 = 0.41 %
AURELIAN & VABALLATH: 3 = 0.13 %
AURELIAN post-reform: 20 = 0.92 %
TACITUS: 3 = 0.13 %
PROBUS: 4 = 0.18 %

B'07A (A103). Commodus yr 30 = AD 189/190
23 + 2 bronze coins (Ptolemaic)
NERO: 5 = 21.73 %
TRAJAN: 1 = 4.34 %
HADRIAN: 1 = 4.34 %
MARCUS AURELIUS pre-reform: 1 = 4.34 %
COMMODUS: 15 = 65.21 %

B'07 B (A103). Aurelian yr 3 = AD 271/272
1,066 + 37 illegible
SEPTIMIUS SEVERUS: 1 = 0.09 %
ELAGABAL: 11 = 1.03 %
SEVERUS ALEXANDER: 17 = 1.59 %
MAXIMINUS: 7 = 0.65 %
GORDIAN I: 1 = 0.09 %
GORDIAN III: 21 = 1.96 %
PHILIP: 46 = 4.31 %
DECIUS: 11 = 1.03 %
TREBONIAN: 12 = 1.12 %
VALERIAN: 133 = 12.47 %
MACRIAN & QUIETUS: 6 = 0.56 %
GALLIENUS: 462 = 43.33 %
CLAUDIUS II: 319 = 29.92%
AURELIAN pre-reform: 17 = 1.59 %
AURELIAN & VABALLATH: 2 = 0.18 %

C'07 (A104). Aurelian yr 3 = AD 271/272
1,803 + 31 illegible and 5 bronze coins (Ptolemaic)
NERO: 38 = 2.1 %
GALBA: 1 = 0.05 %
OTHO: 2 = 0.11 %
VITELLIUS: 3 = 0.16 %
VESPASIAN: 6 = 0.33 %
TITUS: 1 = 0.05 %
TRAJAN: 5 = 0.27 %
HADRIAN: 19 = 1.05 %
ANTONINUS PIUS: 9 = 0.49 %
MARCUS AURELIUS pre-reform: 1 = 0.05 %
COMMODUS: 6 = 0.33 %
ELAGABAL: 2 = 0.11 %
SEVERUS ALEXANDER: 13 = 0.72 %
MAXIMINUS: 4 = 0.22 %
GORDIAN I: 1 = 0.05 %
GORDIAN III: 13 = 0.72 %
PHILIP: 13 = 0.72 %
DECIUS: 7 = 0.38 %
TREBONIAN: 7 = 0.38 %
VALERIAN: 111 = 6.15 %
MACRIAN & QUIETUS: 9 = 0.49 %
GALLIENUS: 504 = 27.95 %
CLAUDIUS II: 978 = 54.24 %
QUINTILLUS: 1 = 0.05 %
AURELIAN pre-reform: 49 = 2.71 %

A'09 (A114). Marcus Aurelius yr 10 = AD 169/170
2,302 + 92 illegible
CLAUDIUS: 73 = 3.17 %
NERO: 1,526 = 66.29 %
GALBA: 76 = 3.3 %
OTHO: 20 = 0.87 %
VITELLIUS: 7 = 0.3 %
VESPASIAN: 79 = 3.43 %
TITUS: 9 = 0.39 %
NERVA: 8 = 0.35 %
TRAJAN: 48 = 2.09 %

TABLE III. DATTARI HOARDS   187

HADRIAN: 360 = 15.64 %
ANTONINUS PIUS: 90 = 3.91 %
MARCUS AURELIUS pre-reform: 6 = 0.26 %

B'09 (A110). Probus yr 4 = AD 278/279
1,956 + 50 illegible
NERO: 4 = 0.2 %
TRAJAN: 1 = 0.05 %
HADRIAN: 2 = 0.1 %
ANTONINUS PIUS: 1 = 0.05 %
MARCUS AURELIUS pre-reform: 7 = 0.35 %
COMMODUS: 38 = 1.94 %
ELAGABAL: 49 = 2.5 %
SEVERUS ALEXANDER: 130 = 6.64 %
MAXIMINUS: 99 = 5.06 %
GORDIAN I: 3 = 0.15 %
PUPIENUS & BALBINUS: 1 = 0.05 %
GORDIAN III: 165 = 8.43 %
PHILIP: 288 = 14.72 %
DECIUS: 57 = 2.91 %
TREBONIAN: 43 = 2.19 %
VALERIAN: 463 = 23.67 %
MACRIAN & QUIETUS: 10 = 0.51 %
GALLIENUS: 451 = 23.05 %
CLAUDIUS II: 132 = 6.74 %
AURELIAN pre-reform: 4 = 0.2 %
AURELIAN & VABALLATH: 3 = 0.15 %
AURELIAN post-reform: 4 = 0.2 %
PROBUS: 1 = 0.05 %

C'09 (A140). Diocletian yr 12 = AD 295/296
4,116 + 4 illegible and 2 bronze coins (Ptolemaic)
MARCUS AURELIUS pre-reform: 1 = 0.02 %
ELAGABAL: 2 = 0.04 %
GORDIAN III: 2 = 0.04 %
PHILIP: 1 = 0.02 %
GALLIENUS: 2 = 0.04 %
CLAUDIUS II: 16 = 0.38 %
AURELIAN pre-reform: 10 = 0.24 %
AURELIAN & VABALLATH: 255 = 6.19 %

VABALLATH: 7 = 0.17 %
AURELIAN post-reform: 37 = 0.89 %
TACITUS: 14 = 0.34 %
PROBUS: 327 = 7.94 %
CARUS and sons: 389 = 9.45 %
TETRARCHY: 3,053 = 74.17 %

[*D'09* (A14). Tiberius yr 7 = AD 20/21
136 (All Tiberius yr 7) + 65 Ptolemaic tetradrachms]

A'11 (A69). Commodus yr 31 = AD 190/191
2,271 + 4 bronze coins (2 Ptolemaic and 2 Alexandrian)
TIBERIUS: 2 = 0.08 %
CLAUDIUS: 189 = 8.32 %
NERO: 1,330 = 58.56 %
GALBA: 86 = 3.78 %
OTHO: 15 = 0.66 %
VITELLIUS: 7 = 0.3 %
VESPASIAN: 98 = 4.31 %
TITUS: 2 = 0.08 %
NERVA: 2 = 0.08 %
TRAJAN: 33 = 1.45 %
HADRIAN: 327 = 14.39 %
ANTONINUS PIUS: 147 = 6.47 %
MARCUS AURELIUS pre-reform: 16 = 0.7 %
COMMODUS: 17 = 0.74 %

B'11 (A159). Diocletian yr 12 = AD 295/296
12,534 + 48 illegible and 7 bronze coins (4 Ptolemaic and 3 Alexandrian)
NERO: 7 = 0.05 %
VESPASIAN: 2 = 0.01 %
TITUS: 1 = 0.007 %
TRAJAN: 1 = 0.007 %
HADRIAN: 3 = 0.02 %
ANTONINUS PIUS: 8 = 0.06 %
MARCUS AURELIUS pre-reform: 9 = 0.07 %
MARCUS AURELIUS post-reform: 1 = 0.007 %
COMMODUS: 80 = 0.63 %

TABLE III. DATTARI HOARDS   189

CARACALLA: 1 = 0.007 %
ELAGABAL: 93 = 0.74 %
SEVERUS ALEXANDER: 325 = 2.59 %
MAXIMINUS: 111 = 0.88 %
GORDIAN I: 3 = 0.02 %
PUPIENUS & BALBINUS: 2 = 0.01 %
GORDIAN III: 147 = 1.17 %
PHILIP: 422 = 3.36 %
DECIUS: 74 = 0.59 %
TREBONIAN: 53 = 0.42 %
AEMILIAN: 1 = 0.007 %
VALERIAN: 551 = 4.39 %
MACRIAN & QUIETUS: 16 = 0.12 %
GALLIENUS: 1,932 = 15.41 %
CLAUDIUS II: 2,907 = 23.19 %
QUINTILLUS: 4 = 0.03 %
AURELIAN pre-reform: 157 = 1.25 %
AURELIAN & VABALLATH: 252 = 2.01 %
VABALLATH: 1 = 0.007 %
AURELIAN post-reform: 431 = 3.43 %
TACITUS: 172 = 1.37 %
PROBUS: 3,633 = 28.98 %
CARUS and sons: 458 = 3.65 %
TETRARCHY: 676 = 5.39 %

A'13 (A54). Antoninus Pius yr 20? = AD 156/157
874 + 7 illegible and 2 bronze coins (Ptolemaic)
CLAUDIUS: 8 = 0.92 %
NERO: 505 = 57.78 %
GALBA: 17 = 1.95 %
OTHO: 2 = 0.23 %
VITELLIUS: 8 = 0.92 %
VESPASIAN: 13 = 1.49 %
NERVA: 2 = 0.23 %
TRAJAN: 9 = 1.03 %
HADRIAN: 275 = 31.46 %
ANTONINUS PIUS: 35 = 4 %

Totals Alexandrian tetradrachms: 30,062 (11 hoards, excluding D'09)
TIBERIUS: 2 (1 hoard) = 0.006 %
CLAUDIUS: 289 (4 hoards) = 0.96 %
NERO: 4,122 (8 hoards) = 13.71 %
GALBA: 207 (5 hoards) = 0.68 %
OTHO: 47 (5 hoards) = 0.15 %
VITELLIUS: 27 (5 hoards) = 0.08%
VESPASIAN: 232 (6 hoards) = 0.77 %
TITUS: 20 (5 hoards) = 0.06 %
NERVA: 15 (4 hoards) = 0.04 %
TRAJAN: 114 (8 hoards) = 0.37 %
HADRIAN: 1,138 (8 hoards) = 3.78 %
ANTONINUS PIUS: 252 (7 hoards) = 0.83 %
MARCUS AURELIUS pre-reform: 59 (8 hoards) = 0.19 %
MARCUS AURELIUS post-reform: 2 (2 hoards) = 0.006 %
COMMODUS: 508 (6 hoards) = 1.68 %
SEPTIMIUS SEVERUS: 5 (2 hoards) = 0.01 %
CARACALLA: 1 = 0.003 %
ELAGABAL: 316 (7 hoards) = 1.05 %
SEVERUS ALEXANDER: 959 (6 hoards) = 3.19 %
MAXIMINUS: 250 (16 hoards) = 0.83 %
GORDIAN I: 9 (5 hoards) = 0.02 %
PUPIENUS & BALBINUS: 3 (2 hoards) = 0.009 %
GORDIAN III: 429 (7 hoards) = 1.42 %
PHILIP: 1,026 (7 hoards) = 3.41 %
DECIUS: 182 (6 hoards) = 0.6 %
TREBONIAN: 131 (6 hoards) = 0.43 %
AEMILIAN: 1 = 0.003 %
VALERIAN: 1,717 (6 hoards) = 5.71 %
MACRIAN & QUIETUS: 48 (6 hoards) = 0.15 %
GALLIENUS: 3,486 (7 hoards) = 11.59 %
CLAUDIUS II: 4,369 (6 hoards) = 14.53 %
QUINTILLUS: 5 (2 hoards) = 0.01 %
AURELIAN pre-reform: 246 (6 hoards) = 0.81 %
AURELIAN & VABALLATH: 515 (5 hoards) = 1.71 %
VABALLATH: 8 (2 hoards) = 0.02 %
AURELIAN post-reform: 492 (4 hoards) = 1.63 %
TACITUS: 189 (3 hoards) = 0.62 %
PROBUS: 3,965 (4 hoards) = 13.18 %

TABLE IV. OTHER SUPPOSED HOARDS   191

CARUS and sons: 847 (2 hoards) = 2.81 %
TETRARCHY: 3,729 (2 hoards) = 12.4 %

Grand totals: 30,418
Alexandrian tetradrachms: 30,062 = 98.82 %
Bronze coins: 23 (7 hoards) = 0.07 %
Illegible coins: 331 (8 hoards) = 1.08 %
Ptolemaic tetradrachms 2 (1 hoard) = 0.006 %

TABLE IV. *Other Supposed Hoards*

Aswan 1962? (A48). Antoninus Pius yr?/Hadrian yr 15 = AD 130/131
45
CLAUDIUS: 3 = 6.66 %
NERO: 24 = 53.33 %
GALBA: 2 = 4.44 %
VESPASIAN: 2 = 4.44 %
TRAJAN: 2 = 4.44 %
HADRIAN: 11 = 24.44 %
ANTONINUS PIUS: 1 = 2.22 %

Cairo Hoard 1895 (A138). Diocletian yr 12 = AD 295/296
822
MARCUS AURELIUS pre-reform: 1 = 0.12 %
COMMODUS: 1 = 0.12 %
ELAGABAL: 1 = 0.12 %
GORDIAN III: 2 = 0.24 %
PHILIP: 2 = 0.24 %
VALERIAN: 5 = 0.6 %
GALLIENUS: 10 = 1.21 %
CLAUDIUS II: 87 = 10.58 %
AURELIAN & VABALLATH: 2 = 0.24 %
AURELIAN post-reform: 10 = 1.21 %
TACITUS: 3 = 0.36 %
PROBUS: 54 = 6.56 %
CARUS and sons: 86 = 10.46 %
TETRARCHY: 558 = 67.88 %

Currelly 1910 (A28). Vespasian yr 2 = AD 69/70
197
CLAUDIUS: 144 = 73 %
NERO: 51 = 25.88 %
VESPASIAN: 2 = 1.01 %

EEF c. 1900 (A27). Vespasian yr 2 = AD 69/70
1,175
CLAUDIUS: 24 = 2.04 %
NERO: 1,128 = 95.99 %
GALBA: 14 = 1.19 %
OTHO: 4 = 0.34 %
VITELLIUS: 1 = 0.08 %
VESPASIAN: 4 = 0.34 %

Faiyûm 1902? (sine numero). Nero yr 12 = AD 65/66
15
CLAUDIUS: 1 = 6.66 %
NERO: 14 = 93.33 %

Faiyûm b. 1929 (A142). Diocletian yr 11 = AD 294/295
237
PROBUS: 18 = 7.59 %
CARUS and sons: 19 = 8.01 %
TETRARCHY: 200 = 84.38 %

Girga 1947 (A113). Carinus yr 1 = AD 282/283
1,058
CLAUDIUS II: 7 = 0.66 %
AURELIAN pre-reform: 20 = 1.89 %
AURELIAN post-reform: 106(?) = 10.01 %
TACITUS: 38 = 3.59 %
PROBUS: 886 = 83.74 %
CARUS and sons: 1 = 0.09 %

Jungfleisch 1972 (A22). Nero yr 13 = AD 66/67
107
NERO: 107 = 100 %

TABLE IV. OTHER SUPPOSED HOARDS   193

El Manshâh 1925 (A29). Vespasian yr 2 = AD 69/70
1,293 + 2 silver ingots and 8 silver bracelets
NERO: 1,292 = 99.9 %
VESPASIAN: 1 = 0.07 %

Tell el-Maskhûta 1 (A87). Valerian yr 3 = AD 255/256
39
CLAUDIUS: 1 = 2.56 %
NERO: 8 = 20.5%
DOMITIAN: 1 = 2.56 %
NERVA: 1 = 2.56 %
TRAJAN: 1 = 2.56 %
HADRIAN: 7 = 17.94 %
ANTONINUS PIUS: 2 = 5.12 %
MARCUS AURELIUS pre-reform: 1 = 2.56 %
COMMODUS: 1 = 2.56 %
ELAGABAL: 2 = 5.12 %
SEVERUS ALEXANDER: 4 = 10.25 %
MAXIMINUS: 1 = 2.56 %
PHILIP: 5 = 12.82 %
TREBONIAN: 2 = 5.12 %
VALERIAN: 2 = 5.12 %

Tell el-Maskhûta 2 (A61). Marcus Aurelius yr 7 = AD 166/167
89
NERO: 46 = 51.68 %
GALBA: 1 = 1.12 %
VESPASIAN: 4 = 4.49 %
TITUS: 1 = 1.12 %
TRAJAN: 1 = 1.12 %
HADRIAN: 22 = 24.71 %
ANTONINUS PIUS: 11 = 12.35 %
MARCUS AURELIUS pre-reform: 3 = 3.37 %

Tell el-Maskhûta 3 (A89). Valerian yr 6 = AD 258/259
131
NERO: 22 = 16.79 %
GALBA: 1 = 0.76 %
TRAJAN: 1 = 0.76 %

HADRIAN: 9 = 6.87 %
ANTONINUS PIUS: 3 = 2.29 %
MARCUS AURELIUS pre-reform: 2 = 1.52 %
COMMODUS: 8 = 6.1 %
ELAGABAL: 11 = 8.39 %
SEVERUS ALEXANDER: 21 = 16.03 %
MAXIMINUS: 4 = 3.05 %
GORDIAN III: 12 = 9.16 %
PHILIP: 16 = 12.21 %
DECIUS: 7 = 5.34%
TREBONIAN: 4 = 3.05 %
VALERIAN: 10 = 7.63 %

Tell el-Maskhûta 4 (A86). Trebonian yr 3 = AD 252/253
162
CLAUDIUS: 1 = 0.61 %
NERO: 58 = 35.8 %
GALBA: 3 = 1.85 %
OTHO: 2 = 1.23 %
VESPASIAN: 9 = 5.55 %
TRAJAN: 3 = 1.85 %
HADRIAN: 34 = 20.98 %
ANTONINUS PIUS: 27 = 16.66 %
MARCUS AURELIUS pre-reform: 6 = 3.7 %
ELAGABAL: 4 = 2.46 %
SEVERUS ALEXANDER: 8 = 4.93 %
MAXIMINUS: 1 = 0.61 %
GORDIAN III: 3 = 1.85 %
PHILIP: 2 = 1.23 %
TREBONIAN: 1 = 0.61 %

Tell el-Maskhûta 5 (A78). Caracalla yr 20 = AD 211/212
312
CLAUDIUS: 3 = 0.96 %
NERO: 128 = 41.02 %
GALBA: 9 = 2.88 %
OTHO: 4 = 1.28 %
VITELLIUS: 2 = 0.64 %
VESPASIAN: 12 = 3.84 %

TABLE IV. OTHER SUPPOSED HOARDS   195

TITUS: 1 = 0.32 %
NERVA: 1 = 0.32 %
TRAJAN: 12 = 3.84 %
HADRIAN: 79 = 25.32 %
ANTONINUS PIUS: 48 = 15.38 %
MARCUS AURELIUS pre-reform: 9 = 2.88 %
COMMODUS: 2 = 0.64 %
SEPTIMIUS SEVERUS: 1 = 0.32 %
CARACALLA: 1 = 0.32 %

Newell 1913 (A58). Marcus Aurelius yr 2 = AD 161/162
427
CLAUDIUS: 15 = 3.51 %
NERO: 202 = 47.3 %
GALBA: 18 = 4.21 %
OTHO: 11 = 2.57 %
VITELLIUS: 3 = 0.7 %
VESPASIAN: 16 = 3.74 %
TITUS: 2 = 0.46 %
NERVA: 1 = 0.23 %
TRAJAN: 15 = 3.51 %
HADRIAN: 104 = 24.35 %
ANTONINUS PIUS: 38 = 8.89 %
MARCUS AURELIUS pre-reform: 2 = 0.46 %

Sanieh 1889 (A26). Galba yr 2 = AD 68/69
481 + 46 illegible
TIBERIUS: 1 = 0.2 %
CLAUDIUS: 151 = 31.39 %
NERO: 328 = 68.19 %
GALBA: 1 = 0.2 %

Totals Alexandrian tetradrachms: 6,590 (16 hoards)
TIBERIUS: 1 = 0.01 %
CLAUDIUS: 343 (9 hoards) = 5.2 %
NERO: 3,408 (13 hoards) = 51.71 %
GALBA: 49 (8 hoards) = 0.74 %
OTHO: 21 (4 hoards) = 0.31 %
VITELLIUS: 6 (3 hoards) = 0.09 %

VESPASIAN: 50 (8 hoards) = 0.75 %
TITUS: 4 (3 hoards) = 0.06 %
DOMITIAN: 1 = 0.01 %
NERVA: 3 (3 hoards) = 0.04 %
TRAJAN: 35 (7 hoards) = 0.53 %
HADRIAN: 266 (7 hoards) = 4.03 %
ANTONINUS PIUS: 130 (7 hoards) = 1.97 %
MARCUS AURELIUS pre-reform: 24 (7 hoards) = 0.36 %
COMMODUS: 12 (4 hoards) = 0.18 %
SEPTIMIUS SEVERUS: 1 = 0.01 %
CARACALLA: 1 = 0.01 %
ELAGABAL: 18 (4 hoards) = 0.27 %
SEVERUS ALEXANDER: 33 (3 hoards) = 0.5%
MAXIMINUS: 6 (3 hoards) = 0.09 %
GORDIAN III: 17 (3 hoards) = 0.25 %
PHILIP: 25 (4 hoards) = 0.37 %
DECIUS: 7 (1 hoard) = 0.1 %
TREBONIAN: 7 (3 hoards) = 0.1 %
VALERIAN: 17 (3 hoards) = 0.25 %
GALLIENUS: 10 (1 hoard) = 0.15 %
CLAUDIUS II: 94 (2 hoards) = 1.42 %
AURELIAN pre-reform: 20 (1 hoard) = 0.3 %
AURELIAN & VABALLATH: 2 (1 hoard) = 0.03 %
AURELIAN post-reform: 116 (2 hoards) = 1.74 %
TACITUS: 41 (2 hoards) = 0.62 %
PROBUS: 958 (3 hoards) = 14.53 %
CARUS and sons: 106 (3 hoards) = 1.6 %
TETRARCHY: 758 (2 hoards) = 11.5 %

Grand totals: 6,646
Alexandrian tetradrachms: 6,590 = 99.15 %
Illegible coins: 46 (1 hoard) = 0.69 %
Other objects: 10 (1 hoard) = 0.15 %

TABLE V. *All hoards. Accumulated numbers.*

Hoard number	End date	Total	Nero	Commodus	Galli-enus	Aurelian Post-reform	Probus	Tetrarchy
A17	65/66	40	23	0	0	0	0	0
CHVII sine numero	65/66	55	37	0	0	0	0	0
A22	66/67	162	144	0	0	0	0	0
A25	68	335	316	0	0	0	0	0
A26	68/69	816	644	0	0	0	0	0
A27	69/70	1991	1772	0	0	0	0	0
A28	69/70	2188	1823	0	0	0	0	0
A29	69/70	3481	3115	0	0	0	0	0
A36	127/128	3543	3159	0	0	0	0	0
A37	128/129	3759	3345	0	0	0	0	0
A48	130/131	3804	3369	0	0	0	0	0
A47	134/135	3817	3379	0	0	0	0	0
A42	138/139	3845	3396	0	0	0	0	0
A43	143/144	4081	3529	0	0	0	0	0
A45	149/150	4183	3595	0	0	0	0	0
A52	155/156	4302	3659	0	0	0	0	0
A54	156/157	5176	4164	0	0	0	0	0
A58	161/162	5603	4366	0	0	0	0	0
A60	164/165	10026	7128	0	0	0	0	0
A62	166/167	10112	7186	0	0	0	0	0
A61	166/167	10201	7232	0	0	0	0	0
A63	169/170	10299	7288	0	0	0	0	0
A114	169/170	12601	8814	0	0	0	0	0
A103 (B'07A)	189/190	12624	8819	15	0	0	0	0
A69	190/191	14895	10149	32	0	0	0	0
A78	211/212	15207	10277	34	0	0	0	0
Ax1	246/247	15436	10285	34	0	0	0	0
A86	252/253	15598	10343	34	0	0	0	0
A87	255/256	15637	10351	35	0	0	0	0
A88	257/258	15643	10351	35	0	0	0	0
A89	258/259	15774	10373	43	0	0	0	0
A92	261/262	16958	10373	299	1	0	0	0
A94	262/263	17430	10373	329	9	0	0	0
A95	263/264	17504	10382	331	13	0	0	0
A96	264/265	17517	10382	331	14	0	0	0
A97	265/266	18467	10382	331	88	0	0	0

Hoard number	End date	Total	Nero	Commo-dus	Galli-enus	Aurelian Post-reform	Probus	Tetrarchy
A98	268/269	19327	10382	375	98	0	0	0
A99	269/270	19350	10382	375	98	0	0	0
A103 (B'07B)	271/272	20416	10382	375	560	0	0	0
A104	271/272	22219	10420	381	1064	0	0	0
A105	272/273	22236	10420	381	1064	0	0	0
A107	274/275	22417	10420	381	1064	181	0	0
A108	274/275	22439	10420	381	1064	189	0	0
A109	276/277	24606	11127	733	1125	209	4	0
A110	278/279	26562	11131	771	1576	213	5	0
A111	282/283	26617	11131	771	1576	217	36	0
A112	282/283	26996	11131	771	1580	243	140	0
A113	282/283	28054	11131	771	1580	349	1026	0
A115	285/286	28058	11131	771	1580	349	1026	3
A117	287/288	30815	11131	771	1580	451	1878	1273
A118	288/289	31474	11131	815	1584	451	1878	1274
A119	289/290	33642	11131	815	1584	466	2845	2247
A132	291/292	34841	11131	815	1584	471	2946	3193
A131	292/293	35303	11131	815	1584	489	3154	3305
A128	292/293	35400	11131	815	1584	489	3165	3384
A130	292/293	35426	11131	815	1584	491	3169	3400
A133	293/294	38559	11131	815	1584	538	4552	4762
A135	293/294	38581	11131	815	1584	538	4552	4783
A136	294/295	38628	11131	815	1584	538	4557	4821
A142	294/295	38865	11131	815	1584	538	4575	5021
A143	295/296	39185	11132	824	1590	538	4575	5024
A144	295/296	41657	11132	824	1590	544	4739	7092
A145	295/296	42936	11132	824	1590	553	4853	8089
A146	295/296	43553	11132	824	1590	556	4911	8565
A147	295/296	44563	11132	824	1590	558	4972	9380
A148	295/296	45584	11132	824	1590	560	5077	10146
A149	295/296	48366	11132	824	1590	569	5256	12382
A150	295/296	49784	11132	824	1590	575	5363	13532
A152	295/296	50715	11132	824	1591	575	5430	14281
A140	295/296	54831	11132	824	1593	612	5757	17334
A159	295/296	67365	11139	904	3525	1043	9390	18010
A138	295/296	68187	11139	905	3535	1053	9444	**18568**

TABLE VI. *Karanis Hoards. Accumulated numbers.*

HOARD NUMBER	END DATE	TOTAL	NERO	COMMO-DUS	GALLI-ENUS	AURELIAN POST-REFORM	PROBUS	TETRARCHY
12 (A17)	65/66	40	23	0	0	0	0	0
30A (A88)	257/258	46	23	0	0	0	0	0
32 (A94)	262/263	518	23	30	8	0	0	0
14 (A95)	263/264	592	32	32	12	0	0	0
15 (A96)	264/265	605	32	32	13	0	0	0
1 (A98)	268/269	1465	32	76	23	0	0	0
28 (A99)	269/270	1488	32	76	23	0	0	0
5 (A105)	272/273	1505	32	76	23	0	0	0
6 (A107)	274/275	1686	32	76	23	181	0	0
7 (A108)	274/275	1708	32	76	23	189	0	0
20 (A111)	282/283	1763	32	76	23	193	31	0
31 (A112)	282/283	2142	32	76	27	219	135	0
26 (A115)	285/286	2146	32	76	27	219	135	3
36 (A117)	287/288	4903	32	76	27	321	987	1273
30 (A118)	288/289	5562	32	120	31	321	987	1274
25 (A119)	289/290	7730	32	120	31	336	1954	2247
22 (A131)	292/293	8192	32	120	31	354	2162	2359
29 (A133)	293/294	11325	32	120	31	401	3545	3721
33 (A136)	294/295	11372	32	120	31	401	3550	3759
17 (A143)	295/296	11692	33	129	37	401	3550	3762
18 (A144)	295/296	14164	33	129	37	407	3714	5830
19 (A145)	295/296	15443	33	129	37	416	3828	6827
21 (A146)	295/296	16060	33	129	37	419	3886	7303
23 (A147)	295/296	17070	33	129	37	421	3947	8118
24 (A148)	295/296	18091	33	129	37	423	4052	8884
34 (A149)	295/296	20873	33	129	37	432	4231	11120
35 (A150)	295/296	22291	33	129	37	438	4338	12270
16 (A152)	295/296	23222	33	129	38	438	4405	13019

TABLE VII. *Other Excavation Hoards. Accumulated numbers.*

HOARD NUMBER	END DATE	TOTAL	NERO	COMMO-DUS	GALLI-ENUS	AURELIAN POST-REFORM	PROBUS	TETRARCHY
A25	68	173	172	0	0	0	0	0
A36	127/128	235	216	0	0	0	0	0
A37	128/129	451	402	0	0	0	0	0
A47	134/135	464	412	0	0	0	0	0
A42	138/139	492	429	0	0	0	0	0
A43	143/144	728	562	0	0	0	0	0
A45	149/150	830	628	0	0	0	0	0
A52	155/156	949	692	0	0	0	0	0
A60	164/165	5372	3454	0	0	0	0	0
A62	166/167	5458	3512	0	0	0	0	0
A63	169/170	5556	3568	0	0	0	0	0
Ax1	246/247	5785	3576	0	0	0	0	0
A92	261/262	6969	3576	256	1	0	0	0
A132	291/292	8168	3576	256	1	5	101	946
A128	292/293	8265	3576	256	1	5	112	1025
A130	292/293	8291	3576	256	1	7	**116**	1041
A135	293/294	8313	3576	256	1	7	116	1062

TABLE VIII. *Dattari Hoards. Accumulated numbers.*

HOARD NUMBER	END DATE	TOTAL	NERO	COMMO-DUS	GALLI-ENUS	AURELIAN POST-REFORM	PROBUS	TETRARCHY
A54	156/157	874	505	0	0	0	0	0
A114	169/170	3176	2031	0	0	0	0	0
A103 (B'07A)	189/190	3199	2036	15	0	0	0	0
A69	190/191	5470	3366	32	0	0	0	0
A97	265/266	6420	3366	32	74	0	0	0
A103 (B'07B)	271/272	7486	3366	32	536	0	0	0
A104	271/272	9289	3404	38	1040	0	0	0
A109	276/277	11456	4111	390	1101	20	4	0
A110	278/279	13412	4115	428	1552	24	5	0
A140	295/296	17528	4115	428	1554	61	332	3053
A159	295/296	30062	4122	508	3486	492	3965	**3729**

TABLE IX. *Other Supposed Hoards. Accumulated numbers.*

HOARD NUMBER	END DATE	TOTAL	NERO	COMMO-DUS	GALLI-ENUS	AURELIAN POST-REFORM	PROBUS	TETRARCHY
CHVII sine numero	65/66	15	14	0	0	0	0	0
A22	66/67	122	121	0	0	0	0	0
A26	68/69	603	449	0	0	0	0	0
A27	69/70	1778	1577	0	0	0	0	0
A28	69/70	1975	1628	0	0	0	0	0
A29	69/70	3268	2920	0	0	0	0	0
A48	130/131	3313	2944	0	0	0	0	0
A58	161/162	3740	3146	0	0	0	0	0
A61	166/167	3829	3192	0	0	0	0	0
A78	211/212	4141	3320	2	0	0	0	0
A86	252/253	4303	3378	2	0	0	0	0
A87	255/256	4342	3386	3	0	0	0	0
A89	258/259	4473	3408	11	0	0	0	0
A113	282/283	5531	3408	11	0	106	886	0
A142	294/295	5768	3408	11	0	106	904	200
A138	295/296	6590	3408	12	10	116	958	758

PLATES

Cleopatra VII Thea yrs 17-22

Nero yrs 11-12

PLATE I. *Egyptian tetradrachms from Cleopatra to Aurelian. (Size 1:1).*

PLATE I   203

Commodus yr 21 (of Marcus Aurelius)

Gallienus yrs 10-12

Aurelian yrs 5-6

Claudius: Size III
(1½ obols?)

Trajan: drachms

Harian: drachms

Incerti: (tesserae?)

PLATE II. *Alexandrian bronze coins. (Size 1:1).*

PLATE III   205

PLATE III. *Augustus as depicted in the temple of Kalabsha.*

Index

No references are given to figures and tables